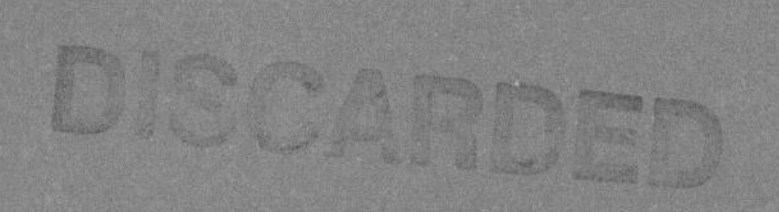
DISCARDED

D0130864

# ITALIAN COOKING

# ITALIAN COOKING

GIANNI SCAPPIN
ALBERTO VANOLI
STEVEN KOLPAN
THE FOODS AND WINES OF ITALY
AND WINE NOTES

PHOTOGRAPHS AND FOOD STYLING
Francesco Tonelli

JOHN WILEY & SONS, INC.

**THE CULINARY INSTITUTE OF AMERICA**

| | |
|---|---|
| President | Dr. Tim Ryan '77 |
| Vice-President, Dean of Culinary Education | Mark Erickson '77 |
| Senior Director, Educational Enterprises | Susan Cussen |
| Director of Publishing | Nathalie Fischer |
| Editorial Project Manager | Mary Donovan '83 |
| Editorial Assistant | Shelly Malgee '08 |

Published by John Wiley & Sons, Inc., Hoboken, New Jersey

Published simultaneously in Canada



Design by Vertigo Design NYC

**Library of Congress Cataloging-in-Publication Data:**

Scappin, Gianni.

Italian cooking at home : with the Culinary Institute of America / by Gianni Scappin, Alberto Vanoli, and Steven Kolpan ; photographs by Francesco Tonelli.

p. cm.

Includes index.

ISBN 978-0-470-18258-1 (cloth)

1. Cookery, Italian. 2. Cookery--Italy. I. Vanoli, Alberto. II. Kolpan, Steven. III. Tonelli, Francesco, photographer. IV. Culinary Institute of America. V. Title.

TX723.S3544 2011

641.5945--dc22

2010016368

Printed in China

10 9 8 7 6 5 4 3 2 1

# Contents

# Acknowledgments

This book is dedicated to our students, whose love of cooking and food always inspires us, and to President Tim Ryan and all of our colleagues here at The Culinary Institute of America, as well as those spread across the globe. We are grateful for your support.

We would all like to thank our families and friends, for all they have done to help make this book a reality. A special note of thanks to Lynn Tonelli for her prop styling and to Shelly Malgee for her hard work managing the photo shoots.

# The foods and wines of Italy

Italians know the foods and wines of their own regions and have learned the customs and traditions of the table thoroughly at a young age. In this chapter, we will review some of the famous foods of various regions in Italy and the wines that help make each meal into a feast.

# Northern Italy

## PIEDMONT (PIEMONTE)

The Piedmont (Piemonte) region of Italy, located in the far northwest and bordered by France and Switzerland, is one of the largest regions in the country. Its provincial capital is Turin (Torino).

Because the Po River—the longest river in Italy—flows through Piedmont, Carnaroli rice, used for risotto, is a very important crop. Other important agricultural products include wheat, fruit, vegetables such as asparagus and onions, honey, hazelnuts and walnuts, and, of course, grapes for wine.

Piedmont is home to the finest white truffles in the world, harvested with the aid of trained dogs during truffle season in the autumn of the year, which is also the best time to hunt for mushrooms and wild game. Incredibly aromatic fungi that cannot be cultivated, tartufi bianchi can sell for more than $2,000 per pound. White truffles, which are served raw, are thinly shaved and served on top of many dishes in Piedmont, especially pasta, risotto, carne cruda—marinated chopped raw beef or veal—and salads.

## Wine notes: Piedmont

The Piedmont region produces some of Italy's finest wines; Piemontese wines are also some of the most food-friendly. The wines span a variety of styles and are sure to lift the appreciation of your cooking to a higher level.

### The Whites

There are two Piemontese whites to look for: Gavi and Arneis. These are considered to be the best dry white wines of the region, and with good reason. Gavi and Arneis are both delicious wines, and both are distinctive.

Gavi (sometimes labeled as Cortese di Gavi or Gavi di Gavi) is made from the Cortese grape and is a light- to medium-bodied dry, refreshing white that is best served with lighter fish dishes, especially freshwater fish such as trout.

Arneis is often labeled as Roero Arneis; Roero is the region. The ancient Arneis grape produces a dry wine that is medium- to full-bodied, with a distinctive hazelnut-tinged aroma. Arneis is a fine foil for fish stews, as well as for Vitello Tonnato (page 97) and the extraordinarily delicate Lardo di Cavour, milky-white strips of cured fat scented with rosemary and served with hazelnuts.

### The Reds

*Il vino è rosso* ("Wine is red") is an old Piemontese expression, and there is no doubt that Piedmont produces some of Italy's greatest red wines.

Barolo and Barbaresco, both made solely from the Nebbiolo grape, are often referred to, respectively (and respectfully), as the king and queen of Piemontese reds, and they certainly live up to their royal titles. Both wines, produced from vineyards in the southern Langhe region of Piedmont, are full-bodied and require a bit of aging to appreciate fully with food. Though not very dark in color, the wines are complex, with assertive, earthy aromas and dark cherry/licorice flavors. Both wines can be moderately to quite expensive and can set the tone for a special-occasion meal. They are best served with hearty red-meat dishes and aged hard cheeses.

Gattinara and Ghemme, made mostly from the Nebbiolo grape in the northern reaches of Piedmont, are a bit softer, and a touch less earthy, than Barolo and Barbaresco in their youth, though by no means do they lack intensity. These are full-bodied wines that, while best with several years of bottle age, can often be enjoyed a few years younger than the more powerful Barolo and Barbaresco.

Barbera is the most widely planted grape in Piedmont, and it yields a delightful red wine, especially in the areas surrounding the towns of Alba, Asti, and Monferrato. The wine, redolent of mature red and black berries, is medium-bodied, but with a searing acidity that refreshes the palate, happily preparing you for another sip of wine, another bite of food. Barbera is a good example of a "crossover wine"; it is equally at home with richer fish dishes (grilled salmon, for example) and white meats and leaner cuts of red meat. Try it with Gnocchi di Zucca con Fonduta Piemontese (page 203); you'll be glad you did.

Dolcetto, the "little sweet one," actually is a grape that makes a light- to medium-bodied dry red wine that is a pleasure to drink. Dolcetto, especially from the towns of Alba, Asti, and Dogliani, is a red wine that can take a bit of a chill, particularly in hot weather, and is a great wine for picnics and barbecues. A terrific pizza wine, Dolcetto is often paired with the Piemontese classic Bagna Caòda (page 67).

## Bubbles

The Piedmont region is famous for its frothy, softly sweet white sparkler Asti (formerly Asti Spumante; *spumante* means "sparkling"), made from Moscato grapes. An appealing, refreshing crowd-pleaser, Asti is low in alcohol—5 percent to 7 percent—and high in pleasure. A nice poolside sipper, Asti, or its frizzante (semi-sparkling) counterpart Moscato d'Asti, is also the perfect foil for cheesecake, as well as Brutti ma Buoni and Bunet all'Astigiana (pages 318 and 307).

More bubbly fun comes from Piedmont in the form of Brachetto d'Acqui, a rosé/light red sweet, low-alcohol sparkler that tastes like red berries—especially strawberries and cherries. This is the perfect match for dark chocolates in any form and is particularly appealing with chocolate and hazelnuts, the signature nut of Piedmont.

## Cheese notes: Piedmont

Piedmont is known for the quality of its milk, as cows, sheep, and goats graze in pastures in the region's hills, mountains, and valleys. Nine of Piedmont's cheeses have earned Italy's prestigious DOP (Denominazione di Origine Protetta). Some of Piedmont's best cheeses include:

**BETTELMATT:** A semi-hard cow's milk cheese ("Toma" is the Italian term for this style), produced only in the summer along the Swiss border in mountainside pastures. The cheese is brined or salted for about two weeks, and must mature for a minimum of two months before sale. Bettelmatt has a thick, brown rind, and the cheese is straw to gold in color.

**BRA DOP:** Made from two milkings—one early in the day, one later—of pasteurized cow's milk, sometimes blended with a bit of sheep or goat's milk. Dry salted every day for six days after being pressed into rounds, there are two styles of Bra: Duro—a hard cheese, and Tenero—a soft, brine-soaked version. Bra Duro has a hard, beige-to-brown rind, while Bra Tenero has a thin, off-white rind.

**BRA D'ALPEGGIO DOP:** Produced only in the mountainous grazing lands of Piedmont's Cuneo province, the best Bra d'Alpeggio is made from a single breed of cow, the Piemontese. The process of cheesemaking is similar to Bra DOP (above), but is more likely to be the artisanal product of small farmers. Made in both the duro and tenero styles.

**CASTELMAGNO DOP:** Made in its namesake town and surrounding areas for the last 800 years, Castelmagno is a blue cheese made from two successive milkings of cows, with a bit of sheep or goat's milk allowed. Making Castelmagno is a labor-intensive process, including about a month of salting every other day, and extensive aging in caves. The rind is smooth and white when the cheese is young, but much harder and clay red when aged.

**GORGONZOLA DOP:** Made from cow's milk in several provinces of Piedmont, Gorgonzola is one of the world's most famous blue cheeses. Gorgonzola is creamy, and the blue-green mold in the cheese gives it a spicy, tangy flavor. The rind is thick and moist, and becomes red in color as the cheese matures.

**GRASSO D'ALPE:** A cow's milk toma, Grasso d'Alpe is a semi-soft cheese with a fairly thick rind; the darker the rind, the more mature the cheese. A Grasso d'Alpe that has gone through extended aging (sometimes more than a year) is called Mezzapasta or Spress.

**MURRAZZANO DOP:** Originally a sheep's milk cheese, today Murrazzano can be made from as much as 40 percent cow's milk. Ready to eat after about 10 days of ripening, Murazzanno should age for another month or so to bring out its mature flavors. The rind is thin, and the cheese is semi-soft with a white to light yellow color.

**RASCHERA DOP:** Made primarily from unpasteurized cow's milk from only two breeds—Bruno-Alpina or Piemontese—in Cuneo province, Raschera ages in cool, damp caves between three weeks and three months. Less mature cheeses have a distinctive smell of grass and hay, while more mature versions take on a nutty aroma. The cheese is semi-soft.

**REBRUCHON:** Similar to the famous French cheese, Rebruchon, the Piemontese version is made from rich cow's milk. A soft, fatty, runny cheese, Rebruchon has a thin rind and is white to off-white in color.

**ROBIOLA DI ROCCAVERANO DOP:** Robiola di Roccaverano is made from 100 percent goat's milk, but legally it can be made from up to 85 percent cow's milk. Robiola di Roccaverano, is a young, soft-ripened cheese, with a very thin, highly edible rind. The cheese is white to straw color, semi-soft, and has a sweet, fresh taste. Sold in small individual rounds, Robiola di Roccaverano should be consumed within a few weeks of purchase.

**TOMA PIEMONTESE DOP:** Produced throughout the Piedmont region and made exclusively from cow's milk, this cheese is aged between two weeks and two months, depending on the size and weight of the "wheel"—anywhere from about four to seventeen pounds, and from six to fourteen inches in diameter. The outer rind is smooth, and varies in color from off-white to brown; the cheese is fairly soft, but firm.

## AOSTA VALLEY (VALLE D'AOSTA)

The Aosta Valley (Valle d'Aosta) in northwestern Italy is bordered by Italy's Piedmont region to the south, France to the west, and Switzerland to the north. The smallest region in all of Italy, Valle d'Aosta is a mountainous region, and Mont Blanc/Monte Bianco and the Matterhorn/Monte Cervino are its highest mountains. Because of its unique geographic position, residents of the Aosta Valley form a trilingual society (predominantly Italian and French, with a small number of German speakers).

### Food notes: Aosta Valley

Traditional foods and dishes of Valle d'Aosta include a variety of salumi (cured meats and sausages), including the famous DOP (Denominazione di Origine Protetta) Jambon de Bosses, a salt-cured aged ham; and Valle d'Aosta Lard d'Arnad (DOP), the regional lardo, which is cured in a marble container and served in a glass jar. Game is another important ingredient in the cooking of Valle d'Aosta. Soups made from rice and barley, bolstered with cabbage and enriched with the region's excellent cheeses, are a mainstay.

### Wine notes: Aosta Valley

Very little wine from this region is imported to the United States, but those wines that do make it out of Europe are generally very good. Wines that are imported on a small scale include the dry, light- to medium-bodied white Petite Arvine and a light, fruity version of Pinot Noir. Rarely, you might find red wines made from the native wine grapes Petit Rouge, Cornalin, and Fumin. The best way to immerse yourself in the wines of this region is to visit the Aosta Valley.

### Cheese notes: Aosta Valley

The Aosta Valley is known for the quality of its milk, much of it sourced from one of the local cow breeds, Valdostana. The region is best known for one cheese with an international reputation, Fontina DOP. Fontina from the Aosta Valley is a soft, buttery cheese made from the milk of Valdostana cows. The cheese is aged for a minimum of three months, until the rind takes on a dark yellow to reddish-brown color. Each wheel of Fontina is stamped with a seal that features an outline of the Matterhorn (Monte Cervino).

## LOMBARDY (LOMBARDIA)

Lombardy is anchored by its capital city of Milan and includes Alpine regions, rolling foothills, and the beautiful lake districts of Como, Garda, Idro, Iseo, Lugano, Maggiore, and Varese. With about ten million people (one third living in Milan), Lombardy is Italy's most populous region and one of the country's most prosperous. Lombardy is bordered by Switzerland to the north, Emilia-Romagna to the south, Piedmont to the west, and the Veneto and Trentino-Alto Adige regions to the east.

Italy's fourth-largest region in total area, Lombardy is, in its major provinces such as Milan, Bergamo, Brescia, and Varese, highly industrialized, but about 40 percent of Lombardy's land is used for agriculture.

### Food notes: Lombardy

Olive Oils: DOP extra-virgin oils whose name will appear on the bottle label: Garda and Laghi Lombardi

Salumi include: Bresaola di Valtellina (salt-cured beef with a buttery texture); Cotechino di Modena (fresh sausage made from pork, fatback, and pork rind); Mortadella di Bologna (finely ground cured pork sausage with pork fat); Salame Brianza DOP and Salame di Varza DOP (cured pork salamis); Salame d'Oca di Mortasa DOP (cured goose salami); Salamini Italiani alla Cacciatore DOP (a small, pocket-sized pork sausage); and Zampone di Modena (similar to cotechino, but includes pig's trotter as an ingredient)

### Wine notes: Lombardy

Lombardy's best wines are still a bit of a secret, except to the neighboring Swiss, who tend to think of these wines as their own.

Lombardy produces the finest sparkling wine in Italy, Franciacorta. The wine, available as a white or rosé sparkler, is spectacular and challenging and sometimes surpasses the quality of true Champagne. Franciacorta is expensive and worth it.

From vineyards located on the steep banks of the Adda River in the Valtellina Superiore region come four of Lombardy's best dry red wines: Inferno, Grumello, Sassella, and Valgella. These wines are made almost entirely from the Nebbiolo grape (locally known as Chiavennasca). In particular, Grumello ($20 to $35) consistently delivers the pleasure of a complex but balanced mélange of both black and red fruits. And how can you ignore the attractive heat of a delicious red named Inferno?

## Cheese notes: Lombardy

Lombardy is known for the quality of its dairy products, especially cheeses made from cow's milk. The pastures of Lombardy's Valtellina are prime grazing land for the region's cattle. Many of Lombardy's cheeses have earned the DOP (Denominazione di Origine Protetta), because they are unique to the region. Lombardy is perhaps Italy's most important region when it comes to cheese. The DOP cheeses of Lombardy include:

**BITTO:** Bitto is made from cow's milk with a maximum of ten percent goat's milk added, which adds aromatics to the cheese. Bitto is a semi-hard cheese that in its youth is quite sweet in flavor, but becomes far more complex and intense as it ages. Bitto must be aged a minimum of 70 days, but some cheeses are matured for years.

**GORGONZOLA:** Also produced in the adjoining Piedmont region, Gorgonzola is one of the world's most famous blue cheeses made from cow's milk. Gorgonzola is creamy, and the blue-green mold in the cheese gives it a spicy, tangy flavor.

**GRANA PADANO:** Produced in Piedmont and Veneto, as well as Lombardy, Grana Padano is often compared to the more famous Parmigiano-Reggiano (see Cheese Notes: Emilia-Romagna, page 10), and with good reason. The cheese-making process, the aging of the cheese, and the flaky, granular ("grana") character of the cheese is quite similar. The flavor of the cheese is also similar, especially when used for grating, but Grana Padano also makes a fine eating cheese. As with Parmigiano-Reggiano, the imprint of the Grana Padano consorzio (the group of registered producers), the code number of the dairy that produced the cheese (no names are used), and the production date must appear on the rind. Grana Padano is somewhat less expensive than Parmigiano-Reggiano.

**MASCARPONE:** A very creamy soft sweet/softly sour triple-cream cheese, almost yogurt-like in texture, mascarpone is often used in the preparation of desserts, most famously tiramisù. Recipes that call for crème fraîche can easily switch to mascarpone.

**PROVOLONE VAL PADANA:** Although most often associated with southern Italy, Provolone cheese has been made in northern Italy since the beginning of the 20th century. Provolone Val Padana is a semi-hard cow's milk cheese that is produced in a variety of sizes and shapes: a pear, a cone, a salami, a melon, among others. The taste of Provolone Val Padana may be anywhere from sweet and mild to tangy and sharp. A good eating cheese, Provolone is also good for cooking, because it melts and stretches.

**TALLEGIO:** Tallegio is a soft cheese made from raw or pasteurized cow's milk, and with a naturally pink-tinged rind, Tallegio is one of Italy's few washed-rind cheeses, and so has a very powerful aroma, which it develops over a minimum of 35 days' ripening time. Tallegio has a mild flavor and a buttery texture, but as it matures, the flavor becomes much more intense.

### TRENTINO-ALTO ADIGE

Trentino-Alto Adige borders Austria and Switzerland to the north and northwest, Lombardy to the west, and Veneto to the south, and combines two cultures: Italian and Austrian. The region is officially bilingual (Italian and German) and was officially recognized as such in 1947, following the end of World War II. Most Italian speakers live in the southern part of the region in the Trento province—the town of Trento is the region's capital—while the German-speaking population lives in the Alto Adige (in German, Südtirol) area in the province of Bolzano (in German, Bozen). In reality, the provinces operate semi-autonomously, with Alto Adige recognized as its own cultural capital. With about a million people in the entire region, the population is divided more or less equally between the southern province and the northern province. Trentino-Alto Adige is a mountainous region, defined by the southern Alps and the Dolomites.

## Food notes: Trentino-Alto Adige

As you might imagine, the Italian and Austrian cooking traditions of Trentino-Alto Adige are historically and culturally different. In Trentino, pasta, such as tagliatelle, gnocchi, and ravioli, is important, but polenta, most often made from cornmeal, is the primary staple of the region. Vegetables, including turnips and potatoes, are found in the soups of the "Italian side" of the region. Game, poultry, pork, salt-cured beef (carne salata), and blood sausages (biroldi), as well as mortadella are popular choices in Trentino. The frittata—a baked omelet with vegetables, meats, or cheeses—is a popular dish in Trentino.

In Alto Adige, the "Austrian side" of the region, the claim to fame is Speck dell'Alto Adige. Speck is an artisanal product: boned ham that is salted and spiced, cold-smoked, and then aged. It is one of the most delicious smoked hams in the world. Speck dell'Alto Adige is an important ingredient in canederli dumplings. True to their culinary heritage, citizens of Alto Adige enjoy such dishes as sauerbraten—pot roast in a sauce of onions, wine, vinegar, and sometimes other ingredients, such as chocolate. Sausages are served with sauerkraut, mustard, and pickles. Streams in Alto Adige provide brook trout, while the forests provide venison. Pasta tends to be spaetzle: small egg noodles or tiny dumplings. Dessert strudel and fritters feature apples, as the region is Italy's apple basket.

In the entire region of Trentino-Alto Adige there is one DOP olive oil, Garda, produced in Trento but which can also be produced in parts of Lombardy and Veneto.

## Wine notes: Trentino-Alto Adige

There is a real cultural divide in the styles of many of the wines produced here. The entire region is known, however, for producing Italy's finest examples of Pinot Grigio.

Unlike the watery or merely serviceable wines that have flooded American markets, fine Pinot Grigio from Alto Adige is sublime: a medium-bodied wine with a nose of tropical fruits wrapped in cashews and hazelnuts and a refreshing, mouthwatering flavor that is not at all simple, but lively and complex.

Alto Adige has made its reputation in the United States on Pinot Grigio, as well as on whites and reds made mostly from popular market-driven varietals such as Chardonnay and Merlot. Raise the bar for Pinot Grigio by tasting a great one from Alto Adige.

Trentino (the traditionally Italian sector of this multicultural region) is best known for its excellent sparkling wines, as well as for Teroldego Rotaliano, a wine that can be made as a rosé; as a light, accessible red; or as a full-bodied, hearty, age-worthy red. And Pinot Grigio from Trentino? Terrific.

## Cheese notes: Trentino-Alto Adige

Trentino-Alto Adige produces a wide variety of cow's milk cheeses unique to the region, but the cheeses are hard to find, and very little cheese from this region is exported to the United States. In addition to their own cheeses, such as Almkäse, Lagundo (Bauernkäse in German), Spressa delle Giudicarie (DOP), and Tosela, the region also produces Asiago (DOP; see Veneto, page 7) and Grana Padano (DOP; see Lombardy, page 4).

### FRIULI-VENEZIA GIULIA

Friuli-Venezia Giulia (commonly referred to as Friuli), located in northeast Italy, is bordered by the Veneto region to the west, the countries of Slovenia and Austria to the east and north, and the Adriatic Sea to the south. The region is home to about a million people. The capital of Friuli is Trieste, which because of its geographic location, diverse population, and history (it was, until 1954, part of the former nation of Yugoslavia), is bilingual, with residents speaking Italian, but even more likely, Slovenian. In addition to Trieste, the other major city in Friuli is Udine, where both Friulian and Italian are spoken. Northern Friuli is mountainous, and the climate there is cool. The plains of central and southern Friuli feature a much warmer and humid climate.

## Food notes: Friuli-Venezia Giulia

Due to Friuli's location and history, its foods combine the best traditions of Venetian cooking with strong influences from Austria and Slovenia (and Slovenia's historic antecedents in the former Yugoslavia). In the Alpine provinces of Friuli, meats such as beef, goat, lamb, poultry, and sausages are traditionally cooked—grilled or roasted—in an open hearth, or fogolar. As in so many Italian regions, polenta is an important staple in Friuli on its own with cheese, or as an accompaniment to meat or game stews. Rabbit, venison, and feathered game are used in braised dishes that feature salmì—intensely seasoned wine sauces.

Along Friuli's Adriatic seacoast, where Trieste is located, seafood rules the food traditions: sardines, squid, scallops, prawns, cuttlefish, turbot, crabs, and eels. Turtle soup is popular, as are fish stews, chowders, and fish-based risotto dishes. Because of its Slavic cultural heritage, paprika-spiced beef goulash (gùlas) and rambasici—cabbage rolls stuffed with meat and spices—are popular dishes in this part of Friuli, as are the sausages of central Europe, often served with sauerkraut and horseradish.

Pumpkin is an important ingredient in Friuli, and it finds its way into breads, fillings for pasta, and desserts. Friulians love to eat soups to ward off the chill of winter and make several variations of vegetable soups, as well as soups focused on mushrooms, barley, and beans.

Perhaps the food for which Friuli-Venezia Giulia is, and will always be, most famous is the cured, aged DOP ham Prosciutto di San Daniele. The carefully selected animals used for this ham must be bred only on approved farms and are fed a highly restricted diet. Sea salt is the only agent used to cure the ham, and even that must be used quite sparingly, as the finished aged ham must have a total salt content of less than 6 percent. Prosciutto di San Daniele is produced only in the province of Udine, in and around the town of San Daniele del Friuli.

The one DOP extra-virgin olive oil from Friuli-Venezia Giulia is Tergeste, made from olives harvested in the provinces of Udine and Pordenone.

## Wine notes: Friuli-Venezia Giulia

Since Friuli borders Austria and Slovenia, its wines, especially its whites, display the influences of those places. Since the 1970s, when Friuli began to embrace the principles of best practices for its vineyards and high-tech methods for its wine production, the region's reputation for clean, delicious, food-friendly wine has been spreading.

International varietals rule in Friuli, especially Pinot Grigio, Pinot Bianco, Riesling, Chardonnay, and, among reds, Merlot. A fine medium- to full-bodied white made from the native varietal Tocai Friulano (the name of which was recently changed to simply Friulano) has a healthy presence in the American market. With a bit of searching you can find a great red made from the Refosco grape, Refosco dal Peduncolo Rosso: a full-bodied, fruit-driven, violet-red wine, with flavors of damson plums and moderate tannins that create a pleasant, slightly bitter aftertaste, something akin to a hint of anise or black licorice.

Today, Friulian whites and reds are major players in the international market. Prices vary, with some true values still available from larger producers along with quite a few expensive artisan wines.

## Cheese notes: Friuli-Venezia Giulia

Montasio: This cheese may be made from either raw cow's milk (the traditional method), or milk that has been heated at the dairy. Montasio is semi-soft and pale yellow, with a thin rind and delicate flavor when young, becoming intensely flavorful and semi-hard as it matures. Aged, grated Montasio is the most important, and sometimes the only, ingredient in Frico, a fried cheese crisp from Friuli that can be served as either a savory or sweet snack.

### VENETO

Anchored by Venice, its capital of many islands, canals, and bridges, the Veneto region of Italy really contains no major population centers in our twenty-first century understanding of that concept. The three largest cities—Venice, Verona, and Padua—each have populations of less than 300,000 people. The region is geographically diverse, with both extensive mountain ranges and plains, and relatively small towns dotting the landscape.

## Food notes: Veneto

Veneto's geographic diversity leads to a diverse food culture. With access to the sea, fish and seafood are important parts of Venetian food culture. With widespread farming—from grain production to livestock to dairies to vineyards—Venetians enjoy pasta, rice, cheeses, and, of course, wines. Various meats, including game, are part of some of the traditional dishes of Veneto.

Traditional foods of the Veneto region include DOP extra-virgin olive oils whose name will appear on the bottle label as either Garda or Veneto.

Salumi include cotechino di Modena (fresh sausage made from pork, fatback, and pork rind), Mortadella di Bologna (finely ground cured pork sausage with pork fat), Prosciutto Veneto Berico-Euganeo (raw, cured ham; DOP), Salamini Italiani alla Cacciatore (a small, pocket-size pork sausage; DOP), Sopressa Vicentina (a very popular semi-hard salami seasoned with peppercorns and cloves; DOP), and Zampone di Modena (similar to cotechino, but includes pig's trotter as an ingredient).

## Wine notes: Veneto

Veneto produces a great deal of wine from vineyards planted throughout the region, but it is best known in the

United States for the dry white wine Soave, the sparkling dry to semi-dry wine Prosecco, and the reds Bardolino, Valpolicella, and Amarone. These are all classic Veneto wines that are made largely from classic Italian grapes. Veneto also produces plenty of Pinot Grigio, as well as whites and reds based on international varietals, especially Merlot.

Soave is a refreshing, pretty, straightforward quaffing white; Soave Classico, for just a few dollars more, can be more complex and provocative. Prosecco is a widely available, charming, and simple sparkler that's highly affordable (often in the $8 to $15 range) a refreshing drink before a meal, or fun when paired with light, simple foods.

Bardolino and Valpolicella are both made from the same grapes; Corvina is the dominant grape type. Both of these light- to medium-bodied reds are equally at home with meat, fish, pasta, and pizza. Look for wines from the Classico districts.

Ironically, Italy's most powerful wine, Amarone, is made from grapes grown in the same vineyards as the much lighter Valpolicella. The difference is that Amarone is made from passito grapes, which are dried in the sun and then indoors over the winter. The grapes shrivel, becoming virtual raisins, and the resulting dry red wine has higher than 15 percent alcohol.

Also, look for the ripasso style of Valpolicella. In this style, Valpolicella juice is "re-passed" over the lees—the spent yeast cells—of Amarone and then fermented, creating a medium- to full-bodied wine with luscious and complex flavors.

## Cheese notes: Veneto

Veneto is known for the high quality of its cheeses, which are overwhelmingly produced from milk from Bruno Alpina cows. Two DOP cheeses, Asiago and Montasio (see Friuli-Venezia Giulia, page 6) cheeses have developed worldwide reputations. Unfortunately, many of Veneto's other delicious cheeses are not widely available in the United States.

Asiago d'Allevo DOP: Produced from raw cow's milk in mountainous regions, Asiago d'Allevo is a semi-hard cheese when relatively young; the cheese becomes harder and more intensely aromatic and flavorful as it ages. The hard aged cheeses can be used for both eating and for grating. The rind is thin, and becomes a light shade of brown as the cheese matures. Asiago Pressato DOP is produced from pasteurized cow's milk at lower elevations and valleys, Asiago Pressato is a soft to semi-soft cheese with a delicate flavor.

Other cheeses from Veneto include:

**CANSIGLIO:** Made from raw milk, Cansiglio is a relatively soft cheese.

**CARNIA:** Made from partially pasteurized milk, the cheese is semi-soft, with a mild flavor and a distinctive herbaceous aroma.

**CASALINA:** A soft, fresh cheese made from pasteurized milk, Casalina's taste is delicate, with a pleasantly sour note on the palate.

**CASATELLA TREVIGIANA:** A fresh cheese made from pasteurized whole milk, Casatella Trevigiana is soft and creamy, almost buttery, with a bit of contrasting tanginess.

**COMELICO:** Produced only from raw milk, the cheese has a thin rind, soft texture, and delicate flavor.

**FODOM:** Made from partially skimmed milk and aged for about two months, Fodom is a delicately flavored, semi-soft to semi-hard cheese.

**FORMAIO EMBRIAGO (OR UBRIACO):** A semi-soft cheese that has been bathed in grape pomace (skins left over from making wine) and freshly pressed red wine for a few days to preserve the dark purple rind of the cheese. This "inebriated" cheese is quite aromatic, with a delicate flavor and an exciting finish of grape and wine.

**MONTE VERONESE D'ALLEVO (DOP):** Relatively low in fat, this cheese has been made for centuries from the raw milk of cows raised on mountainside pastures. When aged between six months and two years, this becomes a perfect cheese for either grating or eating; the flavors become more complex as it ages. Cheese labeled simply as Monte Veronese (DOP) is a full-fat version that is aged for one month, and is much softer in texture and quite delicate in flavor.

**MORLACCO:** Morlacco is a soft cheese with a briny flavor and a soft, thin rind.

**RICOTTA AFFUMICATA:** This smoked ricotta cheese is produced from the whey of cow's milk. During a week's aging, the cheese is smoked over wood fires. When released immediately, this low-fat cheese is soft, with a salty/smoky flavor. After a month of aging, the smoked cheese turns hard and can be used for grating.

## LIGURIA

Liguria, located in northwest Italy, is one of the nation's smallest regions, a thin strip of rocky and mountainous land bordered by Piedmont to the north, Emilia-Romagna to the east, Tuscany to the southeast, and France to the west. Liguria forms a large coastal area resting on the Ligurian Sea. Liguria is somewhat isolated, as it is surrounded by the sea and enclosed by the Alps and Apennines mountain ranges. The major cities in Liguria are its capital, Genoa, as well as La Spezia, Savona, and San Remo.

Liguria is renowned for the Cinque Terre, a particularly rugged section of coastline that includes five cliffside villages ("Five Lands"). From north to south the villages are Monterosso al Mare, Vernazza, Corniglia, Manarola, and Riomaggiore. Cinque Terre has been declared an Italian national park, as well as a UNESCO World Heritage site. Not accessible by car, the terraced lands of the Cinque Terre are connected by trains, boats, and some of the most difficult and beautiful walking paths in the world.

### Food notes: Liguria

Because of its location on the Ligurian Sea, Liguria thrives on seafood, including sea bass, mussels, squid, scallops, oysters, lobsters, prawns, and sardines. The anchovies of Monterosso have received the coveted DOP (Denominazione di Origine Protteta) from the Italian government and European Union. However, the cooking traditions of the region also feature vegetables and greens, mushrooms, and herbs. The most important plants here are basil and garlic, the basis for the world-renowned pesto. In fact, the basil from Liguria is so prized that *basilico genovese* has been awarded its own DOP status.

Pasta in Liguria is based on wheat, and records show that Ligurians were producing *maccheroni* as early as the thirteenth century, even before that famous son of Genoa, Christopher Columbus, sailed to the Americas. Of course, the favorite sauce with pasta in this region is pesto. Liguria is the home of focaccia breads, often flavored with basil and other herbs, sometimes with onions, sometimes with cheeses. They are a common site in Ligurian bakeries and a regional favorite (see recipes, pages 25–27).

Olive Oil: DOP extra-virgin oil whose name will appear on the bottle label: Riviera Ligure.

Salumi include Salame di Sant'Olcese and Salame Felino, salamis produced from pigs fed largely on acorns, hazelnuts, and chestnuts. The ubiquitous "Genoa salami" (which, unlike the two salamis just cited, contains garlic) is a style that may or may not have originated in Genoa, but it is not currently a product of Liguria.

### Wine notes: Liguria

Liguria produces very little wine for export to the United States. Because of the rugged, mountainous terrain, there are few acres of fine vineyards, and those acres are farmed by small producers: artisanal growers and winemakers. Should you visit Liguria, the white wines of the Cinque Terre, as well as the reds and whites from the Colli di Luni area, produced from grapes grown on the border with Tuscany, are worth seeking out and enjoying.

### Cheese notes: Liguria

The classic cheeses of Liguria, most of them made from cow's milk, and some of them from goat or sheep's milk, are not well known in the American market because they are not regularly imported to these shores. There are no DOP cheeses produced in Liguria. Both Parmigiano-Reggiano (see page 10) and Pecorino Romano cheeses (see page 19), produced outside of Liguria, are important components for pesto.

# Central Italy

## EMILIA-ROMAGNA

The region of Emilia-Romagna, considered part of central Italy, is in fact the gateway to northern Italy. Emilia-Romagna is bordered by the Adriatic Sea to the east, Le Marche and Tuscany to the south, Liguria to the west, and Lombardy and Veneto to the north.

When it comes to food, the region is perhaps Italy's most well known, due to the iconic foodstuffs and dishes of Emilia-Romagna: Parmigiano-Reggiano cheese; Prosciutto di Parma; balsamic vinegar (aceto balsamico) from Modena; tagliatelle with Bolognese sauce from Bologna; tortellini from Emilia; cappelletti pasta from Reggio; cappellacci pasta stuffed with squash from Ferrara; garganelli and passatelli pastas from Romagna; and of course, lasagne. Extraordinary pork products include mortadella from Bologna, culatello from Zibello, and zampone from Modena.

## Food notes: Emilia-Romagna

Some of the most important foods of Emilia-Romagna include:

Olive Oils: DOP extra-virgin oils whose name will appear on the bottle label: Brisighella, Cartoceto, Colline di Romagna.

Vinegars (DOP): Aceto Balsamico Tradizionale di Modena and Aceto Balsamico Tradizionale di Reggio Emilia

Salumi (fresh and cured meats) include: Coppa Piacentina (cured pork salami; DOP), Cotechino di Modena (fresh sausage made for slicing from pork, fatback, and pork rind), Culatello di Zibello (cured, aged ham, a variation of Prosciutto; DOP), Mortadella di Bologna (finely ground cured pork sausage with pork fat), Pancetta Piacentina (cured bacon; DOP), Prosciutto di Modena and Prosciutto di Parma (cured, aged hams; DOP), Salame Piacentino (cured pork salami; DOP), Salamini Italiani alla Cacciatore (a small, pocket-size pork sausage; DOP); Vitellone Bianco dell'Appennino Centrale (veal), and Zampone di Modena (similar to cotechino).

## Wine notes: Emilia-Romagna

In the American market, Emilia-Romagna is widely represented by one wine, Lambrusco, made from a red grape of the same name. Lambrusco can be made as a white, rosé, or red wine and is often frizzante (semi-sparkling). A small amount of fine dry red Lambrusco is available in the American market, but you really have to search for it.

While some wine aficionados may not respect the simplicity and popularity of fizzy Lambrusco, the original screw-cap wine, we have found few wines that are a better match for the famous foods of Emilia-Romagna: Prosciutto di Parma and Parmigiano-Reggiano cheese. Try all three—the wine, the ham, and the cheese—with some good bread and see if you don't agree.

Albana di Romagna is a white wine from the region; most often the type sold in the United States is dry. Albana di Romagna is a reliable, medium-bodied, tasty sip, but also make sure to look for Sangiovese di Romagna, a well-made, fruit-forward, medium-bodied red that is extremely food-friendly and extremely well priced.

## Cheese notes: Emilia-Romagna

Although Emilia-Romagna produces several fine cheeses from the milk of both cows and sheep, it also produces the most famous cheese in Italy, and one of the most famous cheeses in the world—Parmigiano-Reggiano (DOP). Much imitated throughout the world, no "Parmesan" cheese comes close to the aroma, texture, and especially the flavor of Parmigiano-Reggiano.

Parmigiano-Reggiano: Made from cow's milk—both the evening milking and the following day's morning milking—Parmigiano-Reggiano is made to exacting standards: tiny granules of cheese curd are set in molds for about three days, in order to drain moisture; the cheese is placed in a salt brine for 24 days, and then is aged for at least one year; many of the cheeses are aged longer.

In the United States, Parmigiano-Reggiano is known mostly as a grating cheese, and it serves that purpose wonderfully. But crumbly, flaky, rough-textured Parmigiano-Reggiano is an extraordinary cheese for the table, to be served after a meal or as a snack with a fine wine—white, red, or sparkling, dry or sweet. As a table cheese, Parmigiano-Reggiano has no equal.

To make sure that you are purchasing the genuine article, look for the imprint of the Parmigiano-Reggiano consorzio (the group of registered producers), the code number of the dairy that produced the cheese (no names are used), and the production date. True Parmigiano-Reggiano is expensive, and worth every penny.

### TUSCANY (TOSCANA)

Tuscany (Toscana), with its extraordinary cities of Florence and Siena, its picturesque towns and villages, its countryside vineyards, and its Maremma seacoast, is the most-visited of any of Italy's twenty provinces. With its culture and history derived from the ancient Etruscans (starting in the sixth century B.C.) and the 200-year rule of the Medici (from 1523 to 1737), Tuscany is a magnet for tourists from all over the world.

Tuscany is famous for its wines, a bit less so for its food, perhaps because the food of Tuscany is so simple, letting the quality of the ingredients stand out in the classical dishes. Cooking in Tuscany is based in cucina povera—the food of the poor—and features soups of vegetables and beans (the Tuscans are known in Italy as mangia fagioli, or bean eaters) drizzled with local olive oil. Tuscany is also known for the use of fresh herbs in its cooking, especially tarragon, rosemary, and sage. Traditionally, bread (pane sciocco) is unsalted, and it creates a blank canvas for soups, stews, and salads, including the famous tomato-bread salad panzanella, one of the world's greatest "leftovers."

## Food notes: Tuscany

Olive Oils: DOP extra-virgin oils whose name will appear on the bottle label: Chianti Classico, Lucca, and Terre di Siena.

Salumi include: Lardo di Colonnata (cured pig fat with rosemary and other herbs), Mortadella di Bologna (finely ground cured pork sausage with pork fat), Prosciutto Toscano (raw, cured ham; DOP), Salamini Italiani alla Cacciatore (a small, pocket-size pork sausage; DOP), Vitellone Bianco dell'Appennino Centrale (veal), Soppressata (dry-cured salami), Biroldo (blood sausage), and wild boar salumi.

## Wine notes: Tuscany

Tuscany produces some of Italy's most famous traditional reds, using the Sangiovese grape as the backbone of the wines. Tuscany is also home to some of Italy's most modern wines, the "Super Tuscans." These wines, which range in price from relative bargains to wildly expensive, focus on Sangiovese as well, but also on international grapes such as Cabernet Sauvignon, Merlot, and Syrah.

The most notable dry white wine from Tuscany is Vernaccia di San Gimignano, produced in the vineyards surrounding San Gimignano, a medieval town perched on top of a hill. A light to medium-bodied wine, Vernaccia di San Gimignano pairs well with seafood and shellfish.

### The Reds

The wines that have made Tuscany famous are its traditional reds, all based on the Sangiovese grape, including the following wines:

**CHIANTI:** The image of this wine was once so bad that the name for the traditional straw-wrapped Chianti bottle, *fiasco*, entered the English language as a term meaning something that's a disaster. Those days are gone. Today's Chianti, especially Chianti Classico, is delicious and food-friendly. You can buy a fruit-forward wine labeled as just *Chianti* from a good producer for $10 to $15 (good with vegetables, fish, or meats); Chianti Classico starts at about $15 and stops before $30 (a little more power and complexity in this wine; food can be a bit heartier); and Chianti Classico Riserva starts at about $20 and climbs to about $40, depending on vintage and producer (a powerful and complex wine, great with braised and grilled meats). Also look for Chianti Rufina, Chianti Colli Senesi, Chianti Colli Fiorentini, and other wines featuring the name of any of the eight Chianti subregions—great wines with extremely reasonable prices.

**VINO NOBILE DI MONTEPULCIANO:** It's a mouthful to say, but Vino Nobile di Montepulciano is also a mouthful of delicious wine at an affordable price, often less than $25. For that money, you get a world-class wine that is irrepressibly delicious. The full-bodied wine is fragrant, with herbal and spice notes, and mature black and red fruits on the palate.

**CARMIGNANO:** With Sangiovese as its base, Carmignano, a wine from the vineyards surrounding Florence, can include as much as 20 percent Cabernet Sauvignon or Cabernet Franc in the finished wine. This is a limited-production, elegant wine, with the aroma of rose petals and black currants, as well as wild black fruit flavors. If you've never tasted Carmignano, it can be a revelation. Carmignano is usually priced less than $30.

**BRUNELLO DI MONTALCINO:** Many people believe that Brunello di Montalcino is consistently the finest red wine produced in Italy. It is an extraordinary wine, certainly the most powerful example of wine made from Sangiovese grapes; this is a wine that can and should age for years, and some of the riserva wines for a lifetime. Big and brawny but at the same time delicately balanced, Brunello di Montalcino is definitely a special-occasion wine, with retail prices starting at more than $60 and rising to the heavens for older, sought-after wines. For those who can afford it, the experience of tasting a great Brunello di Montalcino is priceless.

**ROSSO DI MONTALCINO:** Like Brunello, Rosso di Montalcino is made from 100 percent Sangiovese grapes picked in and around the same vineyards as the more esteemed wine, and it is made only by Brunello di Montalcino producers. For less than $30 at retail, you can enjoy some hints of Brunello in a wine that is enjoyable either right out of the bottle or within a few years—your choice.

**MORELLINO DI SCANSANO:** This red from Tuscany is just now making a bit of a splash in the American market. Morellino di Scansano, from the Maremma—southern coastal Tuscany—is made from Sangiovese grapes and is an earthy, rich, and complex wine. Morellino (one of dozens of alternative names for Sangiovese) is often priced less than $25 and worth a lot more. The riserva wines are more expensive (about $35) and are glorious.

**SUPER TUSCANS:** There are hundreds of these wines produced throughout Tuscany, and some of them represent the most expensive wines produced in all of Italy. There are a few bargains available, however. Following is a list, by no means nearly complete, of some of the best-known "Super Tuscans" (*asterisk indicates a good bargain): Aprelis*, Borgoforte*, Cepparello, Col di Sasso*, Dogajolo*, Excelsus, Guado al Tasso, La Brancaia, Le Pergole Torte, Luce, Lupicaia, Masseto, Oreno, Ornellaia, Promis, Sangioveto, Sassicaia, Sassoalloro, Solaia, Spargolo, Summus, Tignanello, Tinscvil, Villa Pillo*

## Cheese notes: Tuscany

Tuscany is known for its Pecorino cheese; Pecorino Toscano has earned DOP status. Pecorino Toscano is made from sheep's milk and is produced as either a soft cheese (aged for a minimum of 20 days) or a hard cheese (aged for at least four months). Both the soft and hard versions have an edible yellow-tinged rind.

Other artisan cheeses from Tuscany, all made from sheep's milk, include: Caciotta Toscana, Marzolino del Chianti, Pecorino Bacellone, Pecorino della Garfagnana, Pecorino di Montagna, Pecorino di Pienza, Pecorino Senese, and a soft, fresh cheese, Raviggiolo di Pecora.

### UMBRIA

Umbria, in central Italy, is bordered by Tuscany (Toscana) to the north and west, the Marches (Le Marche) to the east, and Latium (Lazio) to the south. The terrain of Umbria is mostly hilly or mountainous. The three major cities in Umbria are Perugia, its capital and home to one of Italy's finest universities; Assisi, famous for St. Francis; and Spoleto, best known for the Festival dei Due Mondi (Festival of the Two Worlds), a famous celebration of music and art held each year. The fourth-smallest region in Italy, with a population of less than a million people, Umbria is known as the "green heart of Italy." This landlocked region is truly green for about 10 months of the year (excepting the dry months of August and September).

## Food notes: Umbria

Because of its location, Umbrians have always relied on the land for their sustenance, be it local produce, herbs, lentils, cardoons, wild mushrooms, meats, cheeses, or olive oils. Umbria is known throughout the culinary world for its egg pasta, tagliatelle, and large loaves of unsalted bread baked in wood-fired ovens (pane casareccio).

Olive Oil: DOP (designated and protected origin) extra virgin oil whose name will appear on the bottle label: Umbria. The region produces some of Italy's finest olive oils.

Salumi include: Mazzafegati (spicy liver sausages flavored with pine nuts, raisins, and orange rinds), Prosciutto di Norcia; Salamini Italiani alla Cacciatore (a small, pocket-size pork sausage; DOP), and Vitellone Bianco dell'Appennino Centrale (veal).

## Wine notes: Umbria

Although Umbria lives in the shadow of its neighbor Tuscany when it comes to discussions of fine Italian wines, Umbria produces excellent wines of its own, the best of which are still a secret to the American wine public.

One white wine from Umbria has had great success in the United States: Orvieto. Look for Orvieto Classico, easy to find and a great bargain—generally $12 to $17.

Lungarotti is a producer who has had great success with its Rubesco, a reasonably priced Sangiovese-Canaiolo red blend from the Torgiano wine district. Rubesco is a full-bodied, hearty, complex, but food-friendly red. The wine is reasonably priced at retail, usually less than $20.

Sagrantino di Montefalco is just beginning to gather steam in the American market. This extraordinary red is unique thanks to its singular grape, Sagrantino. Inky, full, and rich, with just the right acidity, it is one of the world's great wines. It is expensive and can be found mostly on fine Italian restaurant wine lists and in some better wine stores.

## Cheese notes: Umbria

Umbria does not have a rich cheese-making tradition. Parts of Umbria (and Latium) are included in the Pecorino Toscano DOP (see Tuscany, page 11), and this sheep's milk cheese is used both for eating and for cooking as a grating cheese.

### LATIUM (LAZIO)

The region of Latium (Lazio) is named for the ancient Latin tribe that became the Romans. It is located in Italy's center and is anchored by the nation's capital, Rome. Latium is bordered by the Tyrrhenian Sea to the west, Abruzzo, Molise, and The Marches to the east, Campania to the south, and Umbria and Tuscany to the north. About six million people live in the region; more than four million of them live in Rome.

The food culture of Latium is based on its agricultural heritage. Historically, Latium, which is relatively wide and flat, focused on animals raised on pasture lands, particularly lamb. Fruits, vegetables, herbs, and spices are an important part of the traditional diet and traditional cooking. Artichokes are a particularly important vegetable in Latium, along with beans, peas, and lettuces. Strawberries and watermelons from the region are superb. Mint, cloves, and rosemary can be found in many traditional dishes. Since Vatican City is located within Rome, religious and spiritual life has historically had an impact on the cooking of Latium, in particular on fish and vegetable dishes. The Jewish community of Rome has also had an impact on the classic dishes of the region (such as carciofi alla giudea: deep-fried artichokes).

## Food notes: Latium

Important foods produced in Latium include:

Olive Oils: DOP extra-virgin oils whose name will appear on the bottle label: Canino, Sabina, and Tuscia.

Salumi include: Mortadella di Bologna (finely ground cured pork sausage with pork fat); Salamini Italiani alla Cacciatore (a small, pocket-size pork sausage; DOP); and Vitellone Bianco dell'Appennino Centrale (veal).

## Wine notes: Latium

In the American market, just as it is in the Italian capital city of Rome, Latium is all about Frascati, an inexpensive, fruity, fragrant, simple, crisp, light, and dry white wine. Frascati works well as an accompaniment to light, simple dishes, especially fish or deep-fried artichokes, a historic staple of Rome's Jewish ghetto. Often overlooked, Frascati is a favorite for warm weather, when you want to sip something that does not demand your attention but is tasty, especially when dining al fresco.

Est! Est!! Est!!! di Montefiascone is the stuff of Italian legend. This refreshing white wine has lovely aromatics, and those found in the American market are pleasant, especially with fried foods.

## Cheese notes: Latium

Consistent with its culinary history, most cheeses from Latium are produced from sheep's milk. Surprisingly, Pecorino Romano, one of Italy's best-known cheeses is not produced commercially in Latium (or its capital, Rome), but in Latium. Although the sheep's whey-based ricotta cheese that is produced throughout Italy is known by many as "Ricotta Romana," the original fresh ricotta is still made here. Cacciotta Romana, a fresh, semi-soft sheep's milk cheese, can sometimes be found in the United States.

### THE MARCHES (LE MARCHE)

The Marches (Le Marche) region is mostly hilly and mountainous, but with a dramatic eastern border on the Adriatic Sea. To the north of The Marches lies Emilia-Romagna, to the west are Tuscany and Umbria, with Abruzzo to the south. About 1.5 million people live in the region, mostly in small towns. Though much of The Marches is industrial, with many small, family-owned businesses as well as large manufacturers, there are lovely villas and resorts found on the region's coastline, as well as picturesque restored towns and villages throughout the region.

## Food notes: The Marches

The region is known for its fine seafood provided by the bounty of the Adriatic Sea. Sardines, red mullet, sole, mollusks, crustaceans, and baccalà—dried cod—are important ingredients in the cuisine of The Marches. The region's recipes are influenced by its neighbor, Emilia-Romagna, especially where pasta and salumi are concerned. The Marches is second only to the Piedmont region for the hunting and gathering of tartufi bianchi—white truffles—which abound in the late autumn and winter.

The Ascolana olives—olive ascolane del Piceno—that thrive in the groves of the province of Piceno are so prized that they have received their own DOP (Denominazione di Origine Protetta) from the Italian government. The giant olives—historically known as Picenae, for their home province—are sold either in brine or stuffed, often with meat, cheese, and bread, and deep-fried.

Salumi include: Mortadella di Bologna (finely ground cured pork sausage with pork fat), Prosciutto di Carpegna (a salt-cured ham; DOP), and Vitellone Bianco dell'Appennino Centrale (veal).

## Wine notes: The Marches

The most famous wine in The Marches is Verdicchio; about 20 million bottles are produced each year, and Verdicchio is second only to Soave (from Veneto) as the most imported Italian white wine in the American market. Verdicchio is an accessible, reasonably priced, and high-quality wine. A medium-bodied dry white with an herbaceous nose and green apple acidity to refresh the palate, Verdicchio at its best shows off a bit of hazelnut in the finish to add some complexity. It's a great match for fish and poultry.

Two reds from The Marches have made some small inroads in the United States, Rosso Conero and Rosso Piceno. Based on the Montepulciano grape, both are appealing, medium-bodied wines meant to be drunk young, within three to five years of their vintage date. These are great pasta wines that would also be wonderful accompanying grilled salmon or white or red meat dishes.

## Cheese notes: The Marches

The region is best known for its DOP cheese with ancient origins: Casciotta d'Urbino. Traditionally made from two milkings or raw sheep's milk (about 75 percent) and raw cow's milk (about 25 percent), Casciotta d'Urbino has a mild flavor with a crumbly but soft, fatty texture.

Other cheeses produced in The Marches are mostly made from sheep's milk, including the unusual Cacio a Forma di Limone, molded in the shape of lemons, and dry-cured with salt and lemon zest, which after brushing with flour and water, adheres to the rind. The lemony tang is immediately apparent in the flavor of the cheese.

# Southern Italy

### ABRUZZI (ABRUZZO) AND MOLISE

Abruzzo, a mountainous region of Italy, is located in south-central Italy, about 40 miles east of Rome, on the Adriatic seacoast. The capital of Abruzzo is the village of L'Aquila; a little more than a million people live in the region. There are several preserved and picturesque historic hill towns of both the medieval era and the Renaissance era in this region, some of which are protected as part of a national and regional park system.

Molise, a very small region, was until 1963 part of the combined region of Abruzzo-Molise; it features a mountainous and hilly landscape. Bordered by Abruzzo to the northwest, Latium to the west, and Campania and Puglia to the south, Molise has a dramatic seacoast on the Adriatic. With no major cities, Molise contains several hilltop provinces, the best known of which are Campobasso, Isernia, and Termoli. A total of about 320,000 people live in Molise; only the Valle d'Aosta region has a smaller population.

## Food notes: Abruzzo and Molise

The important foods produced in the Abruzzo and Molise regions include:

Olive Oils: DOP extra-virgin oils whose name will appear on the bottle label: Molise, and from Abruzzo: Aprutino Pescarese, Colline, Teatine, and Pretuziano delle Colline Teramane

Salumi include: Vitellone Bianco dell'Appennino (veal produced from calves that graze in mountain pastures), Mortadelline di Campotosto (a smoked pork salami with a vein of lardo running through it, flavored with wild fennel, and packaged in a hand-sewn casing), prosciutto affumicato (smoked ham), Salamini Italiani alla Cacciatore (a small, pocket-size pork sausage; DOP), and soppressata (dry-cured salami).

## Wine notes: Abruzzo and Molise

Montepulciano d'Abruzzo is a red wine that is enjoyable in its youth; it's quite fruity and easy to drink. Widely available in the United States, this wine is developing a good reputation among wine drinkers who enjoy a good, food-friendly wine (especially with barbecue and roasts) at a very reasonable price. Montepulciano d'Abruzzo is also available as a dry but refreshing rosé (rosato), too.

Trebbiano d'Abruzzo is a simple, straightforward white wine that will work well when paired with lighter fish dishes.

Molise produces very little wine, and most of it is consumed in the region. When visiting, look for Biferno, which is made as either a blended red or blended white wine.

## Cheese notes: Abruzzo and Molise

Some of Abruzzo's best cheeses are several Pecorino cheeses made from sheep's milk. The cheeses include:

**PECORINO ABRUZZESE:** This is a firm cheese that is aged for about two months before release.

**PECORINO DEL PARCO:** Produced only in those towns included in Abruzzi's national park districts, this is a semi-hard cheese that is aged a minimum of two months before release.

**PECORINO DI CAPRACOTTA:** This is an ancient cheese that is semi-soft, aromatic, and flavorful.

## CAMPANIA

The region of Campania is where southern Italy begins. With the vital seaside city of Naples, the looming presence of Mount Vesuvius, the Amalfi Coast, and the islands of Capri and Ischia, Campania is a magnet for tourists. The soil is mostly volcanic (tufo), and it is highly productive in the coastal zones of Campania, where tomatoes, eggplants, lettuces, garlic, potatoes, peas, figs, apricots, lemons, and cherries are just some of the produce that grows in abundance. The Tyrrhenian Sea provides the shellfish and mollusks that are so important in the cooking of Campania.

### Food notes: Campania

Perhaps the best known tomato for canning and cooking is grown in the shadow of Mount Vesuvius: the San Marzano tomato (pomodoro di San Marzano). This tomato, grown mostly on small family farms, is canned locally and exported all over the world. Lemon groves dot the steep terraces of the Amalfi Coast, and lemons (limoni Costa d'Amalfi) are harvested throughout the year. Lemons from the Sorrentine Peninsula and from Capri—limoni di Sorrento—find their way into the popular Italian liqueur, limoncello, a delicious sweet-sour syrupy drink that is increasingly popular in the United States as a digestivo after a fine Italian meal.

In Cilento, some of the finest figs in the world are cultivated and are later dried for eating and enjoying all year round. In the province of Avellino, chestnuts are grown in the mountains, and those from the Giffoni area are especially prized for their flavor and fragrance. Artichokes (carciofi) from Campania also enjoy a stellar reputation.

DOP extra-virgin oils whose name will appear on the bottle label: Cilento, Colline Salernitane, and Penisola Sorrentina. Campania's best olive oils have recognizable fruity notes (especially apples) and a moderately black pepper finish on the palate.

### Wine notes: Campania

Campania produces less than 5 percent of Italy's wines, but what beautiful wines they are. Taurasi, made from the Aglianico grape, is known for its power and complexity. The two best-known white wines of Campania, Greco di Tufo and Fiano di Avellino, are medium- to full-bodied white wines that marry well with fish stews, shellfish, and white meats. Also look for varietal-labeled Falanghina from Campania, a wonderfully refreshing and mineral-driven medium-bodied white that is quite reasonably priced.

### Cheese notes: Campania

Campania is best known for its very special fresh mozzarella made from buffalo's milk (Mozzarella di Bufala Campana DOP). This is a very white, very soft, moist cheese sold in its own liquid. Buffalo mozzarella has a tangy, almost yogurt-like taste, with a grassy aroma. It is an extraordinary delicacy that is completely different in taste and texture than mozzarella made from cow's milk.

## BASILICATA

Basilicata is a mountainous region located in southern Italy, with coastlines on the Tyrrhenian Sea to the west and the Ionian Sea to the east. With less than 600,000 people, Basilicata's citizenry makes up only about 1 percent of Italy's population.

### Food notes: Basilicata

Salumi include: capocollo (air-dried ham made from pork head (capo) and shoulder (collo), and seasoned with sweet or hot peppers), luganica (very spicy sausages), salsiccia (a fresh sausage made from pork meat and pork fat), salame, and prosciutto.

### Wine notes: Basilicata

Basilicata, a region that produces only 1 percent of Italy's wine, is known in the United States for one wine made solely from one grape, the Aglianico, which is grown on the steep slopes of Mount Vulture. That wine is Aglianico del Vulture. A full-flavored, deeply colored, often age-worthy red, this earthy wine can be a powerhouse, but it's always food-friendly with hearty dishes. Many producers currently offer American wine consumers great value, because the wine is not yet widely appreciated in the American market. Aglianico del Vulture is most often priced under $20.

## Cheese notes: Basilicata

Basilicata does not produce many varieties of cheese, but their best cheeses are unique in character. Fresh cheeses—Fior di Latte (Mozzarella) and Ricotta—are made throughout the region, as they are in much of Italy. Basilicata's most-prized cheeses include:

**BURRINO:** This is a double-layered cheese with an almost-round shape, often with a knob at the top of the cheese. Made from the whey of cow's milk, the outside layer of Burrino is a soft cheese with an almost white rind. The inside layer really is butter made from the whey; quite creamy and aromatic.

**CASIEDDU:** Made from goat's milk (two milkings) that has been filtered through fern fronds and a sachet of aromatic herbs, Casieddu can be served fresh (wrapped in brilliantly green fern fronds) or aged. The cheese, soft when young, hardens with age.

**PECORINO DI FILIANO AND PECORINO DI MOLITERNO:** Both cheeses are made from either sheep or goat's milk, or both. Both cheeses have hard rinds and firm consistencies. Pecorino di Moliterno is richer in flavor.

### APULIA (PUGLIA)

Apulia (Puglia) forms the "heel" of the Italian "boot." This southern region is warm and dry, and its land is mostly plain, except for mountains in the north. Farming, especially for olives, wine grapes, almonds, and figs, is the backbone of the local economy, along with commercial fishing; Apulia borders both the Adriatic and Ionian seas. Here, you will find unique buildings (i trulli), which are whitewashed stone structures of ancient design in the shape of beehives that are used both as storage barns and as homes. There are entire communities of trulli homes; probably the most famous is Alberobello, in the province of Bari, where more than 1,000 trulli are situated on terraced land. The trulli of Puglia were declared as protected under the UNESCO World Heritage laws in 1996.

## Food notes: Puglia

The produce of Puglia, an important part of the daily diet, includes broccoli, broccoli rabe, cauliflower, chickpeas, eggplant, fava beans, lentils, and tomatoes. Pasta, made from durum wheat, is a mainstay in Puglia, where there are more types eaten at home and in restaurants than in any other part of Italy.

Puglia is known for the quality of its olive oils, which have a noticeably fruity taste. Five of Puglia's growing regions have been granted DOP status; extra-virgin oils whose name will appear on the bottle label are Colline di Brindisi, Dauno, Terra di Bari, Terra d'Otranto, and Terre Tarentine. Olive oil from Puglia can be some of Italy's best, and it is definitely worth seeking out.

## Wine notes: Puglia

A southern region that not long ago was known as Italy's largest producer of indifferent wine, Puglia is going through a sea change in the way it thinks about and produces wine for the international market. Puglia's two best-known medium- to full-bodied reds are Salice Salentino and Primitivo di Manduria, the former made mostly from Negroamaro grapes, the latter from 100 percent Primitivo (which is actually the same grape as California's Zinfandel). Both wines are excellent values.

Puglia also produces white wines made from Chardonnay, Sauvignon Blanc, and other "international" wine grapes. Many of Puglia's export wines, both white and red, offer tremendous value and quality.

## Cheese notes: Puglia

Puglia produces cheeses from cow, goat, and sheep's milk, and its best-known cheeses in export markets are Cacioricotta, Burrata, and Scamorza.

**BURRATA:** Made from cow's milk, this is a cheese in a knotted "ball," which is made from stretched curds. The cheese inside the ball is made from both curds and whey and the finished cheese is smooth, buttery, and delicate in flavor.

**CACIORICOTTA:** Made from goat's milk, Cacioricotta is similar to the better-known ricotta, and when served fresh is soft in texture and mild in flavor. Aged cacioricotta is used for grating.

**SCAMORZA:** A sheep's milk cheese, Scamorza is formed in the shape of an oval with a knob on top. Fresh scamorza is a semi-soft cheese, with a slightly buttery flavor. After a bit of aging, the cheese becomes harder, with more concentrated flavor.

## CALABRIA

The region of Calabria forms the toe of the "boot" of Italy, and it is the southernmost region on the Italian mainland. Calabria is bordered by Basilicata to the north, the Ionian Sea to the east, the Tyrrhenian Sea to the west, and the island of Sicily to the southwest. About two million people live in the region, which is about 5,800 square miles. Calabria is mostly mountainous, defined by three mountain regions—Aspromonte in the south, La Sila in central Calabria, and Pollino in the north. The two major cities in the region are Reggio Calabria (only a few miles from the northwest coast of Sicily) and Catanzaro, the capital of Calabria, located on the central-east coast of the region, bordering the Ionian Sea.

### Food notes: Calabria

Calabria grows citrus fruits, wine grapes, olives, and chestnuts. The region is famous for its aromatic and tasty red onions (cipolla rossa di Tropea). DOP status has been granted to Calabria's extraordinary bergamot oranges, bergamotti di Reggio Calabria. Porcini mushrooms grow in abundance, especially throughout the Sila mountain range. Popular meats are lamb, pork, and goat, as well as a wide variety of fish caught in the surrounding oceans. Preserved meats and fish are an important part of traditional Calabrian cuisine (anchovies preserved in olive oil, for example). As in so many other regions of Italy, pasta is a culinary mainstay, and pasta dishes are often paired with local and regional vegetables, especially eggplant, tomatoes, peppers, artichokes, potatoes, asparagus, and beans (fagioli).

Olive Oils: DOP extra-virgin oils whose name will appear on the bottle label: Alto Crotonese, Bruzio, and Lemezia.

Salumi include: dry-cured pork salumi, each of which has been awarded DOP status: Capocollo di Calabria; Pancetta di Calabria; Salsiccia di Calabria; and Soppressata di Calabria.

### Wine notes: Calabria

While the Greeks had Calabria in mind when they called this part of the world Oenotria (Land of the Vine), modern Calabria bears little resemblance to that ancient land of wine. Wine takes a backseat in Calabria's struggling economy to olive oil, grains, citrus, and vegetables. This province produces about 1.5 percent of Italy's wine, and an infinitesimal amount of that wine is exported. However, if you visit Calabria, do as the locals and relaxed tourists do, and enjoy the local vino da tavola served from utilitarian demijohns, oversize glass bottles that hold five gallons of wine that get refilled on a regular basis.

About 90 percent of Calabria's wine is red, and a lot of that wine is based on the Gaglioppo grape, introduced to Calabria by the ancient Greeks. The best-known wine region is Cirò, which produces dry whites, rosés, and reds. Cirò is the stuff of legend, drunk by the athletes celebrating their victorious performances in the ancient Olympics. Cirò whites, made from the Greco grape, are dry, quite fresh, and appealing. The reds and rosés, made from the Gaglioppo grape, tend to be strong and alcoholic. Cirò is exported in tiny amounts to the United States.

### Cheese notes: Calabria

Calabria produces quite a few true artisan cheeses, but very few find their way to the American market. The best-known and widely-available cheese from the region is Caciocavallo Silano (DOP). Caciocavallo Silano is a cow's milk cheese, often pear-shaped, sometimes with a knob formed at the top of the oval. The cheese, which is salted in brine and then aged for at least fifteen days is semi-soft to semi-hard, and a bit stringy. The best cheeses take on a crumbly texture and distinct aromatics. Caciocavallo Silano is most often eaten fresh as a table cheese, but does appear in some classic recipes of Calabria.

## SICILY (SICILIA)

Sicily (Sicilia), the largest region in Italy, is a triangle-shaped island located in the middle of the Mediterranean Sea. Sicily is mountainous, with plains along the southern coastline. The largest volcano in Europe, Mount Etna, is located in northeast Sicily. About five million people live on the island, about 65 percent of them in small towns. Large cities in Sicily include the capital, Palermo, as well as Catania, Messina, and Siracusa.

Agriculture and fishing are very important occupations in Sicily. Fruits and vegetables, such as tomatoes, olives (and some excellent olive oils), artichokes, eggplants, beans, onions, lemons, oranges, and raisins are grown on the island. Prickly pears, grown on the cactus plants found on the slopes of Mount Etna (fichidindia dell'Etna) are famous as a hand fruit, a pastry ingredient, and the basis for an aperitivo liqueur, Ficodì.

Seafood, including sardines, anchovies, tuna, swordfish, cuttlefish, and sea bass, is an important part of Sicilian cuisine. Meat dishes are prepared from rabbit, goat, turkey, lamb, and goose. Pasta and rice, as well as spices—

pepper, cinnamon, nutmeg, clove—and cheeses, especially Pecorino Siciliano, Ragusano, and ricotta, are important elements in Sicilian gastronomy.

Perhaps no region of Italy is as well known for its sweets and desserts as Sicily, where gelato, ice cream, and ices, as well as pastries and cookies, are produced and consumed in abundance. One of the most famous pastries in the world was born in Sicily: cannoli, fried pastries filled with sweet ricotta cheese, sometimes with candied fruits or chocolate bits.

## Food notes: Sicily

Olive Oils: DOP extra-virgin oils whose name will appear on the bottle label: Monte Etna, Monti Iblei, Val di Mazara, Valdemone, Valle del Belice, and Valli Trapanesi. A table olive from the Trapani province, Oliva da Tavola Nocellara del Belice, has also received its own DOP designation.

Bottarga: Salt-cured roe of either tuna, swordfish, or mullet, bottarga is a delicacy that is often called the "caviar of the Mediterranean." Roe is placed in brine for anywhere from eight to twenty hours, and then it is salted on all sides. The roe sacks are tied together, placed under a weight, and salted each day for 40 days, drying the roe. The roe pouches, which shrink in size, are then tied again and sun-dried for about a month. Bottarga is sold in jars, like caviar, and as solid blocks for slicing, and it is also sold as a salty/briny powdered condiment.

## Wine notes: Sicily

Sicily is the largest producer of wine in Italy and over the past decade or so has become one of the country's most exciting wine regions. This excitement becomes real when you taste fine examples made from Sicily's own grape varietals–Nero d'Avola, Frappato, Nerello Mascalese, Catarratto, Inzolia, and Grillo, among many others. Sicily also produces other fine examples of wines made from popular international varietals, especially Chardonnay, Cabernet Sauvignon, and Merlot. Some of the most interesting wines are produced from blends of traditional grapes or from blends of those traditional varietals with the "international" grape varieties.

The reds of Sicily are rustic: earthy, full-bodied, and excellent when paired with red meats and hearty pasta dishes. Nero d'Avola from Sicily has become popular in the American market, and it's easy to see why. A big, earthy, inky, food-friendly red that reflects the sunshine of Sicily in its ripe flavors, Nero d'Avola is a perfect match for hearty dishes such as rich stews.

Sicily's best whites are usually medium-bodied and display a distinctive seaside minerality that makes for an attractive match with fish stews and many other soulful seafood dishes.

Lately, we've also seen quite a bit of Inzolia, a white grape from Sicily, in the American market. The best Inzolia wines have a fresh, fruit-driven flavor, with a subtle finish of hazelnuts. If we've piqued your interest, ask a knowledgeable wine merchant or sommelier to help you find a delicious Inzolia wine. We love Inzolia-based wines with a wide variety of seafood.

The region is famous for its fortified wine, Marsala, available in a wide range of styles (from bone dry to quite sweet). Sicily's best Marsalas can be hard to find in the U.S. export market.

Sicily's export wines are moderately expensive to very expensive, but there are many values to be had in both good whites and reds.

## Cheese notes: Sicily

Sicily is famous for a cheese with ancient origins, Pecorino Siciliano (DOP), made from raw sheep's milk. This pecorino is uncooked, and may be eaten as a fresh cheese (tuma), as a minimally aged salt-cured cheese, or as a cheese that has been aged for a minimum of four months, sometimes with black peppercorns imbedded in the cheese. After aging, Pecorino Siciliano is hard and solid, with a pungent aroma and sharp flavor; perfect for eating or for grating.

Another esteemed cheese from Sicily is Ragusano (DOP), made from cow's milk. Ragusano is uncooked, and shaped into distinctive large blocks, known as scaluni. The cheese is aged for as little as one week, producing a soft cheese with a delicate flavor, or as long as four months, enhancing the intensity of flavor. Ragusano can be used as an eating cheese, a grating cheese, or served in thick slices that have been coated in bread crumbs and deep-fried.

### SARDINIA (SARDEGNA)

Sardinia (Sardegna) is the second-largest island in the Mediterranean; Sicily is the largest. Sardinia's terrain is hilly and rocky, especially along its coasts, but there are relatively few high mountains on the island due to hundreds of thousands of years of erosion of ancient rock formations. The island's climate is mild but in some ways extreme: About 300 days of sunshine are complemented by about two months of rain, mostly in the autumn and winter.

Sardinia's population is relatively small, about 1.65 million people, but life on Sardinia is long, a testament, at least in part, to the Mediterranean diet. The average lifespan of a Sardinian is longer than 80 years, and the island boasts the highest ratio of people over 100 years old in the world when compared to the total island population (about 360 centenarians live on Sardinia). The beaches and coastal towns of Sardinia make the island an active hub for relaxed tourism, and on some parts of this windy island, for surfing.

## Food notes: Sardinia

Because of its varied island flora, Sardinia is known for its honey, the most well known being arbutus, produced by bees attracted to the wild shrub of the same name (also known as corbezzolo, the strawberry tree). In addition, Sardinia is also known for the extraordinary quality of its eucalyptus and chestnut honeys.

Olive Oil: DOP extra-virgin oil whose name will appear on the bottle label: Sardegna

Salumi include: Agnello di Sardegna (tender lamb raised solely on sheep's milk), prosciutto di cinghiale (cured ham made from wild boar), capocollo (also known as coppa; cured pork made from the shoulder and neck of the pig)

As with Sicily, Sardinia is also known for the delicacy bottarga (see page 18), as well as for excellent sea salt and saffron.

## Wine notes: Sardinia

Winemakers on the island of Sardinia have, over the past 10 to 15 years, begun to produce some very fine wines, and American wine consumers have begun to enjoy them. Sardinia's most highly regarded white wine is Vermentino di Gallura, a dry wine from the far north that is the perfect accompaniment to the local pesce alla griglia, grilled fish in olive oil with fresh herbs. Vermentino di Sardegna is just a bit less expensive and easier to find.

Earthy, fruit-driven, full-bodied Sardinian red wines often feature the Cannonau grape (called Grenache in France and the United States). Cannonau di Sardegna and other Cannonau-based reds, sometimes blended with 15 to 20 percent Merlot or Cabernet Sauvignon, are now widely available in the United States. These are great wines to enjoy with pasta, pizza, and meat-based dishes.

With steady improvement in whites and reds for the export market, Sardinia is now on the wine world's map as a region to watch for quality and for excellent value.

## Cheese notes: Sardinia

The cheeses of Sardinia are based largely on the milk of sheep, and secondarily, goats. There are millions of these animals grazing the hardscrabble terrain of the island. The three cheeses for which Sardinia is best known are Pecorino Romano, Pecorino Sardo, and Fiore Sardo, all of them sheep's milk cheeses and all of them registered as DOP (Denominazione di Origine Protetta) food products.

It may surprise many that Pecorino Romano is identified as a Sardinian cheese, since Rome is in the Lazio region, not Sardinia. Starting in the late nineteenth century, due to extraordinary demand for Pecorino Romano, many cheese makers moved their base of operations from Latium to Sardinia, because Sardinia had millions of sheep and a history and culture of making cheese from the milk of those sheep.

Pecorino Romano is made from the morning and evening milkings of the sheep; the milk is filtered and heated. Cheese curds are drained of all whey, and when dry, placed into molds and pressed. The cheese is then dry-salted several times, after which it is aged. Table cheese is aged a minimum of five months, while cheese to be used for grating is aged a minimum of eight months. Pecorino Romano is a hard cheese with a granular, almost rocky appearance, with an intense aroma and a sharp taste.

Pecorino Sardo is made from partially cooked sheep's milk, and is made into either a "sweet" version (a soft cheese) or a "ripened" cheese (a semi-soft to semi-hard cheese that may also be made as a smoked cheese). Most of the milk of Sardinia's seven million goats is utilized for the production of Pecorino Sardo.

Traditionally made from uncooked raw milk, Fiore Sardo is truly an artisinal cheese; its aging takes place in three different areas: the pinnetta—the shepherd's hut—where the cheese is exposed to open fires, creating a delicately smoky aroma and taste; then the cheese rests under dairy roofs; and finally the cheese is sent to cellars, where it is turned and oiled on its rind. Aging lasts anywhere from two months to eight months. The more mature cheeses are extremely hard and crumbly. Fiore Sardo cheeses have an irregular, cylindrical shape.

# Spuntini

Spuntini are little snacks meant to be enjoyed during the day, either before a meal or simply to hold you over until it is time to gather around the table. These tempting dishes include fritters served with salumi, pizza by the slice, bruschetta with a wide array of toppings, piadini, frittatas, and savory pies filled with rice and vegetables.

Focaccia is served on its own, with various toppings, or split and stuffed to make panini sandwiches. Panzanella, a bread salad, and frittatas, a special type of omelet eaten hot or room temperature, epitomizes some important aspects of the Italian ethic when it comes to cooking: enjoy everything, make every bite delicious, and waste nothing.

# Types of spuntini

There are literally hundreds of snacks enjoyed up and down the country. Here, we've gathered some of our favorites.

## FOCACCIA

Focaccia are snack breads typically from Liguria but present in some variations throughout the regions. Because of their richness and various seasonings, they are normally enjoyed, cold or warm, as a stand-alone snack, as a quick meal accompanied with a fresh salad, or as part of any antipasto. Besides being enjoyed as is, focaccia can also be accompanied by salumi and cheeses or split and stuffed to make into flavorful sandwiches. The Focaccia al Rosmarino (see page 27) is perfect for making into panini.

## PANZANELLA

Panzanella may be very popular in restaurants today, but this summer dish is actually very simple and humble. It is moistened bread flavored with ingredients from the garden.

There are different local names for different versions of panzanella, such as:

ricca (for the rich), made by adding black olives, celery heart, boiled carrot, wild fennel, arugula, and Pecorino Toscano to the basic recipe.

del prete (of the priest), made by adding raw sliced carrot, diced prosciutto, diced mozzarella, Italian tuna in oil or mackerel in oil, and capers to the basic recipe.

For something more contemporary and unusual and very refreshing, you might want to try adding cubed watermelon and shredded ricotta salata to the basic recipe.

## FRITTERS

Panissa Fritta (see page 29) and Gnocco Fritto (see page 33) are classic examples of fritters. Panissa is typical of the "street food" that you may find all over the country and may be served along with different types of salumi (Italian cold cuts in general), a fresh ricotta, eggplant stew, zucchini, and so on. Gnocco fritto are a type of savory fried dough from Bologna in Emilia-Romagna, where they are typically served with cold cuts.

## PIZZA

If you have a baking stone, place the pizza directly on the preheated stone. If you don't have the wooden paddle you see in your favorite pizzeria, you can use a flat baking sheet, one with no sides. First, scatter a bit of cornmeal on the pan, and then put the shaped pizza onto the pan. Put the edge of the pan on the far side of the stone and quickly pull (actually, jerk) the pan from underneath the pizza. It should slide right onto the stone, although this maneuver does require a little bit of practice.

## BRUSCHETTA

At its most elemental, bruschetta is a simple piece of good bread (the better the quality of the bread, the better the result will be), grilled or toasted, rubbed with a piece of broken garlic and a generous drizzle of extra-virgin olive oil. Choose a topping according to the season, what you have on hand, what you like, and how much money you'd like to spend!

# Techniques for making spuntini

## SQUASH PUREES

This method works for any hard-skinned squash, including pumpkin, Hubbard, and acorn. The draining step removes extra water from the squash for a richer, deeper flavor and a better texture in dishes like Gnocchi di Zucca (see page 203) and Torta di Riso e Zucca (see page 36).

1. Preheat the oven to 350 degrees F. Cut the squash in half, scoop out the seeds and fibers, and rub the cut sides with a little olive oil. Put them, cut side down, in a roasting pan. Cover the pan with foil and roast the squash until the flesh is very tender (you'll be able to pierce it easily with the tip of a paring knife), about 1 hour.
2. Scoop the tender flesh out of the skin and transfer to a bowl. Use a fork to mash and crush the squash into a coarse puree.
3. Transfer the puree to a strainer lined with a coffee filter or cheesecloth. Set the strainer over a bowl and let the puree drain for at least 2 hours. The puree is ready to be used in other dishes, or it can be stored in a covered container in the refrigerator for up to 5 days.

## BLANCHING GREENS

You can use this basic blanching technique to prepare spinach, kale, chard, escarole, arugula, and other greens. Once the greens are blanched and squeezed dry (see below) , simply sauté them with olive oil and garlic for a delicious side dish.

1. Trim the stems, and remove any split or bruised portions. Remove any wilted or bruised leaves.
2. Some greens, like collards or chard, may have stems that should be either cooked separately from the greens or started in the boiling water before the leaves. To prepare them, cut the stems away from the leaves, and keep them separate. Rinse the stems and cut them into pieces of the size required in your recipe.
3. Clean the leaves in plenty of cold water until there are no more traces of sand or grit. Drain them in a colander.
4. Bring a large pot of salted water to a rolling boil over high heat. If you are cooking greens with study stems like chard, add them to the pot first and cook for 2 to 3 minutes before adding the leaves.
5. Add the cleaned greens all at once and stir to submerge them. Cook uncovered until tender and a deep color, 3 to 4 minutes. Lift the greens out of the water with a sieve or slotted spoon and transfer to a bowl of ice water. After the greens are chilled, drain in a colander for several minutes.
6. If necessary, squeeze the greens as follows: Drape a clean dish towel or a large piece of cheesecloth in a colander. Put the greens in the center of the cloth and gather the edges of the towel around the greens. Tighten the cloth by twisting the edges with one hand. Use the other hand to twist the ball of greens in the opposite direction. Once you have squeezed out the extra liquid, unwrap the greens and chop them as coarse or fine as your recipe requires.

Focaccia Genovese, Focaccia al Rosmarino (page 27), and Focaccia alle Cipolle (page 26).

# Focaccia alla genovese

## GENOESE-STYLE FOCACCIA

The most basic of focaccias, alla Genovese, is seasoned only with olive oil and salt.

**SERVES 8 (MAKES 8 LARGE PIECES)**

DOUGH

**1 cup milk**

**1 tsp sugar**

**1 envelope active dry yeast**

**4 cups all-purpose or "00" flour, plus as needed for dusting dough and work surface**

**¾ cup water, about 70 degrees F**

**5 tbsp olive oil**

**1 tsp kosher salt**

TOPPING

**2 tbsp olive oil**

**1 tbsp water**

**1 tsp kosher salt**

1. To make the dough, warm the milk to about 100 degrees F over very low heat (this will happen quickly; don't let it boil). Remove it from the heat, let it cool slightly, and then add the sugar and yeast. Stir until dissolved. Let the mixture rest for 15 minutes; you will see a thick foam form on the surface.
2. Combine the flour, yeast mixture, water, 2 tablespoons of the olive oil, and salt in a large bowl and mix by hand or with a dough hook using a stand mixer until a smooth, elastic dough forms, 10 to 15 minutes.
3. Dust the surface of the dough with a sprinkling of flour, cover the bowl tightly with plastic wrap, and let the dough rise at room temperature until it doubles in bulk, about 1 hour.
4. Transfer the dough to a floured work surface. Press the dough out into a rough square, and then pull the 4 corners in toward the center. Turn it over so the upper surface is smooth. Drape the ball of dough with the plastic you used during the first rise and let it rest until it has relaxed, about 30 minutes.
5. Brush a baking sheet (with sides) or a jelly-roll pan liberally with 2 tablespoons of the olive oil. Uncover the dough and spread and pull it into a rectangle about the same dimensions as your pan. Lift the dough into the pan and brush the surface with the remaining 1 tablespoon of olive oil. Drape the plastic wrap over the surface and let the dough rise until it has nearly doubled in volume, about 30 minutes.
6. Preheat the oven to 500 degrees F. Position a rack in the bottom third of the oven.
7. To make the topping, whisk together the olive oil, water, and salt; it should thicken. Remove the plastic from the dough and pour the oil mixture over the dough. Use your fingertips to press dimples into the dough in a random pattern.
8. Bake the focaccia until the edges are slightly golden in color, 10 to 12 minutes. Remove from the oven and cool on a rack for about 10 minutes. The focaccia is ready to cut into squares and serve.

# Focaccia alle cipolle

## FOCACCIA WITH ONIONS

This is another version of a focaccia, this time adding potatoes and onion for a rich, moist bread. (See the photograph on page 24.)

**SERVES 8 (MAKES 8 LARGE PIECES)**

DOUGH

**1¾ cups water, about 70 degrees F, added as needed**

**1 envelope active dry yeast**

**5 cups bread flour, sifted, plus as needed for dusting dough and work surface**

**3 cups Potato Puree (page 186)**

**2 tsp kosher salt**

**2 tbsp olive oil**

TOPPING

**1 tbsp olive oil**

**12 thick slices yellow onion (about 1 medium)**

**2 tsp kosher salt**

1. To make the dough, combine the water and yeast in the bowl of a stand mixer. Stir to distribute the yeast, and let the mixture rest for a few minutes to rehydrate the yeast.
2. Add the flour, potato puree, and salt. Mix on low speed with a dough hook until a smooth, elastic dough forms, 10 to 15 minutes.
3. Dust the surface of the dough with a sprinkling of flour, cover the bowl tightly with plastic wrap, and let the dough rise at room temperature until it doubles in bulk, about 1 hour.
4. Transfer the dough to a floured work surface. Press the dough out into a rough square, and then pull the 4 corners in toward the center. Turn it over so the upper surface is smooth. Drape the ball of dough with the plastic you used during the first rise and let it rest until it has relaxed, about 30 minutes.
5. Brush a baking sheet (with sides) or a jelly-roll pan liberally with the olive oil. Uncover the dough and spread and pull it into a rectangle about the same dimensions as your pan. Lift the dough into the pan and stretch it out into an even layer that fills the pan.
6. To make the topping, brush the surface of the dough with the olive oil. Cover the surface with the onion (separate the slices into rings). Drape the plastic wrap over the surface and let the dough rise until it has nearly doubled in volume, about 30 minutes.
7. Preheat the oven to 350 degrees F. Position a rack in the bottom third of the oven.
8. Before the focaccia goes into the oven, use your fingertips to gently press dimples into the dough in a random pattern. Sprinkle the salt over the surface.
9. Bake the focaccia until the edges are slightly golden in color, 10 to 12 minutes. Remove from the oven and cool on a rack for about 10 minutes. The focaccia is ready to cut into squares and serve.

# Focaccia al rosmarino

## FOCACCIA WITH ROSEMARY

This is another version of a focaccia, this time adding rosemary, that is perfect to serve, cold or warm, as a snack or as part of any antipasto. (See the photograph on page 24.)

**SERVES 8 (MAKES 8 LARGE PIECES)**

DOUGH

**2 cups water, about 70 degrees F, added as needed**

**1 envelope active dry yeast**

**5 cups bread flour, sifted, plus as needed for dusting dough and work surface**

**2 tsp kosher salt**

**2 tbsp olive oil**

TOPPING

**1 tbsp olive oil**

**1 tbsp coarsely chopped rosemary**

**1 tsp kosher salt**

1. To make the dough, combine the water and yeast in the bowl of a stand mixer. Stir to distribute the yeast, and let the mixture rest for a few minutes to rehydrate the yeast.
2. Add the flour and salt. Mix on low speed with a dough hook until a smooth, elastic dough is formed, 10 to 15 minutes.
3. Dust the surface of the dough with a sprinkling of flour, cover the bowl tightly with plastic wrap, and let the dough rise at room temperature until it doubles in bulk, about 1 hour.
4. Transfer the dough to a floured work surface. Press the dough out into a rough square, and then pull the 4 corners in toward the center. Turn it over so the upper surface is smooth. Drape the ball of dough with the plastic you used during the first rise and let it rest until it has relaxed, about 30 minutes.
5. Brush a baking sheet (with sides) or a jelly-roll pan liberally with the olive oil. Uncover the dough and spread and pull it into a rectangle about the same dimensions as your pan. Lift the dough into the pan and stretch it out into an even layer that fills the pan.
6. To make the topping, brush the surface of the dough with the olive oil. Cover the surface evenly with the rosemary. Drape the plastic wrap over the surface and let the dough rise until it has nearly doubled in volume, about 30 minutes.
7. Preheat the oven to 350 degrees F. Position a rack in the bottom third of the oven.
8. Before the focaccia goes into the oven, use your fingertips to press dimples into the dough in a random pattern. Sprinkle the salt over the surface.
9. Bake the focaccia until the edges are slightly golden in color, 10 to 12 minutes. Remove from the oven and cool on a rack for about 10 minutes. The focaccia is ready to cut into squares and serve.

# Panissa fritta o panelle

## CHICKPEA FRITTERS

This is a chickpea "polenta" cooked slowly and then left to cool. Once it cools, it's firm enough to cut into pieces to fry or grill.

**SERVES 4 (MAKES 12 PIECES)**

- 1¼ cups chickpea flour, sifted
- 3 tbsp extra-virgin olive oil
- 1½ tsp kosher salt, plus more as needed
- 1½ cups cold water
- ¼ cup thinly sliced green onions, white part only
- 1 tbsp chopped flat-leaf parsley
- ½ tsp chopped sage
- ½ tsp chopped rosemary
- Freshly ground black pepper, as needed
- Frying oil (mild olive, canola, peanut, or blend), as needed for frying

1. Put the flour in a large bowl. Add 1 tablespoon of the olive oil and the salt. Stir the batter as you pour in the water, mixing well to prevent any lumps from forming. Let the batter rest at least 30 minutes before making the fritters. Leave the batter at room temperature if you plan to continue within 1 hour; refrigerate the batter if you want to continue later than that or even the next day.
2. Heat the remaining olive oil in a small skillet over medium heat. Add the green onions and cook, stirring frequently, until limp and tender, about 3 minutes. Add the parsley, sage, and rosemary; remove the pan from the heat, season with a little salt and pepper, and reserve.
3. Skim away any foam on the surface of the batter and pour the batter into a heavy-bottomed pan. Put the pan over medium heat and cook, stirring constantly as though you were making polenta. Cook until the mixture gets quite stiff, about 7 minutes. Meanwhile, oil a baking sheet. Add the scallion-and-herb mixture and stir until blended. Pour the batter out onto the baking sheet. Press it into an even layer about ¼ inch thick, and let it cool completely (you can keep it in the refrigerator for a couple of days).
4. Heat the oil in a deep-fat fryer or a deep pot to 375 degrees F.
5. Cut the chickpea mixture into 2- or 3-inch squares. Cut the squares in half diagonally to make triangle-shaped fritters. Lower the fritters in batches into the hot oil with a slotted spoon or frying basket. Fry until crisp and golden brown, about 2 minutes. Lift the fritters from the oil, drain on paper towels, season with salt, and serve at once.

# Panzanella

## TOMATO-BREAD SALAD

Panzanella may be very popular in restaurants today, but this summer dish is actually very simple and humble. It is day-old bread moistened and flavored with ingredients from the garden.

SERVES 4

1 loaf day-old Tuscan bread (about 1 pound)

1 small red onion

1 seedless cucumber

4 ripe tomatoes (about 12 oz)

½ cup basil leaves, plus more for garnish

Salt and freshly ground black pepper, as needed

½ cup extra-virgin olive oil

3 tbsp red wine vinegar

1. Put the bread, in one large piece, into a bowl that can hold it comfortably. Add enough cold water to cover the bread almost completely. Let it soak until the bread is very moist. Drain away the water and squeeze the bread and break it up with your fingertips. It should look like a very thick soup.
2. Slice the onion and cucumber very thinly and add them to the bread. Cut the tomatoes into small wedges and add them to the bread, reserving a few to top the salad when serving it. Tear the basil in small pieces directly into the bowl. Season the salad with salt and pepper and dress it with the olive oil, tossing gently to blend. Keep the salad at room temperature if you will be serving it within an hour or two; otherwise, cover the salad and store it in the refrigerator.
3. Just before serving the panzanella, add the vinegar and blend it into the salad. Serve the panzanella with additional fresh basil and the reserved tomato wedges on top.

Wine notes: Panzanella is a satisfying salad with lighter whites or reds. If adding tuna or mackerel, stay with a white; otherwise choose the wine you like.

**White:** Vernaccia di San Gimignano from Tuscany; Sauvignon Blanc from Friuli-Venezia Giulia; Gavi or Arneis from Piedmont

**Red:** Chianti from Tuscany; Merlot from Veneto; Dolcetto or Barbera from Piedmont

# Gnocco fritto con prosciutto

## CRISPY DOUGH WITH PROSCIUTTO

Some recipes call for San Pellegrino sparkling water instead of yeast, but we have found that yeast gives you a more consistent result.

**SERVES 6 TO 8**

**1 cup water, about 70 degrees F, added as needed**

**1 envelope active dry yeast**

**3⅔ cups all-purpose or "00" flour, sifted, plus as needed for dusting dough and work surface**

**¼ cup lard or 6 tbsp (¾ stick) unsalted butter**

**1 tsp kosher salt, plus as needed**

**Frying oil (mild olive, canola, peanut, or blend), as needed for frying**

**8 oz sliced prosciutto or other salumi, for serving**

1. Combine the water and the yeast in a small bowl. Stir to distribute the yeast, and let the mixture rest for a few minutes to rehydrate the yeast.
2. Mound the flour on a clean work surface and make a well in the center. Add the yeast mixture, the lard (or butter), and the salt. Use your fingertips to drag the flour into the wet ingredients and mix them until a soft, ragged dough forms. Gather the dough into a ball and knead it until a soft but elastic dough forms, about 5 minutes. Dust the dough, your hands, and the work surface with additional flour as you knead to keep the dough from sticking, but use the least amount possible.
3. Gather the dough into a ball and transfer to a clean bowl (it should be large enough to hold the dough after it doubles in volume). Dust the surface of the dough with a sprinkling of flour, cover the bowl tightly with plastic wrap, and let the dough rise at room temperature until it doubles in bulk, about 30 minutes.
4. Set up a pasta machine and set it to the largest opening. Dust a work surface with flour. Cut off pieces of dough about the size of an egg. Working with one piece of dough at a time, roll the dough into sheets about ⅛ inch thick. (For more information about rolling dough in a pasta machine, see page 151.)
5. Cut the dough sheets into gnocco; we like diamonds that measure about 2 inches on a side, and we use a pasta cutter to create a ruffled edge. (See next page.)
6. Heat about 1 inch of oil in a deep skillet or pot to 325 degrees F. The surface should look hazy and ripple, but you should not see smoke rising from the surface.
7. Gently slide 2 or 3 of the gnocco into the hot oil. As they fry, they will puff up and blister. You may need to turn them so they fry evenly. When they are golden brown, after about 2 minutes, lift them from the oil and drain them briefly before you season them with salt. Continue frying the gnocco until they are all finished.
8. Serve the gnocco while they are very hot, accompanied by the prosciutto.

Wine notes: A bit of fruity sparkle and sweetness will be like adding a berry or melon to the prosciutto and will make this snack a lot of fun.

**Sparkling White:** Extra-dry Prosecco from Veneto

**Lightly Sparkling Sweet Red:** Lambrusco from Emilia-Romagna

**Sparkling Sweet Red:** Brachetto d'Acqui from Piedmont

Making gnocco fritto (page 33)

1. If you need to reposition the dough during rolling, flip the dough over the pin so that the dough doesn't get stretched or misshapen.

2. Make sure to flour generously so the dough does not stick to the work surface.

3. Cut the rolled dough into diamonds measuring about 2 inches on each side. You can use a pasta cutter to create ruffled edges.

4. After about 2 minutes of frying, when the gnocco are golden brown, very carefully lift them out of the oil and drain briefly before seasoning.

# Torta pasqualina

## EASTER TART

*Pasqua* is Italian for "Easter." Torta pasqualina, as the name implies, is typically made during the Easter season; it hails from Liguria.

**SERVES 6 TO 8**

CRUST

**2¼ cups all-purpose or "00" flour, plus as needed for dusting dough and work surface**

**2 tbsp extra-virgin olive oil**

**½ tsp kosher salt, plus as needed**

**¾ cup water**

FILLING

**1 lb spinach, cooked and chopped (page 23)**

**1 lb mixed Swiss chard and borage leaves, cooked and chopped (page 23)**

**1 lb ricotta**

**½ cup grated Parmigiano-Reggiano (2 oz)**

**8 large eggs**

**2 tbsp marjoram**

**½ teaspoon kosher salt**

1. To make the crust, put the flour in a large bowl. Add the oil and salt. Use a pastry cutter to mix the oil into the flour enough to make a mixture that resembles cornmeal. Add the water and mix the dough briefly, just enough so that it will hold together when you press it into a ball. Wrap the dough and chill it in the refrigerator at least 1 hour before rolling it out.
2. Preheat the oven to 350 degrees F. Position a rack in the bottom third of the oven.
3. To make the filling, stir together the spinach, chard and borage leaves, ricotta, Parmigiano-Reggiano, 2 eggs, marjoram, and salt.
4. Unwrap the dough and set it on a floured work surface. To line a 10-inch tart pan, cut the dough into 2 almost equal balls; one should be slightly bigger than the other. Working with the large ball first, roll the dough out into a 14-inch-diameter round about ⅛ inch thick. Lift the dough gently into the tart pan. Add the filling and spread it in an even layer. Use a serving spoon or a small ladle to make 6 wells large enough to hold an egg. Crack the remaining 6 eggs, putting 1 egg into each of the wells.
5. Roll out the smaller ball of dough into an 11-inch-diameter round; it should be the same thickness as the bottom layer. Transfer the top crust to the tart. Pinch the edges together with your fingertips or crimp them together with the tines of a fork.
6. Bake the tart until the crust is golden brown, 50 to 60 minutes. Cool the tart for at least 15 minutes on a rack before cutting and serving it.

Wine notes: To cleanse and refresh the palate of the bitterness of the greens and the richness of the cheese, choose a light, simple, off-dry sparkler.

**Sparkling White:** Extra-Dry Prosecco from Veneto

# Torta di riso e zucca

## SAVORY TART OF RICE AND SQUASH

Another famous savory pie, this torta is perfect in the fall, when squash are ripening.

**SERVES 8 TO 10**

DOUGH

**2¼ cups all-purpose or "00" flour, sifted, plus as needed for dusting dough and work surface**

**10 tbsp cold unsalted butter, cut into small cubes**

**1 tsp kosher salt**

**6 tbsp cold water**

FILLING

**1¼ cups short-grain white rice**

**½ cup (1 stick) unsalted butter**

**2 cups chopped leeks (about 4), white and light green portions only**

**4 sage leaves**

**1⅔ cups Butternut Squash Puree (page 23)**

**1½ cups grated Parmigiano-Reggiano (6 oz)**

**Pinch of ground cinnamon**

**Salt and freshly ground black pepper, as needed**

1. Preheat the oven to 350 degrees F. Position a rack in the bottom third of the oven.
2. To make the dough, put the flour in the bowl of a stand mixer or a large bowl. Add the butter and salt. Use the paddle attachment of the mixer or a pastry cutter to mix the butter into the flour enough to make a mixture that resembles cornmeal. Add the water and mix the dough briefly, just enough so that it will hold together when you press it into a ball. Wrap the dough in plastic wrap and chill it in the refrigerator for at least 4 hours before rolling it out.
3. To make the filling, bring a saucepan of salted water to a full boil over high heat and add the rice. Stir to separate the grains, and let the rice cook uncovered until the grains are tender, about 15 minutes. Lower the heat if necessary to keep the rice from boiling over. Drain the rice in a sieve or colander and transfer to a large bowl.
4. Heat the butter in a large skillet over medium heat. Add the leeks and sage leaves and cook them gently over low heat until the leeks are tender, about 5 minutes.
5. Add the squash puree, cheese, and the leek-and-sage mixture to the rice. Stir until evenly blended. Season with a pinch of cinnamon and salt and pepper.
6. Unwrap the dough and set it on a floured work surface. To line a 10-inch tart pan, cut the dough into 2 almost equal balls; one should be slightly bigger than the other. Working with the large ball first, roll the dough out into a 14-inch-diameter round about ⅛ inch thick. Lift the dough gently into the tart pan. Add the filling. Roll out the smaller ball of dough into an 11-inch-diameter round; it should be the same thickness as the bottom layer. Transfer the top crust to the tart. Pinch the edges together with your fingertips or crimp them together with the tines of a fork.
7. Bake the tart until the crust is golden brown, about 40 minutes. Cool the tart for at least 15 minutes on a rack before cutting and serving it.

Wine notes: This dish calls for a medium-bodied, fresh white wine to bring out the savory richness of the squash.

**White:** Oltrepò Pavese from Lombardy; Roero Arneis from Piedmont; Vernaccia di San Gimignano from Tuscany

# Pizza alla napoletana

## NEAPOLITAN-STYLE PIZZA

To get the authentic taste and texture of a classic Neapolitan pizza, you would need a wood-burning oven that can reach about 800 degrees F. That might not be too practical in most homes, but a pizza stone can improve your results. Let it heat up while the oven preheats.

**SERVES 8**

DOUGH

**1½ cups warm water, about 70 degrees F**

**1 envelope active dry yeast**

**4½ cups all-purpose or "00" flour, sifted, plus as needed for dusting dough and work surface**

**¼ cup extra-virgin olive oil**

**1 tsp kosher salt**

TOPPING

**2 cups canned San Marzano tomatoes**

**1 lb fresh buffalo mozzarella, sliced**

**1 tsp crumbled dried Sicilian oregano**

**2 tbsp olive oil**

**Salt and freshly ground black pepper (optional)**

1. To make the dough, combine the water and yeast in a small bowl. Stir to distribute the yeast, and let the mixture rest for a few minutes to rehydrate the yeast.
2. Mound the flour on a clean work surface and make a well in the center. Add the yeast mixture, oil, and salt. Use your fingertips to drag the flour into the wet ingredients and mix them until a soft, ragged dough forms. Gather the dough into a ball and knead it until a soft but elastic dough forms, about 10 minutes. Dust the dough, your hands, and the work surface with additional flour as you knead to keep the dough from sticking, but use the least amount possible.
3. Gather the dough into a ball and transfer to a clean bowl (it should be large enough to hold the dough after it doubles in volume). Dust the surface of the dough with a sprinkling of flour, cover the bowl tightly with plastic wrap, and let the dough rise at room temperature until it doubles in bulk, about 1 hour.
4. To make the topping, drain the tomatoes and sliced mozzarella on several thickness of paper towels while the dough rises to remove any excess moisture.
5. Preheat the oven to 450 degrees F. Position a rack in the bottom third of the oven, with a pizza stone if available.
6. Transfer the dough to a floured work surface. Press the dough out into a rough square, and then pull the 4 corners in toward the center. Turn it over so the upper surface is smooth. Drape the ball of dough with the plastic you used during the first rise and let it rest until it has relaxed, about 30 minutes.
7. Brush a pizza pan liberally with olive oil. Uncover the dough and spread and stretch it into a circle about the same dimensions as your pan. Lift the dough into the pan and stretch it out into an even layer that fills the pan. Crush the tomatoes between your fingertips and distribute them evenly over the surface. Top with the mozzarella slices. Sprinkle with the oregano and drizzle the olive oil over the pizza. Season with salt and pepper if you wish.
8. Bake the pizza until the edges are golden in color and the cheese is bubbly, about 20 minutes (depending on how high your oven will go). Remove from the oven, cut into wedges, and serve at once.

*Traditionally, the dough for this pizza included a little shortening in the dough, but we substitute olive oil.*

*Use San Marzano tomatoes if you can find them; if not, use the best-quality tomatoes you can find.*

Wine notes: The wine should act as a refreshing background flavor to the pizza. Choose a wine with good acidity to match the flavors of the tomatoes.

**White:** Falanghina from Campania; Pinot Grigio from Trentino-Alto Adige; Sauvignon Blanc from Friuli-Venezia Giuiia

**Red:** Chianti from Tuscany; Valpolicella Classico or Merlot from Veneto; Dolcetto or Barbera from Piedmont; Sangiovese di Romagna from Emilia-Romagna

# Pizza al taglio

## PIZZA BY THE SLICE

These are pizzas that you commonly find in bread bakeries in Italy; they are cooked in trays and cut into squares or rectangles. In fact, the name literally means "pizza by the slice." Almost any savory tidbit makes a good topping if you want to try something different than what we suggest here.

**SERVES 4**

- 1⅔ cups water
- 1 envelope active dry yeast
- 3⅔ cups all-purpose or "00" flour, sifted, plus as needed for dusting dough and work surface
- 3 tbsp olive oil, plus 3 tbsp for greasing baking sheet
- 1 tsp kosher salt, plus as needed
- 2 cups canned Roma tomatoes, seeded, juices drained
- 2 tbsp coarsely chopped basil
- 1 tsp crumbled dried oregano
- Freshly ground black pepper, as needed
- 8 oz fresh mozzarella, thinly sliced

1. Combine the water and yeast in the bowl of a stand mixer. Stir to distribute the yeast, and let the mixture rest for a few minutes to rehydrate the yeast.
2. Add the flour, olive oil, and salt. Mix on low speed with a dough hook until a smooth, elastic dough forms, 10 to 15 minutes.
3. Dust the surface of the dough with a sprinkling of flour, cover the bowl tightly with plastic wrap, and let the dough rise at room temperature until it doubles in bulk, about 1 hour.
4. Transfer the dough to a floured work surface. Press the dough out into a rough square, and then pull the 4 corners in toward the center. Turn it over so the upper surface is smooth. Drape the ball of dough with the plastic you used during the first rise and let it rest until it has relaxed, about 30 minutes.
5. Crush the tomatoes by pushing them through a sieve or a food mill into a bowl. Add the basil and oregano and season with a little salt and pepper. Set aside.
6. Preheat the oven to 400 degrees F. Position a rack in the bottom third of the oven.
7. Brush a baking sheet (with sides) or a jelly-roll pan liberally with about 3 tablespoons of olive oil. Uncover the dough and spread and pull it into a rectangle about the same dimensions as your pan. Lift the dough into the pan and stretch it out into an even layer that fills the pan.
8. Bake the untopped pizza until it rises, about 10 minutes, and then remove it from the oven. Spread the tomato mixture over the pizza (leave a ½-inch-wide border on the edges) and top with the cheese. Return the pizza to the oven and bake until the crust is a light golden color on the edges and bottom, the tomatoes are cooked, and the mozzarella is melted and has browned a little. Remove from the oven, cut into squares, and serve at once.

Wine notes: A light- to medium-bodied fresh white will bring out the savory character of the pizza and highlight the flavors of the herbs.

**White:** Frascati from Lazio; Orvieto from Umbria; Vernaccia di San Gimignano from Tuscany

# Erbazzone

## HERB PIE

This rich, savory pie is filled with Swiss chard and pancetta.

**SERVES 8 TO 10**

DOUGH

**2¼ cups all-purpose or "00" flour, sifted**

**2 tbsp lard or unsalted butter, room temperature**

**1 tsp kosher salt**

**2 cups water, added as needed**

FILLING

**1 tbsp olive oil**

**8 oz pancetta, finely chopped or ground**

**2 cups onion julienne (2 medium or 3 small)**

**1 tsp minced garlic (about 1 clove)**

**2 lb Swiss chard, cooked and coarsely chopped (keep stems and leaves separate; page 23)**

**1½ cups grated Parmigiano-Reggiano (6 oz)**

**Salt and freshly ground black pepper, as needed**

1. To make the dough, put the flour in a large bowl. Add the lard (or butter) and salt. Use a pastry cutter to mix the lard into the flour enough to make a mixture that resembles cornmeal. Add the water and mix the dough briefly, just enough so that it will hold together when you press it into a ball. Wrap the dough in plastic wrap and chill it in the refrigerator for at least 4 hours before rolling it out.
2. To make the filling, heat a skillet over medium heat. Add the olive oil and pancetta. Cook, stirring to cook the pancetta evenly, until the pancetta is just starting to get crisp. There should be 2 tablespoons of rendered fat and olive oil in the pan.
3. Add the onions and stir to coat them with the pancetta fat. Sauté, stirring often, until the onions are tender without any browning, about 6 minutes. Add the garlic and stir well. Continue to cook until the garlic loses its harsh aroma, another 3 minutes. Add the chard leaves and stems and cook, stirring well, until the chard is flavored and heated through, 2 to 3 minutes. Transfer the mixture to a bowl and cool to room temperature.
4. Preheat the oven to 350 degrees F. Position a rack in the bottom third of the oven.
5. To finish the filling mixture, stir in the cheese and season the filling with salt and pepper to taste.
6. Unwrap the dough and set it on a floured work surface. To line a 10-inch tart pan, cut the dough into 2 almost equal balls; one should be slightly bigger than the other. Working with the large ball first, roll the dough out into a 14-inch-diameter round about ⅛ inch thick. Lift the dough gently into the tart pan. Add the filling. Roll out the smaller ball of dough into an 11-inch-diameter round; it should be the same thickness as the bottom layer. Transfer the top crust to the tart. Pinch the edges together with your fingertips or crimp them together with the tines of a fork.
7. Bake the tart until the crust is golden brown, 50 to 60 minutes. Cool the tart for at least 15 minutes on a rack before cutting and serving it.

Wine notes: A medium-bodied white or a light-bodied red will work well with this dish, as either will highlight the contrast between the bitter flavors of the chard and the sweetness of the pancetta.

**White:** Albana di Romagna from Emilia-Romagna; Soave Classico from Veneto

**Red:** Sangiovese di Romagna from Emilia-Romagna; Chianti from Tuscany

# Piadine con cicoria e formaggio

## EMILIAN FLATBREAD FILLED WITH CHICORY AND CHEESE

Piadine are sold in the streets throughout Italy, from specialized stands known as *piadinerie*. They are served as soon as they are cooked, filled with a variety of cheeses and vegetables, as in our recipe, or with various sliced meats, but you might also find them stuffed with sweet fillings such as jam or Nutella.

**SERVES 4 TO 6**

**3⅔ cups all-purpose or "00" flour**

**½ tsp baking powder**

**½ tsp salt, plus as needed**

**2½ oz strutto (rendered pork fat or lard)**

**1 cup milk**

**1 lb escarole, trimmed**

**1 tbsp olive oil**

**1 garlic clove, peeled**

**Freshly ground black pepper, as needed**

**6 oz sliced Fontina**

1. Put the flour, baking powder, and salt in a large bowl. Add the strutto. Use a pastry cutter or fork to mix the strutto into the flour enough to make a mixture that resembles cornmeal. Add the milk and mix the dough until it holds together in a ball. Turn the dough out onto a lightly floured surface and knead until smooth. Wrap the dough and let it rest for 30 minutes before rolling it out.
2. Bring a large pot of salted water to a rolling boil over high heat. Add the greens all at once and stir to submerge them. Cook uncovered until tender and a deep color, 3 to 4 minutes. Lift the greens out of the water with a sieve or slotted spoon and transfer to a colander to drain for several minutes.
3. Heat a large skillet over medium heat. Add the olive oil and garlic clove. When the garlic clove starts to brown, add the drained escarole and roll the escarole in the garlic-infused oil until it is very hot and any extra liquid has cooked away. Season well with salt and pepper. Keep hot while preparing the piadine.
4. To roll out the piadine, divide the dough into 6 equal pieces. Shape each piece into a ball, and then, working on a lightly floured surface, roll each piece into an 8-inch circle about ⅜ inch thick. As each piece is rolled out, dust it with a little flour and transfer it to a baking sheet.
5. Heat a cast-iron griddle (testa) or skillet over medium heat. When the pan is quite hot, brush it with a little oil. Put one piece of dough on the skillet and cook on the first side until the dough blisters on top and browns on the bottom, about 2 minutes. Use the tines of a fork to break any very large bubbles, turn the piadina over, and cook on the second side until the piadina is cooked through and brown on both sides, another minute or two. Repeat with the remaining dough pieces.
6. Lay cheese and some of the escarole on each of the piadine. Fold the piadine in half, cut into pieces, and serve at once.

(continued)

Making piadine (page 43)

1. Place the rolled dough on a hot testa, or cast-iron griddle.

2. Cook the first side until it is brown and the dough blisters on top, about 2 minutes. You can use a fork to pop any very large bubbles.

3. Turn the piadina over and cook the second side until it is brown and the dough is cooked through.

Wine notes: You want to choose a white wine that will create a fruit-driven background flavor to mediate between the escarole and the cheese and soften the smoky char of the piadine.

**White:** Albana di Romagna from Emilia-Romagna; Friulano from Friuli-Venezia Giulia; Roero Arneis from Piedmont

# Bruschette miste

## A VARIETY OF BRUSCHETTE

You can just let your imagination go when it comes to creating any type of bruschetta. Use the list of suggested toppings following this recipe or make up your own combinations.

**SERVES 4**

**4 bread slices (¼ inch thick)**

**2 garlic cloves, lightly crushed**

**¼ cup extra-virgin olive oil**

**Salt and freshly ground black pepper, as needed**

Heat a broiler or a grill to high heat (or a grill pan over high heat, if you wish). Grill or broil the bread on both sides until it is crisp and very slightly charred. Rub a crushed garlic clove over the bread to season it (1 clove will season 2 slices) and drizzle the slices with the olive oil. Season with salt and pepper to taste and serve the bruschetta at once with a topping.

*Here are some topping ideas to get you started:*

*Tomato, basil, and oregano*

*Mozzarella and roasted peppers*

*Peas and watercress*

*Chickpeas and olives*

*Asparagus and Parmigiano-Reggiano shavings*

*Cauliflower and anchovies*

*Beans, shrimp, and rosemary*

*Prosciutto and figs*

*Toma cheese and black truffle*

*Caponata (Sicilian-style eggplant)*

*Sheep's milk ricotta, pear, and honey*

*Grilled flank steak and arugula*

# Frittata con asparagi

## ASPARAGUS FRITTATA

A frittata is a popular egg dish eaten as a light dinner, for a snack, or at lunch in a sandwich.

**SERVES 4**

**8 oz green or white asparagus**

**Kosher salt as needed**

**5 large eggs**

**3 tbsp whole milk**

**2 tbsp grated Parmigiano-Reggiano**

**2 tbsp unsalted butter**

1. Preheat the oven to 325 degrees F.
2. Trim the asparagus by snapping off the hard portion of the stalk. Peel the stems. Bring a large pot of salted water to a boil over high heat. Add the asparagus and cook until just barely tender, about 3 minutes. Drain and rinse with cold running water. Cut each stalk in half lengthwise.
3. Whisk together the eggs, milk, and cheese in a medium bowl.
4. Melt the butter in a large ovenproof skillet over medium-low heat. When the butter has stopped foaming, pour in the egg mixture and place the asparagus on top of the eggs.
5. Transfer the skillet to the oven and bake until the eggs are set, 10 to 12 minutes. Cut into wedges and serve hot, or chill the frittata and serve it cut into cubes as a snack or into wedges as a sandwich filling.

Wine note: **White:** Soave Classico from Veneto

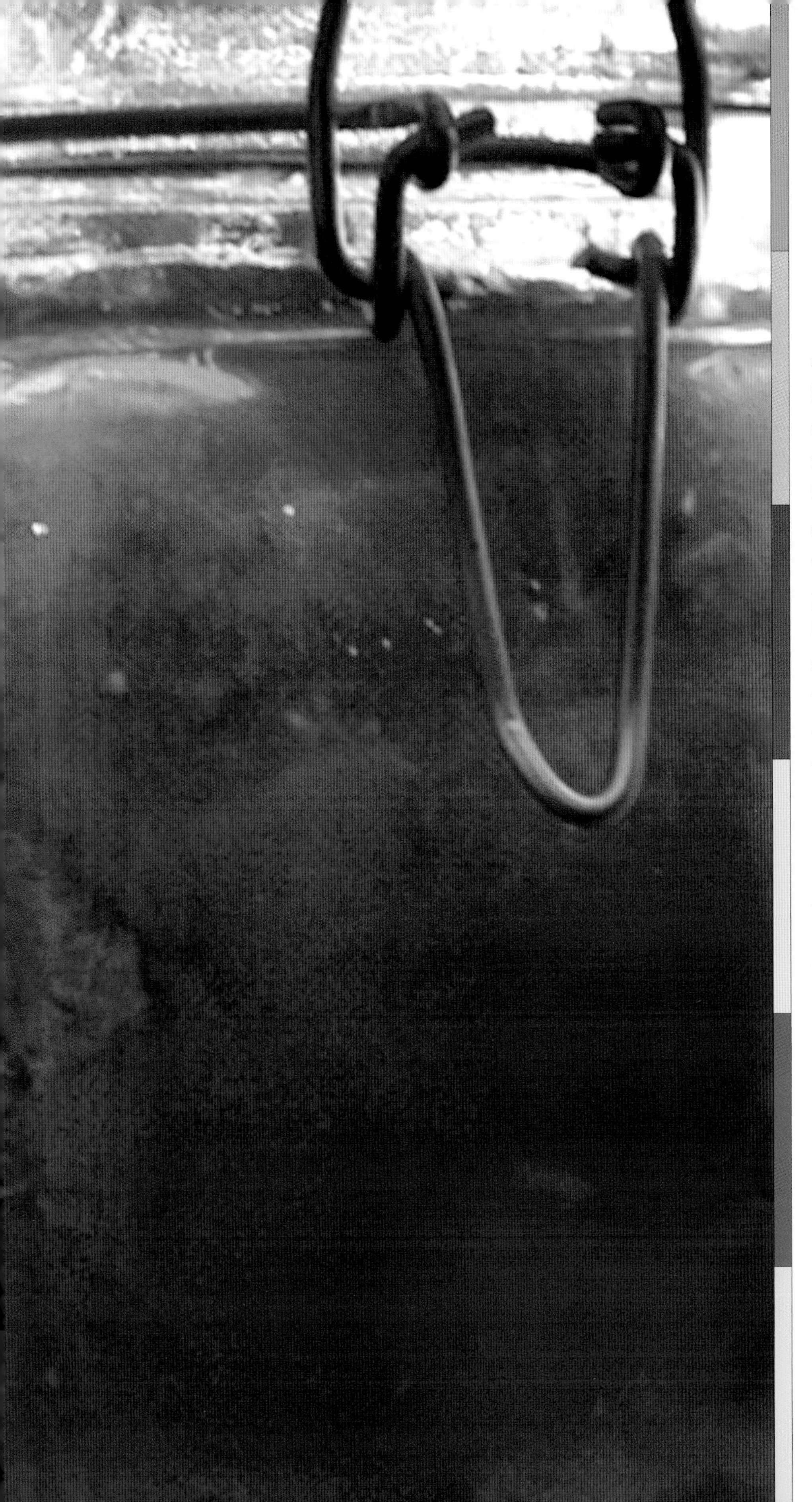

# Conserve

Any great cuisine builds itself out of the foods that even poor families would find on their tables. When you don't have much, you treasure what you do have all the more and you certainly don't waste anything. Frugality is not just a nice virtue; it usually points to a long history of poverty. But the Italians meet the challenge of keeping themselves fed with style. Nowhere is this triumph of great flavor over limited resources more apparent than in the vivid collection of dishes featured on an Italian antipasti platter.

Italian foods are everywhere in the global culinary scene, so you might imagine that there are no surprises left for the American cook. This chapter introduces some of the dishes that might not be at the tip of your tongue when you think of Italian food. They represent the recipes used by generations of cooks to capture and preserve the flavors of a special season and a fleeting flavor—le conserve. These pickled, brined, and oil-preserved foods can be found lining the shelves of any good Italian deli and even some larger supermarkets.

The tradition of putting foods up in the summer to last throughout the winter is still strong. You will find plenty of options here for ingredients like tomatoes, mushrooms, peppers, onions, and celery. Fish and seafood have seasons as well, and you can find techniques for pickling anchovies and herring, and even a recipe for fresh tuna that is gently simmered in oil with fresh herbs.

Our conserve recipes make batches small enough to enjoy over the course of a couple of weeks, and most of them last beautifully in the refrigerator with no special processing or handling necessary. On the other hand, you may want to double or even triple some of our recipes and then use the canning instructions below to safely store them in jars. Once they are safely processed, these preserves will last throughout the winter.

## Peeling and seeding tomatoes

To remove the peel from tomatoes, blanch them first in boiling water, then cool them quickly to stop the cooking. Once the peel is removed, they can be cut in half, seeded, and cored. To cook just the skin, the water needs to stay at a full boil, so only add 3 or 4 tomatoes to the pot at a time; otherwise, the water will cool down too much.

1. Bring a pot of water to a rolling boil over high heat. Fill a large bowl half full with ice water to cool the tomatoes.
2. Cut an X in the bottom of the tomato (the end opposite the stem end). Use a slotted spoon to lower a few tomatoes into the boiling water. Boil for 10 to 20 seconds, just long enough to loosen the skin. Lift them from the water and immediately put them into the ice water for a few minutes. Continue until all of the tomatoes have been blanched in the boiling water.
3. Take them out of the ice water, pull the peel away from the tomatoes, and discard. Cut them in half, scoop out the seeds, and cut out the core. Continue until all of the tomatoes are peeled, seeded, and cored.

## Preparing anchovies and sardines

If you can find fresh sardines or anchovies at the market, they are usually sold whole, which means that you will need to clean them to remove the innards and the bones. It is a fairly simple task that calls for nothing more elaborate than a paring knife and your fingers.

First, make a slit through the fish's belly. Use your index finger to pull out the insides. Flatten the fish to open it (skin side down) by running the tip of your thumb along the entire spine; this opens out the fish and will also loosen the bones from the flesh. You may be able to pinch the spine between your fingers and pull it cleanly away from the fish, or use a paring knife to pull out the backbone and any of the rib bones that come along with it. Once the guts and bones are removed, cut away the head and gills. Finally, to clean the fish, wipe them with a paper towel inside and out, but do not rinse them in water.

# Pickling mushrooms

The smaller the mushrooms, the better for pickling. The most popular are white and cremini mushrooms, but any soft-fleshed type may be used. Mushrooms that are especially spongy (like oak) can absorb too much pickling water or oil. If the mushrooms are very big, quarter them before pickling. If you mix different varieties, keep in mind their different thicknesses, sizes, and weights.

# Sterilizing jars for preserving

You will need a pot deep enough to hold the tallest jar you plan to use with another 3 to 4 inches of space between the top of the jar and the top of the pot.

1. Clean the jars, lids, and rings well with hot, soapy water and rinse well in hot water.
2. Put the pot on a burner and place a canning rack or folded towel in the bottom of the pot.
3. Fill the jars with hot water and put them in the pot (they should sit steadily on the rack or towel and should not touch each other). Add enough additional hot water to cover the jars by 1 inch. Add the lids and rings to the pot.
4. Bring the water to a boil over high heat. After it reaches a boil, continue to boil for 10 minutes longer.
5. Use canning tongs to lift the jars out of the hot water, pour out the water, and set them on a flat, towel-lined surface. Remove the lids and rings and put them on the towel too. The jars are ready to fill.

# Processing jarred preserves and conserves

Many of the preserves in this chapter can be packed in canning jars and processed for longer storage, which is especially useful when you have a bumper supply of something like tomatoes or other fresh garden vegetables.

1. Use the same pot you used to sterilize the jars, add the rack or a folded towel as before, and put the pot on a burner. Put the filled and sealed jars into the pot. (If the jars are small and might bang against each other as you process them in boiling water, you may want to wrap a cloth around each jar to keep them safe.) Add enough hot water to completely cover the jars.
2. Bring the water to a boil and process for the appropriate length of time (the time will vary depending upon the ingredient you are processing; refer to your recipe). Turn off the heat under the pot. Let the jars cool in the hot water bath for 1 hour. Lift the jars from the water with canning tongs and set them on a towel-lined counter.
3. Check the seals to be sure that they are tight. Leave the jars undisturbed. As they cool, you may hear a pop as a vacuum seal forms.If a jar doesn't seal, keep it refrigerated and eat within a week.
4. Label the jars with the name of the contents and store in a cool, dark cupboard for up to 6 months. Once opened, most preserves will keep in the refrigerator for up to 1 week or more.

Wine notes: Most of the dishes in this chapter include ingredients that don't always lend themselves easily to a wine-food pairing. The tricky part is matching a wine with the sweet/sour vinegar-based conserve. The easy choice is a light, fruity sparkler that will help balance all the flavors in the dish.
**Sparkling White:** Prosecco from Veneto

# Giardiniera

## PICKLED GARDEN VEGETABLES

This is a popular Italian pickled vegetable. A giardiniera can be made with any vegetables you enjoy, depending upon what is currently available at the market or from your garden, but celery, carrots, and onions are almost invariably part of the mix.

**MAKES FOUR 1-PINT JARS**

BRINE

8 cups white vine vinegar

4 cups water

½ cup sugar

6 tbsp kosher salt

SACHET

2 tsp black peppercorns

1 tsp allspice berries

1 bay leaf

1 thyme sprig

GIARDINIERA

½ head cauliflower

2 carrots, peeled

2 celery stalks, peeled

1 red bell pepper, seeded

1 yellow bell pepper, seeded

2 baby turnips, peeled

10 pearl onions, peeled

1. To make the brine, combine the vinegar, water, sugar, and salt in a deep nonreactive pot. Bring the liquid to a simmer over medium heat. To make the sachet, tie up the peppercorns, allspice, bay leaf, and thyme in a piece of cheesecloth and add this sachet to the brine.
2. To make the giardiniera, break the cauliflower apart into pieces and cut into small florets. Cut the carrots, celery, and peppers into sticks or strips. Cut the turnips into small wedges. Add the prepared vegetables and the pearl onions to the simmering brine and cook until they are tender but not too soft, about 10 minutes; the time will vary depending upon how tender or tough your vegetables are as well as the sizes of the pieces.
3. Use a slotted spoon to transfer the vegetables to clean jars (use sterilized jars if you plan to process the giardiniera for longer storage; see page 51). Strain the pickling brine over the vegetables to completely cover them. The giardiniera is ready for processing now, or you may simply let the brine cool to room temperature and then seal the jars and refrigerate them. Let unprocessed giardiniera pickle for at least 24 hours before serving, and use within 1 week.

*Processing note: Instructions for sterilizing jars and processing preserves can be found on page 51. Processing time for giardiniera is 20 minutes after the water returns to a boil. Label the jars and store processed giardiniera in a cool, dark place for up to 6 months. Once the jar is opened, the giardiniera will keep in the refrigerator for up to 1 week.*

# Pomodori pelati

## PRESERVED PEELED TOMATOES

These preserved tomatoes are meant to be used in cooked dishes, so choose tomatoes with a lot of thick pulp, such as Roma or plum tomatoes, or, ideally, Italian San Marzano tomatoes.

**MAKES FOUR 1-QUART JARS**

**6 lb ripe Roma or plum tomatoes**

**16 to 20 basil leaves, or as needed**

**1 to 2 tbsp sea salt, or as needed**

1. Sterilize four 1-quart canning jars and their lids (see page 51).
2. Bring a large pot of water to a rolling boil to peel and seed the tomatoes (see page 50). As soon as the tomatoes are peeled and while they are still hot, pack the tomatoes into the jars, pressing them into an even layer about 2 inches thick. Add a few leaves of basil and a pinch of sea salt on top of each layer.
3. Seal the jars, closing them tightly. Wrap the jars in some cloth so the jars won't crack while they are boiling and process the tomatoes as described on page 50. Processing time for pomodori pelati is 45 minutes from the time the water returns to a boil. Label the jars with the name of the contents and store in a cool, dark cupboard for up to 6 months.
4. Once opened, these tomatoes will keep in the refrigerator for up to 1 week.

# Pomodori a pezzetti in conserva

## PRESERVED CHUNKY TOMATOES

Pomodori pelati have been peeled and seeded before being preserved. Here, the tomato is not subjected to any heat at all until it is put into jars and processed. We particularly like this recipe because it is very easy, but we like it even more for the many ways in which you can use the tomatoes. We add them to stews of all kinds, make them into a quick tomato sauce, or even enjoy them right out of the jar on top of a piece of grilled bread.

**MAKES FOUR 1-PINT JARS; ABOUT 6 SERVINGS AS PART OF AN ANTIPASTO**

**3 lb ripe tomatoes**

**10 basil leaves**

**1 tbsp kosher salt**

1. Sterilize four 1-pint canning jars and their lids (see page 51).
2. Cut the tomatoes in half. Remove and discard the core and the seeds.
3. Pack the tomatoes into the jars, pressing them into even layers and adding few leaves of basil and some salt between the layers.

4. Seal the jars, closing them tightly. Process the tomatoes as described on page 51. Processing time is 30 minutes from the time the water returns to a boil. Label the jars with the name of the contents and store in a cool, dark cupboard for up to 6 months.
5. Once opened, these tomatoes will keep in the refrigerator for up to 1 week.

# Pesce di lago in carpione

## VINEGAR-MARINATED FRESHWATER FISH

This method of preparation has been used for a very long time. It is a way to preserve foods by submerging them in vinegar. The traditional fish for this recipe comes from freshwater lakes: trout, pike, pickerel, catfish, and tilapia.

**SERVES 6 TO 8**

2 lb freshwater fish fillets, skin on

1 carrot, peeled

1 celery stalk, peeled

½ small yellow onion, peeled

4 cups white wine vinegar

2 cups white wine

2 cups water

8 to 10 thyme sprigs

3 bay leaves

1 tbsp black peppercorns

1 tbsp kosher salt

SERVING

Lettuce leaves

Extra-virgin olive oil, as needed

Salt and freshly ground pepper, as needed

1. Place the fish, skin side down, in a 2-quart glass or earthenware casserole dish, ideally one with a lid.
2. Slice the carrot, celery, and onion very thinly and put them into a 3-quart saucepan with the vinegar, wine, water, thyme, bay leaves, peppercorns, and salt. Bring the liquid to a simmer over medium heat. Immediately pour the marinade with the vegetables and herbs over the fish.
3. Once the marinade has cooled to room temperature (about 30 minutes), cover the dish and let the fish marinate in the refrigerator for at least 2 days and up to 5 days before serving.
4. To serve the fish, lift the fillets out of the marinade. Serve on a bed of lettuce with some of the pickled vegetables from the marinade. Dress the dish lightly with some extra-virgin olive oil and season with salt and pepper.

# Sarde in saor

## SWEET AND SOUR SARDINES

For this preserved fish, we like to dust the fish in flour and fry it before combining it with a vinegar-and-onion pickle. There are many variations on this particular dish all over Venice and the surrounding areas. For a lighter version, you might prefer to grill the sardines before you cover them with the onion-vinegar mixture.

**SERVES 6 AS AN APPETIZER, 12 AS PART OF AN ANTIPASTO**

PICKLE

**½ cup extra-virgin olive oil**

**2 lb yellow onions, very thinly sliced (5 to 6 onions)**

**2 bay leaves**

**½ tsp freshly ground black pepper**

**2½ cups white wine vinegar**

**½ tsp kosher salt**

**2 cups olive or peanut oil, or as needed**

**2½ lb sardines, filleted (page 50)**

**Flour, as needed, for coating the fish**

SERVING

**Red and yellow bell pepper strips**

**Raisins, plumped in water and drained**

**Toasted pine nuts**

**Salt and freshly ground black pepper, as needed**

1. Heat half of the olive oil in a large skillet over medium heat. Add the onions, bay leaves, and pepper. Stir to coat them with the olive oil and sauté, stirring often, until the onions are tender but not browned, about 15 minutes. Add the vinegar and continue to cook until the vinegar reduces slightly and loses its harsh aroma, 5 minutes longer. Remove the pan from the heat, season with the salt if necessary, and set aside.
2. Heat about 1 inch of frying oil in a deep skillet or pot over medium heat to 350 degrees F. The surface should look hazy and rippled, but you should not see smoke rising from the surface.
3. Coat the sardines inside and out with flour, shaking off any excess. Gently lower two or three of them at a time into the hot oil. Fry them on the first side until they are golden brown, about 2 minutes. Turn them and continue to fry until the second side is brown, another minute. Transfer the sardines to paper towels to drain. Season them with a little salt. Continue frying the sardines in this way until they are all cooked.
4. Arrange about one-third of sardines in a single layer in a 2-quart glass or earthenware casserole dish, ideally one with a lid. Spread one-third of the reserved onions over the fish. Continue to layer the fish and onions until they are all in the casserole dish. Pour any liquid remaining from the onions over the top of the dish. Drizzle the remaining ¼ cup olive oil over the surface of the casserole. Cover the dish and let it rest in the refrigerator for at least 2 days and up to 1 week.
5. Serve the sardines either chilled or at room temperature. Top with a small amount of bell pepper strips, plumped raisins, and toasted pine nuts. Season with salt and pepper.

# Carciofini sott'olio

## BABY ARTICHOKES IN OLIVE OIL

Artichokes are much more commonly served in Italy than in the United States. In addition to being a delicious vegetable that can be pickled, as well as stuffed or steamed or even enjoyed raw, artichokes are also prized for their many health benefits, especially in regard to certain stomach complaints. These pickled artichokes may be served as an appetizer, added to sandwiches, or used to top fish dishes, bruschetta, pizza, or salad.

**MAKES FOUR 1-PINT JARS; ABOUT 8 SERVINGS AS PART OF AN ANTIPASTO**

**Juice of ½ lemon**

**20 baby or 12 medium artichokes, trimmed (page 225)**

**2 cups white wine vinegar**

**2 cups dry white wine**

**1 lemon, sliced**

**5 cloves**

**8 bay leaves, or as needed**

**2 garlic cloves, peeled**

**1 tbsp kosher salt**

**Extra-virgin olive oil, as needed, to cover artichokes**

1. Add the lemon juice to a large bowl of water. Trim and peel the artichokes, keeping them submerged in the water. Cut the artichokes in halves, quarters, or wedges, depending upon their size. Very small baby artichokes can be left whole.
2. Combine the vinegar, wine, lemon, cloves, 4 of the bay leaves, the garlic, and salt in a deep saucepan to make the brine. Bring the liquid to a simmer over medium heat. Add the artichokes to the simmering brine. To keep the artichokes submerged, put a small plate or dish on top of them. (You can cook the artichokes in batches if necessary; they should be completely covered with the brine as they cook.)
3. Cook the artichokes until you can pierce the base or the stem end of the artichoke easily with the tip of a paring knife, 4 to 12 minutes, depending upon the size of your artichokes.
4. Lift the artichokes from the brine with a slotted spoon and let them drain and cool upside down on several layers of paper towels. When the artichokes are cool, transfer them to jars (see page 51) or a crock and add olive oil to cover the artichokes. Don't pack them too tightly; the olive oil should be able to surround each artichoke. Add a fresh bay leaf to each jar (use 2 per jar if the jars are large, and 4 if you are using a crock). Pour enough oil over the artichokes to cover them completely. Let the artichokes rest for about 2 hours before sealing the jars, as the level of oil in the jars may drop as the oil is drawn up into the artichokes. Add more olive oil to keep the artichokes covered.
5. Seal the jars or cover the crock and let the artichokes marinate in the refrigerator for at least 2 days before serving. To serve, lift the artichokes out of the oil, letting the oil drain away. Serve them as part of an antipasto, use them in salads and other dishes, or top grilled bread with them for bruschetta. Any unused artichokes will keep in the refrigerator for up to 2 weeks.

# Funghi sott'olio

## MARINATED MUSHROOMS IN OIL

Marinated mushrooms are a traditional offering in any antipasto. White mushrooms are perfect for this recipe. Look for meaty caps with plump, taut skins and moist stems to be sure they are very fresh. You can also choose a variety of different mushrooms. If you are using a variety of mushrooms, keep them separated by type and add the sturdiest or thickest mushrooms first. Simmer for 2 to 3 minutes, and then add the smaller or more delicate mushrooms and cook for 3 to 4 minutes longer.

**MAKES 6 CUPS; ABOUT 12 SERVINGS AS PART OF AN ANTIPASTO**

PICKLING BRINE

**8 cups water**

**2 cups white wine vinegar**

**¾ cup lemon juice**

**1 tbsp kosher salt**

**1½ lb mushrooms**

**3 garlic cloves, halved**

**3 bay leaves, broken in half**

**6 black peppercorns**

**½ tsp dried oregano**

**2 cups extra-virgin olive oil, or as needed, to cover mushrooms**

1. To make the brine, combine the water, white wine vinegar, lemon juice, and salt in a deep pot. Bring the brine to a simmer over medium heat.
2. Add the mushrooms to the simmering brine. Cook the mushrooms until tender, 3 to 4 minutes. The mushrooms should be completely covered with liquid throughout the cooking time. Add more water to the brine as necessary to keep them submerged.
3. Remove the pot from the heat and let the mushrooms cool to room temperature in the brine. Drain the mushrooms in a colander and then place them on several layers of paper towel to blot up any excess moisture, about 1 hour. The mushrooms are ready for processing now (see below), or transfer them to a 1-quart crock with a lid. Add the garlic, bay leaves, peppercorns, and oregano and pour enough olive oil over the mushrooms to cover them completely.
4. Cover the crock and let the mushrooms marinate in the refrigerator for at least 24 hours before serving. They will keep in the refrigerator for up to 10 days.
5. To serve, lift the mushrooms out of the olive oil with a slotted spoon and let the marinade drain away. Serve them as part of an antipasto, use in other dishes, or use as a topping for bruschetta or pizza.

Processing note: *If you want to preserve the mushrooms for longer than a few days, divide them between 2 sterilized 1-pint jars after they have dried (step 3). Divide the garlic, bay leaves, peppercorns, and oregano between the jars, and add enough olive oil to completely cover the mushrooms.*

*Process the jars for 15 to 20 minutes and then cool, label, and store the jars as described on* *page 51.* *They can be stored in a cool, dark cupboard for up to 4 months. Once opened, the mushrooms will keep for up to 4 days in the refrigerator.*

# Melanzane sott'olio al peperoncino

## PRESERVED EGGPLANT WITH HOT PEPPER

Choosing an eggplant can be a challenge if you aren't sure what to look for. Purple eggplants, including large eggplants sometimes known as "globe," and smaller ones, known as "Italian" eggplant or simply "small globe" eggplant, should have a glossy, shiny skin. If the skin is dull, or worse, wrinkled, the eggplant is older. If you want to avoid eggplants with too many seeds, you can sometimes determine the difference by weighing two similar-size eggplants. The one that weighs less has fewer seeds and may be less bitter. White eggplants typically have a tougher skin than purple varieties; we prefer purple eggplant for this dish.

**MAKES FOUR 1-PINT JARS**

2 lb purple eggplant

½ cup sea salt

1 cup white wine vinegar

Olive oil, as needed

2 tsp crushed hot red pepper, or as needed

4 bay leaves, or as needed

1. Wash the eggplant and slice away the stem and blossom ends. Cut the eggplant into ¼-inch-thick slices. Stack 4 or 5 slices and cut them crosswise into ¼-inch-wide strips.
2. Put the eggplant strips into a colander. Sprinkle the salt over the eggplant and toss to coat it evenly. Set the colander inside a large bowl to catch the liquid that will be released by the eggplant. (If you have a pan with a stacking steamer insert, you can use that instead of a colander and bowl.)
3. To make a weight, find a plate large enough to press down directly onto the top surface of the eggplant. Set a few cans of tomatoes on the plate or dish so that it presses the eggplant as it drains. Press and drain the eggplant in the refrigerator for 24 hours.
4. The next day, taste a piece of the eggplant. If you find it too salty, rinse the eggplant under cold water and then gather the eggplant in a towel and twist to remove the water. Transfer the eggplant to a bowl. Drizzle the vinegar over the eggplant, cover, and let it marinate overnight in the refrigerator.
5. The next day, squeeze the eggplant to remove any extra vinegar and transfer the eggplant to the jars, making even layers about 1 inch thick that you alternate with a drizzle of olive oil, a pinch of crushed hot red pepper, and a bay leaf. Use the back of a spoon to press the eggplant down into the jar and remove any air pockets. Add enough olive oil to completely submerge the eggplant. Cover the jars tightly and refrigerate for at least 7 days before eating. They will keep for up to 2 weeks.

# Acciughe sotto sale

## PRESERVED SALTED ANCHOVIES

The most important issue when you are preserving anchovies is their freshness, so make sure you have a good source for fish and purchase those that have a fresh smell of the ocean, firm flesh, bright eyes, and bright red gills. It is important to keep the fish completely covered in salt. If the anchovies are exposed around the edges of the weight, dissolve salt in water and add the salted water to the crock to cover the fish completely. The longer you preserve your fish directly in the salt, the more volume they will lose and the saltier they will taste. Remove them from the crock once they have reached the state you like, rinse and drain them well, and store them in jars covered with oil. Add a few cloves of garlic, if you wish, and keep them in the refrigerator. If the oil solidifies, let the jars sit at room temperature for about 30 minutes to "melt" the oil.

**MAKES 2 LB; 8 TO 10 SERVINGS AS PART OF AN ANTIPASTO**

2 lb fresh anchovies, cleaned (page 50)

2 lb sea salt (about 6 cups)

Extra-virgin olive, as needed (optional)

Garlic cloves as needed (optional)

1. Blot the anchovies dry with paper towels.
2. Make a layer of salt about ¼ inch deep in a 3-quart casserole or crock. Add the first layer of anchovies, arranging them in rows pointing all in one direction (this is done so that the anchovies will pack together tightly and so that there will be no big air pockets). Sprinkle the first layer generously with salt. Add the second layer of anchovies with the fish arranged in the opposite direction of the first layer. Make another generous layer of salt. Continue layering the anchovies into the crock and covering each layer well with salt. Don't leave any uncovered spots; tap the casserole as you add layers to settle the anchovies and salt. Finish with a layer of salt.
3. To make a weight, use a glass pie plate or ceramic baking dish or something similar that fits snugly into the casserole or crock. It should fit so that it is completely inside the crock and directly on top of the fish. Set something heavy, like a foil-wrapped brick or a few cans of tomatoes, on the plate or dish so that it presses directly on the anchovies.

(continued)

### THE MOON AND ANCHOVIES

There is some controversy in Italy about the best time of the year to harvest and preserve anchovies. According to most people, the moon is one of the biggest factors. The full moon of May is acceptable, but you might find that you have a mix of small and large anchovies then. June is a little better, but nearly everyone agrees that the best time to harvest and preserve anchovies is during the full moon of July, because that is when the anchovies reach their largest size.

The combination of a full moon and the hot weather of July encourages the anchovies to come to the surface, so they are easier to catch. Typically when more fish are easier to catch, the price goes down. In Italy, however, the best prices are usually in May, because the seaside restaurants are not yet open for the season. When the beach-going season starts, the prices go up.

4. Leave them to cure in the refrigerator until they have the flavor you like, at least 2 and up to 4 weeks. (To check, take one anchovy an rinse it well to remove the excess salt, then blot dry and taste.) If liquid rises to the surface as the fish cures, remove it by wicking it away with cheesecloth. If the anchovies don't seem to be covered, however, dissolve some salt in an equal volume of warm water and pour it into the crock (try to do this without disturbing the lid, if possible).
5. Rinse and blot dry the anchovies before either serving or using them in another dish or storing htem in jars as follows: Place the rinsed and dried fish in clean jars. Add a garlic clove or two (depending upon the size of the jar) and enough olive oil to completely cover the fish. Store under refrigeration for up to 2 weeks and drain before using.

# Tonno sott'olio

## TUNA PRESERVED IN OLIVE OIL

You can use this preserved tuna in any dish that calls for oil-packed tuna.

**MAKES FOUR 1-PINT JARS**

- 3 lb fresh tuna fillets or steaks
- 2 qt water
- 4 cups white wine vinegar
- 2 bay leaves, plus more as needed
- 1 thyme sprig
- 2 garlic cloves, peeled
- 2 tbsp sea salt
- 2 cups extra-virgin olive oil, as needed, to cover tuna

1. Place the fish, skin side down, in a 2½- to 3-quart glass or ceramic baking dish.
2. Combine the water, vinegar, bay leaves, thyme, garlic, and salt in a stockpot over medium heat and simmer for 5 minutes. Add the tuna and continue to simmer very gently, partially covered, over low heat for 1 hour. Lift the tuna from the brine and let it drain on several layers of paper towels.
3. Break the tuna apart into large chunks with your fingers. Layer the chunks into the jars, pouring on a little olive oil and placing a bay leaf between layers. (This isn't really a precise science; the layers of tuna should be around 2 inches thick; use the back of a wooden spoon to press the tuna into more compact layers as you work.) Once the jar is filled, add enough additional olive oil to completely cover and submerge the tuna. Seal the jars tightly. The tuna is ready for processing now (see below), or store the jars in the refrigerator and let the tuna marinate for at least 12 hours and up to 48 hours before serving. The tuna will keep for up to 1 week in the refrigerator.

*Processing note: If you want to preserve the tuna for longer than a few days, place the fish in sterilized jars after draining the pieces on paper towels (step 2). Process the jars for 30 minutes and then cool, label, and store the jars as described on page 51. They can be stored in a cool, dark cupboard for up to 6 months. Once opened, the tuna will keep for up to 1 week in the refrigerator.*

# Mostarda di pere

## PEAR MUSTARD

This is a product typical of Mantua, in the Lombardy region. The type of pear you choose really doesn't matter, but what does matter is their ripeness. They should be quite firm but still have enough fragrance to let you know they are ripe. Mustard oil is not always easy to find, but you may be able to locate it in Italian or Indian markets or through an online source such as Amazon.com. If you absolutely cannot find it anywhere and want to get a flavor that comes close, you can dissolve a teaspoon of ground mustard seed in a tablespoon of dry white wine and use that instead.

**MAKES EIGHT ½-PINT JARS**

**5 lb firm but ripe pears**

**Zest and juice of 2 lemons**

**½ cup sugar**

**4 to 6 drops mustard oil**

1. Wash the pears lightly under cold running water. Cut them in half and trim the stem. Use a melon scoop or a grapefruit spoon to remove the seeds and core.
2. Slice the pears very thinly and put them in a heavy saucepan with the lemon juice, lemon zest, and sugar.
3. Place the pears over very low heat and cook, stirring occasionally, until the syrup is very thick; this can take up to 4 hours. Keep the heat as low as possible to avoid browning the syrup; put the pan on a heat diffuser if you have one.
4. Sterilize eight ½-pint canning jars and their lids (see page 51).
5. Remove the pears from the heat. Stir in the mustard oil and pack the pears into the hot sterilized jars. Seal the jars tightly. The jars are ready for processing now (see below), or let the mostarda cool completely, then store in the refrigerator for up to 3 weeks.

*Processing note: If you wish to keep the mostarda for longer than a week, process the jars for 10 minutes, then cool, label, and store the jars in a cool, dark cupboard for up to 3 months. Once opened, the mostarda will keep in the refrigerator for up to 3 weeks.*

# Crudi

*I crudi* refers to a selection of fresh, raw foods. These foods are among the most elemental dishes in the Italian repertoire, full of flavor, texture, and color. Fresh, uncooked meats and seafood are also part of the crudo tradition. You need a butcher and a fishmonger you trust to be sure that your tartares and carpaccios are not only delicious but also safe to serve. Many of the recipes in this chapter are made from the first fresh vegetables of the season, including wild and foraged foods.

Foraging is a time-honored custom throughout Italy. A basket of wild greens picked in the early morning, mushrooms hunted on the forest floor, and wild fennel stalks collected from the edge of a field are just some of the special foods that Italians look for out in the wild. Even Italians have had to curtail unchecked foraging for food in recent years, however. Mushrooms, especially, are protected from overpicking by the requirement that foragers obtain a license or permit. Wild ingredients may be harder to source in the United States, but they are increasingly available in general and specialty markets, farmer's markets, or from your own garden or backyard.

If you can find or forage wild ingredients, remember two important points. First, wild foods are vastly more unpredictable than commercially grown foods. They don't arrive at the market in standard sizes and shapes. The flavor can range from extremely mild to overpowering, even if you picked them all from the same patch of ground. Traditional recipes for wild foods usually pair them with other assertive flavors like anchovies, cured meats, olives, capers, and aged cheeses.

A second and equally important point is this: Wild ingredients can make you sick if you aren't careful. Some foods need to be trimmed, soaked, or even blanched before you cook with them. Mushrooms may look safe to eat and yet still be poisonous. In European countries, you can take your basket of mushrooms to the pharmacy to have someone advise you. In this country, there is no simple way to check them. Our best advice is to know your source and don't take chances.

## MUSHROOMS

You may be able to find a number of different fresh mushrooms in the market beyond the familiar white (or button) mushrooms, including shiitake and oyster mushrooms. Portobello and cremini mushrooms are basically white mushrooms that have been left to mature so that the colors and flavors deepen. Cremini mushrooms are even sometimes labeled *baby portobellos*. Italians love to enjoy mushrooms fresh or pickled. The porcini mushroom is a special variety that is prized for its flavor. A classic presentation is to slice them very thinly and then dress them with olive oil, lemon juice, salt, and pepper.

Each mushroom has a short season, but many varieties respond beautifully to drying. If the only type of mushrooms in your market are mild white mushrooms, you can intensify their flavor by adding dried mushrooms. Before you add dried mushrooms to a dish, you need to soak them long enough to rehydrate them.

1. Put the dried mushrooms in a small dish or bowl.
2. Add enough warm water to cover them generously and let them sit. It may take as little as 10 minutes or as long as 1 hour to soften a mushroom, depending on how old it is.
3. Remove the mushrooms from the soaking liquid, and trim them if necessary. Some stems will never soften, no matter how long you soak them.
4. Strain the soaking liquid through a coffee filter or decant it and use the liquid in another dish, such as a sauce, a stew, a braise, or a broth. To decant the liquid, pour it slowly and carefully out of the bowl into a clean dish. When the sediment is close to the edge of the bowl, stop pouring. Discard whatever is left in the bowl.

# Bagna caôda

## ANCHOVY AND OLIVE OIL DIPPING SAUCE

This sauce, typical throughout the region of Piedmont, is made from three ingredients in equal parts—garlic, anchovies, and olive oil. This version also includes wine. Everyone gathers around the table. The sauce is served in a heated clay pot (a fondue pot is a good substitute). A platter of raw or cooked and chilled vegetables comes to the table with the dip for all to share. Choose an olive oil with a mild flavor for this dish, such as one from the Liguria region.

**SERVES 4 TO 6**

- 2 oz garlic (about 20 cloves)
- 2 oz salt-cured anchovies
- ½ cup dry white wine
- 4 white cardoon stalks
- Juice of ½ lemon
- ¼ cup extra-virgin olive oil
- 2 sweet bell peppers (red, yellow, or orange), cut into large strips
- ½ head small cauliflower, cut into florets or slices
- ½ head small green cabbage, cut into small wedges
- 8 carrots, cut into strips or sticks
- 8 celery heart stalks, cut into large strips
- 8 Jerusalem artichokes, cut into large strips
- 1 fennel bulb, sliced

1. Peel the garlic and slice it very thinly. This recipe calls for a lot of garlic; if you want to tone down the bite, you can put the garlic in a colander and rinse it under cold running water for 10 minutes.
2. Remove the bones from the anchovies, place the anchovies in a bowl, and add the wine and enough water to submerge them completely. Let the anchovies soak for at least 30 minutes and up to 1 hour.
3. Trim the cardoons, making sure to remove any thorns or leaves. Peel the cardoon to remove the heavy fibers and cut into strips or bite-size pieces. Place the cut cardoons in a bowl of cold water that you've added the lemon juice to so the cardoons will stay white. Cook the cardoons in a pot of boiling salted water until they are just tender to the bite, about 5 or 6 minutes. Drain the cardoons and chill them in a bowl of ice water. Drain and blot dry before serving.
4. Combine the olive oil, garlic, and anchovies in a clay pot or fondue pot over very low heat. Stir the bagna caòda as it cooks; the anchovies will break down and the sauce will thicken into a creamy paste. This usually takes 20 to 30 minutes; be sure the sauce does not get hot enough to boil.
5. Arrange all of the vegetables on a large platter. Serve the bagna caôda very hot and dip the vegetables into it.

*If your cardoons are very young and tender, you might be able to eat them raw (after trimming and peeling).*

**Wine notes:** This classic "warm bath" of Piedmont calls for wines that can handle the impact of celery, cardoons, fennel, and Jerusalem artichokes, which will make liquids taste somewhat sweeter. So choose a light- to medium-bodied fruit-driven white or a light, fruity red that can handle the change in flavor without losing its simple character.

**White:** Roero Arneis or Gavi from Piedmont

**Red:** Grignolino, Dolcetto, or Freisa from Piedmont

# Insalata di pere, parmigiano, e noci

## PEAR SALAD WITH PARMESAN AND WALNUTS

This autumn salad of pears can be served on a bed of any bitter baby greens for a nice start to any meal. You may add some radishes if you have some on hand. Be sure to use a good-quality aged balsamic vinegar.

**SERVES 8**

- 4 ripe pears (soft but not mushy)
- 2 cups Prosecco or any dry or lightly sweet sparkling wine
- 2 cups baby arugula leaves
- 1 tbsp julienned mint leaves
- Salt and freshly ground black pepper, as needed
- 4 to 5 tsp balsamic vinegar (at least 3 to 4 years old)
- 3 tbsp olive oil
- One 4-oz chunk Parmigiano-Reggiano, for shaving
- ½ cup chopped toasted walnuts

1. Peel the pears if the skin is tough; if it is tender you may leave it on the fruit. Cut them in half and trim the stem. Use a melon scoop or a grapefruit spoon to remove the seeds and core.
2. Slice the pears very thinly and put them in a bowl. Pour the Prosecco over the fruit.
3. Combine the arugula in a small bowl with the mint. Season with salt and pepper. Add the vinegar and oil and toss until the arugula is evenly coated.
4. Put the dressed arugula on chilled plates or a platter. Use a vegetable peeler to pare thin slices or curls of cheese on top of the salad, and top with the walnuts. Lift the pear slices from the Prosecco and arrange on the plates or platter. Serve at once.

*Balsamic vinegars are not all the same. Choose a well-aged balsamic vinegar, if you have an option. The vinegar will have been aged for at least 3 or 4 years in a succession of different barrels. At the end of this aging process, which is similar to the way that fortified wines are aged, the vinegar has a syrupy consistency and a rich, savory-and-sweet flavor.*

Wine notes: You want to choose a wine that will harmonize with all the flavors in this salad and invigorate the palate. Try a sparkling, fruity, brut or extra-dry Prosecco with cleansing bubbles and refreshing acidity.

**Sparkling White:** Prosecco from Veneto

# Insalata d'arance e finocchi

## ORANGE AND FENNEL SALAD

This very simple salad, typical of Sicily, could be composed of only orange segments, olive oil, salt, and pepper, if you prefer. We like to add some thinly sliced raw fennel, endive, and olives for a more distinctive taste.

**SERVES 4**

2 fennel bulbs

3 navel oranges

4 Belgian endives

2 tbsp orange juice (or lemon juice), or as needed

Sea salt and freshly ground black pepper, as needed

¼ cup extra-virgin olive oil

¼ cup black olives, pitted and coarsely chopped

1. Trim the tops from the fennel bulbs (you may reserve some of the fronds to garnish the dish, if you like). Cut the fennel in half and remove the core. Slice the fennel very thinly, cutting across the stalks. (If you have a mandoline or similar slicer, it will make this step much easier and quicker.) Place in a large bowl.
2. Cut the ends off the oranges and use a paring knife to cut away the skin and the white pith just under the skin. Slice the orange thinly to make rounds, or, if you prefer, cut the orange from between the membrane that separates the orange into segments. If you cut them into segments, work directly over a bowl to catch the juices. You can use the juice to make the dressing. Set the orange pieces aside.
3. Separate the endive leaves from the heads. Cut them crosswise into thin strips and add them to the bowl with the fennel.
4. Make a dressing by blending the orange juice with the salt and pepper in a small bowl. Add the olive oil in a slow stream while whisking. Add the olives and adjust seasoning.
5. Add the dressing to the bowl with the fennel and endive and toss to combine. Place on chilled plates or a platter, top with the orange slices or segments, and serve at once.

Wine notes: The combination of oranges and fennel creates a compelling contrast of light sweetness and light bitterness. What better wine to mediate these two opposites than a dry but fruity light-bodied white from southern Italy?

**White:** Inzolia from Sicily; Vermentino di Sardegna from Sardinia; Falanghina from Campania

# Puntarelle con salsa d'acciughe

## ROMAN CHICORY WITH ANCHOVY DRESSING

Roman-style chicory, known as *puntarelle*, is becoming quite popular in lots of good Italian restaurants in the United States. It has long been a winter favorite in Rome. We like the sharp bite of lemon juice as a counterpoint to the puntarelle, but you may wish to add 2 teaspoons of Dijon mustard to the dressing to mellow the flavors a bit, or you may substitute red wine vinegar for the lemon juice.

**SERVES 4**

**1 head puntarelle (1½ to 2 lb)**

**4 salt-cured anchovy fillets, rinsed well and boned**

**1 garlic clove, peeled**

**2 tbsp lemon juice**

**¼ cup extra-virgin olive oil**

**Freshly ground black pepper, as needed**

1. Trim the chicory stems and remove any split or bruised portions. Remove any wilted or bruised leaves. Separate the outer leaves and the shoots. Rinse the leaves well, spin them dry, and reserve.
2. Slice the shoots lengthwise into thin strips and put them in a bowl of very cold water. Let them soak for at least 30 minutes and up to 2 hours. The shoot strips should curl and become quite crisp. Drain the shoots when you are ready to assemble the salad.
3. Put the anchovies into your salad bowl. Use a fork to mash them into a paste. Add the garlic and crush it with the fork, rubbing the clove right into the bowl. Add the lemon juice and olive oil while whisking with the fork.
4. Add the puntarelle leaves and shoots to the dressing and toss until the leaves and shoot strips are evenly coated. Serve at once with pepper.

Wine notes: Chicory and anchovy, garlic, and lemon dressing provide the balanced flavors of bitter, salty, savory, sweet, and sour. To refresh the palate for this Roman dish, choose a "local" white wine that's charming in its simplicity and effective in quenching thirst.
**White:** Frascati or Est! Est!! Est!!! from Lazio

# Insalata di porcini crudi con parmigiano-reggiano

## RAW PORCINI SALAD WITH PARMIGIANO-REGGIANO

If you can't find fresh porcini, use chanterelle, oyster, cremini, white, or any mushrooms with soft flesh. Serve grilled bread with this simple salad to enjoy it on its own.

**SERVES 6**

- 2 celery hearts or 5 celery stalks
- 8 oz fresh porcini mushrooms
- 2 tbsp extra-virgin olive oil
- 1 tbsp lemon juice
- 1½ tsp thinly sliced chives
- 1½ tsp kosher salt, or as needed
- ⅛ tsp or freshly ground black pepper, or as needed
- 2 cups arugula leaves
- One 8-oz chunk Parmigiano-Reggiano

1. If you are using large celery stalks, they may have tough strings. You can remove them with a vegetable peeler, the same way you would peel a carrot. It is not necessary to peel the tender, smaller ribs from the heart. Trim the celery and cut it into 2- or 3-inch-long pieces. Cut the pieces into thin strips. Set aside.
2. Trim the stem end of the mushrooms (you may completely cut away very tough stems or stems that have softened or been bruised). Use a very sharp knife to cut them into the thinnest slices possible. If you have a mandoline, you could use that.
3. Combine the olive oil, lemon juice, chives, salt, and pepper in a large bowl. Add the sliced porcini and celery and gently toss to coat evenly with the dressing. Place the arugula in a salad bowl and mound the mushroom mixture on top of the arugula. Shave the cheese over the mushrooms with a vegetable peeler and serve.

Wine notes: The combination of arugula and mushrooms creates truly earthy flavors in this salad, and the cheese adds sweet and salty components. Choose a dry, medium-bodied white or a light, fruity rosé to bring out those earthy flavors in the dish, which will in turn bring out the fruitiness of the wine.

**White:** Fiano di Avellino from Campania

**Rosé:** Bardolino Chiaretto from Lugano

# Carpaccio di manzo alle erbette

## BEEF CARPACCIO WITH TENDER GREENS

The simplest approach to this dish is just this: a piece of quality beef, thinly sliced, served with fresh greens, lemon juice, olive oil, and shavings of Parmesan cheese. Different toppings may be added to this dish. Here are just a few suggestions: diced fresh mozzarella, tomato, and basil; grilled vegetables; raw artichokes with marjoram, lemon, and olive oil; and black olives, capers, anchovies, parsley, garlic, and olive oil. Carpaccio may also be served warm: Preheat a broiler to high and set your oven rack as close to the broiler as possible. Put the (ovenproof) plates under the broiler for few seconds and then serve at once.

**SERVES 4**

**12 oz beef tenderloin or New York strip steak**

**6 oz arugula, mâche, purslane, or other soft greens (about 3 cups)**

**Sea salt and freshly ground black pepper, as needed**

**One 6-oz chunk Parmigiano-Reggiano, shaved into thin slices**

**4 tbsp extra-virgin olive oil, as needed**

**2 lemons, halved**

1. Trim any visible fat or sinew from the tenderloin, and then wrap it in plastic wrap. Freeze the meat for 2 hours. If should feel very firm but not be frozen solid.
2. Remove the plastic wrap. Use a very sharp knife with a long, narrow blade to slice the meat into paper-thin slices.
3. Arrange the sliced meat on cold plates or a platter. Top the carpaccio with the greens. Season the carpaccio and greens with salt and pepper. Top with cheese shavings and drizzle with the olive oil. Serve the carpaccio at once with the lemon wedges. (Each person may add lemon juice as desired at the table.)

Wine notes: A medium-bodied dry red wine from Piedmont would be the authentic match for this dish, especially those wines made from the Barbera or Dolcetto grape. (If serving raw artichokes with the carpaccio, go for something lighter and fruitier, like a white Roero Arneis.)

**Red:** Barbera d'Asti or Dolcetto d'Alba from Piedmont

# Carne cruda all'albese

## RAW BEEF IN THE STYLE OF ALBA

We recommend that you seek out a good-quality, tender cut of organic beef, even though in Italy you might find this dish made from a mature veal, the stage at which the meat gets darker and turns from pinkish-gray to a more pronounced red. You want to buy a tender piece of meat, and if you are concerned that there could be bacteria present on the surface of the piece of meat, you may also sear just the outside of the meat very quickly, and then remove the seared part and chop the meat.

**SERVES 4 TO 6**

1 lb beef tenderloin, trimmed

1 garlic clove, lightly crushed but left whole

Juice from 2 lemons

½ salt-cured anchovy fillet, rinsed well and boned (optional)

Salt and freshly ground black pepper, as needed

2 tbsp extra-virgin olive oil, or as needed

1. Trim any visible fat or sinew from the tenderloin, and then wrap it in plastic wrap and chill thoroughly. Use a sharp knife to mince the meat fairly finely. Transfer the meat to a clean, cold bowl. Keep the minced tenderloin very cold if you are not planning to serve it right away.
2. Pierce the garlic clove on the tines of a table fork. Stir the garlic through the meat to "scent" it with the garlic. Gently blend in the lemon juice, anchovy (if you are using it), and salt and pepper. Let the meat rest (leave the fork with the garlic clove in the meat) for about 5 minutes before serving (do not leave it any longer or the meat will lose its attractive red color).
3. Add the olive oil to the cruda, stir once more, and serve at once on chilled plates. Some options for garnishing and serving the cruda follow.

*Here are several garnish options for topping the carne cruda:*

*Shave some fresh white truffle on top if you are ever lucky enough to have some, or try some perfectly fresh, very thinly sliced white mushrooms.*

*Chop or slice some tiny pickles (such as cornichons), or leave them whole.*

*Scatter a few shavings of Parmigiano-Reggiano around the plate.*

*Drizzle a bit more of an exceptional extra-virgin olive oil on top of the meat.*

Wine notes: Alba and Asti are towns in Piedmont and two of the most important wine hubs in the region. There, the locals would choose a medium-bodied Barbera to pair with this dish, especially because the high acidity in the wine will match the refreshing lemon flavors, and together the wine and lemon will enhance the background richness of the carne cruda and Parmigiano.

**Red:** Barbera d'Alba or Barbera d'Asti from Piedmont

# Insalatina di ricci

## SEA URCHIN SALAD

Sea urchins are very popular in the Puglia region, where they are usually eaten raw with a little lemon freshly squeezed on top. We serve the sea urchin in this recipe with a cooked spinach salad because the texture of the cooked spinach is a perfect complement to the sea urchins and spinach's flavor stands up well to their briny, savory taste.

**SERVES 4 TO 6**

1 lb baby spinach

2 fresh green onions, sliced thin on an angle

Extra-virgin olive oil, as needed

12 to 18 sea urchins

Lemon juice, as needed

1. To prepare the spinach, trim the stems and remove any wilted or bruised leaves. Clean the spinach in plenty of cold water until there are no more traces of sand or grit. Drain in a colander.
2. Fill a large pot with water and add enough salt to be able to barely taste it. Cover the pot and bring the water to a rolling boil over high heat.
3. Add the cleaned spinach all at once and stir to submerge. Cook uncovered until the spinach turns a deep green color, about 15 seconds. Lift the greens out of the water with a sieve or slotted spoon and transfer to a bowl of ice water. After the greens are chilled, drain in a colander for several minutes. Squeeze the spinach in your hands to wring out some of the extra water. Arrange the spinach on a plate or platter. Top the spinach with the sliced onion and pour olive oil over the spinach to coat it evenly.
4. Use kitchen scissors to cut the bottom away from each sea urchin. Crack the shell in half and scoop the urchin out of the shell directly onto the spinach. Sprinkle the lemon juice over the urchins and the spinach and serve at once.

Wine notes: The white wines from Puglia may be hard to find, but the Soave Classico and the rosés should be a lot easier to locate. What this dish needs is a dry but fruity wine that will assist in bringing out the briny sweetness in the sea urchin and at the same time will mute the bitterness of the spinach.

**White:** Castel del Monte or Salice Salentino Bianco from Puglia; Soave Classico from Veneto

**Rosé:** Dry rosato from Sicily; Montepulciano d'Abruzzo Cerasuolo from Abruzzo

# Alici marinate con soncino

## MARINATED ANCHOVIES WITH MÂCHE

Fresh anchovies are commonly found in any fish market in Italy. They are prepared in many ways. Here we just marinate them and serve them with buttery sweet lettuce.

**SERVES 4 TO 6**

- 1 lb fresh whole anchovies
- 2 lemons
- ¼ cup dry white wine
- 1 garlic clove, sliced
- 3 fresh bay leaves
- 1 hot red chile, sliced thin
- ½ cup extra-virgin olive oil, plus more as needed
- Mâche (or other tender young green), for serving
- Sea salt, as needed

1. Prepare the anchovies by removing the head and the bones as described on page 50.
2. Place the fish, skin side down, in a 2-quart glass or earthenware dish (large enough to hold the fish in a single layer).
3. Squeeze the lemons into a small bowl; remove any seeds. Add the white wine and pour this mixture over the fish. Let the fish marinate for about 10 minutes.
4. Lift the anchovies from the marinade and transfer to a bowl or crock. Top with the garlic, bay leaves, and hot chile. Pour the olive oil over the fish and let them marinate for 1 hour. Remove and discard the bay leaves.
5. Arrange the mâche on a platter and drizzle the mâche with enough olive oil to just coat the leaves. Season the leaves with salt.
6. Lift the anchovies from the olive oil and serve them on the bed of mâche.

Wine notes: This delicate dish, redolent of the sea and the flavor of fresh lemons, needs a medium-bodied white wine with good acidity and a touch of fruit. Avoid any oak-aged wines and opt instead for the "green" flavors of simpler, more straightforward whites.

**White:** Vermentino di Sardegna or Vermentino di Gallura from Sardinia; Sauvignon from Friuli-Venezia Giulia

# Carpaccio di pesce spada

## SWORDFISH CARPACCIO

Fish carpaccio is very common in regions where fresh fish is available. It is often cured with an acid, usually lemon juice, and marinated with extra-virgin olive oil and herbs.

**SERVES 6 TO 8**

1½ lb swordfish

Sea salt and freshly ground black pepper, as needed

2 lemons, halved

1 orange, halved

¼ cup extra-virgin olive oil

6 green olives

3 tbsp salt-cured capers, rinsed and drained

Mint leaves, as needed

1. Use a sharp knife with a long thin blade to cut the swordfish into very thin slices. (To make them very thin, you may also put the slices between 2 sheets of plastic wrap and pound them very lightly.)
2. Arrange the sliced swordfish on cold plates or a platter. Season with salt and pepper, and then squeeze the lemon and orange juices over the fish (use a small strainer to catch any seeds as you squeeze). Pour the olive oil over the swordfish. Let the swordfish rest for 4 or 5 minutes. As it sits, the fish will begin to turn opaque and get a bit firmer. The longer you let the fish sit, the sharper the flavor and the firmer the fish.
3. Sprinkle the olives, capers, and mint over the top. Serve at once.

Wine notes: This briny, sweet-sour dish requires a medium-bodied dry white or rosé. Since this is a dish from southern Italy, try it with wines from that part of the country, if possible. You want the wine to have enough body to match the intensity of the swordfish but also enough delicate fruit to match the citrus and cleanse the palate of the salt.

**White:** Falanghina from Campania; Vermentino di Gallura from Sardinia; Inzolia from Sicily
**Rosé:** Lacrymarosa from Campania

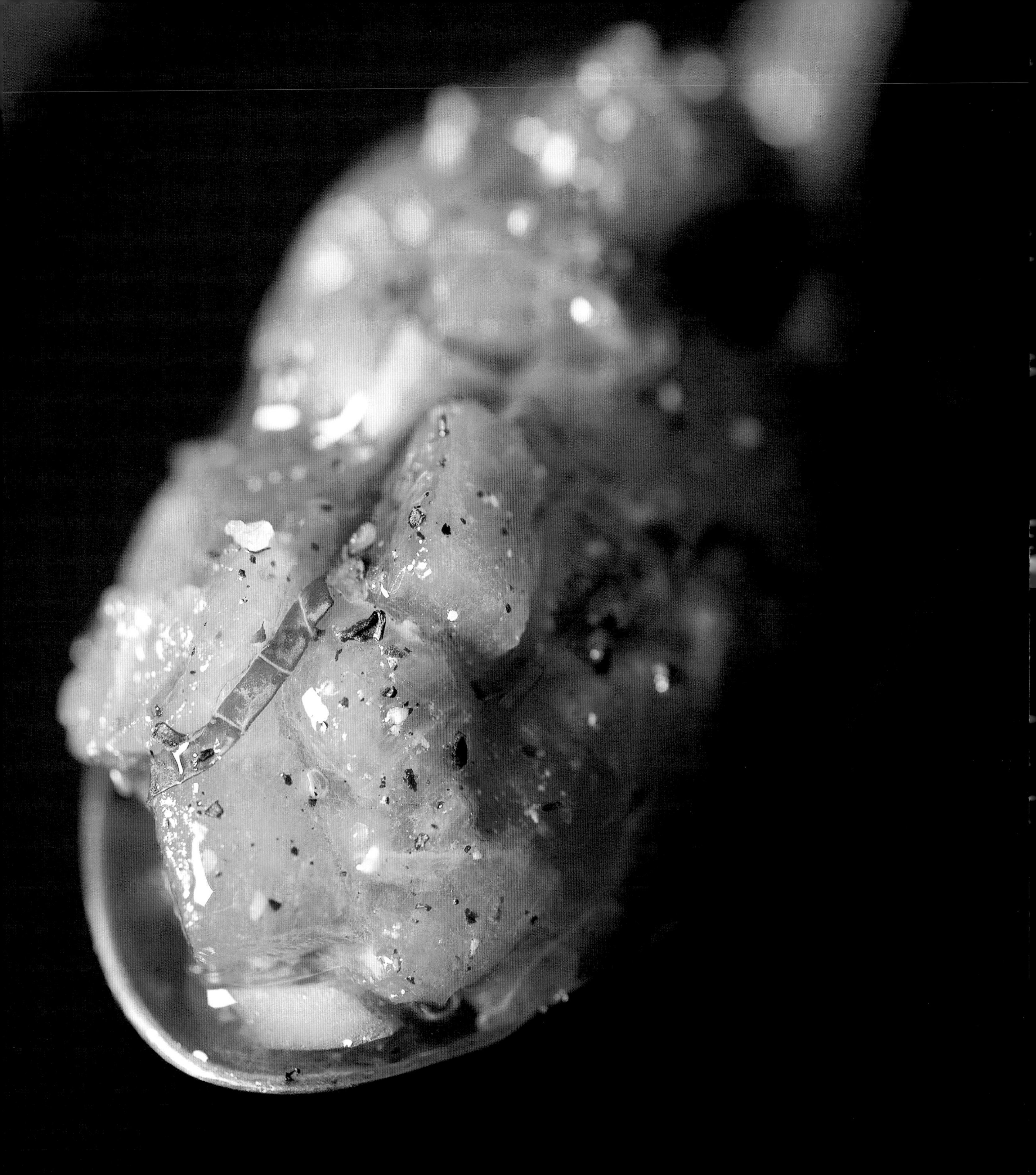

# Tartaro di tonno

## TUNA TARTARE

Tuna is a very popular fish in the south of Italy. We prepare this recipe with a few simple ingredients also typical in that area, including capers, lemon, and red onion. Since the tuna remains partially raw, it must be as fresh as possible. Serve this with bruschetta (see page 45).

**SERVES 4 TO 6**

1 lb tuna
1 tbsp chopped red onion
1 tsp capers in salt
1 tsp chopped mint leaves
2 tbsp olive oil
1 tbsp lemon juice
Sea salt, as needed
Lettuce leaves, for serving

1. Trim the tuna to remove any skin or very dark portions. Use a sharp knife to cut the tuna into very small dice. Transfer the tuna to a clean, cold bowl. Keep it very cold if you are not planning to serve it right away.
2. If you want to tame the bite of the red onion (taste a piece first!), put it in a bowl of cold water and let it soak for about 15 minutes.
3. To prepare the salt-packed capers, put them in a small bowl with enough warm water to cover them generously. Let them soak for 10 minutes, and then rinse them under cold running water. Mince the capers.
4. Add the onions, capers, mint leaves, olive oil, lemon juice, and salt to the tuna just before serving it. Stir them in gently and serve on a bed of lettuce.

---

Wine notes: Pair this southern Italian dish with a medium-bodied dry white wine from southern Italy, if possible: local food, local wine.

**White:** Inzolia from Sicily; Vermentino di Gallura from Sardinia; Falanghina from Campania

# Bresaola con robiola fresca e rucola

## AIR-DRIED BEEF WITH ROBIOLA AND ARUGULA

Bresaola is a typical product of the Valtellina, an area in the north of the Lombardy region. It has the richest flavor if it has a little time to come to room temperature; 15 to 20 minutes is enough. The traditional complement is arugula dressed with oil, lemon juice, and Parmigiano-Reggiano. In this recipe we added Robiola, a creamy, milky cheese from the Lombardy region.

**SERVES 6 TO 8**

1 lb bresaola, very thinly sliced

4 to 5 cups arugula leaves

4 to 5 tbsp extra-virgin olive oil

2 to 3 tbsp lemon juice

Salt and freshly ground black pepper, as needed

1 ball Robiola (about 8 oz), cut into bite-size pieces

1. Arrange the bresaola slices on a platter and allow them to come to room temperature, about 15 minutes.
2. Place the arugula in a large bowl. Drizzle with just enough of the olive oil to lightly coat the leaves. Season the arugula with the lemon juice and salt and pepper.
3. Mound the salad in the center of the slices of bresaola. Top with the cheese and serve at once.

Wine notes: The two reds listed here are made from grapes grown in Lombardy's Valtellina, the origin of the dish as well. Essentially, however, you're seeking a medium- to full-bodied dry red wine to match the intensity of the bresaola and cheese. In a pinch, Chianti Classico, Merlot, or Pinot Noir will work just fine.

**Red:** Inferno or Grumello from Lombardy; Barbera from Piedmont

# Prosciutto e fichi

## PROSCIUTTO AND FIGS

It doesn't matter whether you make this dish with Black Mission, Kadota, Brown Turkey, Celeste, or Calimyrna figs. What's most important is that they are perfectly ripe. If the fresh figs you find are small, you may need only to halve them (cut them lengthwise to show off their beautiful flesh). If they are average size, cut them into quarters.

**SERVES 4**

8 black or green ripe figs

4 to 5 oz prosciutto, thinly sliced (about 3 large slices per person)

4 slices peasant bread (¼ inch thick)

1 garlic clove, peeled and crushed

2 tbsp olive oil

Sea salt, as needed

1. If the figs have very thick skin, as may be in larger fruit, cut away the peel with a very sharp paring knife. Cut the figs into quarters after peeling. If the figs are smaller and the skins are tender and soft, just cut the figs into halves or quarters without peeling them.
2. Arrange the figs on a plate or platter and arrange the prosciutto slices around them.
3. Heat a broiler or a grill to high heat (or a grill pan over high heat). Grill or broil the bread on both sides until it is crisp and very slightly charred. Rub a crushed garlic clove over the bread to season it (1 clove will season 2 slices) and drizzle the slices with the olive oil. Season the bread with a few grains of salt and serve at once with the figs and prosciutto.

Wine notes: Have some fun with this dish and pair it with a lightly sparkling—frizzante—sweeter white or red, such as the traditional Lambrusco, or the fully sparkling—spumante—Brachetto. These wines are slightly sweeter than the dish, and this will help to bring out the richness of the prosciutto and the ripe fig flavors.

**Sparkling White:** Lambrusco Bianco Spumante from Emilia-Romagna
**Sparkling Red:** Lambrusco Reggiano from Emilia-Romagna
**Sparkling Semisweet Rosé:** Brachetto d'Acqui from Piedmont

## SERVING PROSCIUTTO

Prosciutto is one of those ingredients you can eat with pretty much everything...well, almost everything. The most traditional pairing is prosciutto with melon, but figs, kiwi, persimmon, pear, and peaches also complement prosciutto very well. You can also serve prosciutto with fresh mozzarella or another soft and delicate cheese or with Parmesan.

Make sure you buy a good-quality prosciutto. Look for a soft reddish color. The fat should be creamy white, and the slices should drape well. Great prosciutto has a silky texture and a rich, pleasantly salty flavor.

You may also create a salad from figs and prosciutto by adding little bit of greens to the plate (such as radicchio, endive, and arugula cut in small pieces). Lay the figs on top of the greens, and then tear slices of prosciutto into small pieces and add them to the plate. Scatter bits of fresh mozzarella on top, and season with shreds of mint and basil. Dress this salad simply with a drizzle of extra-virgin olive oil, salt, and pepper.

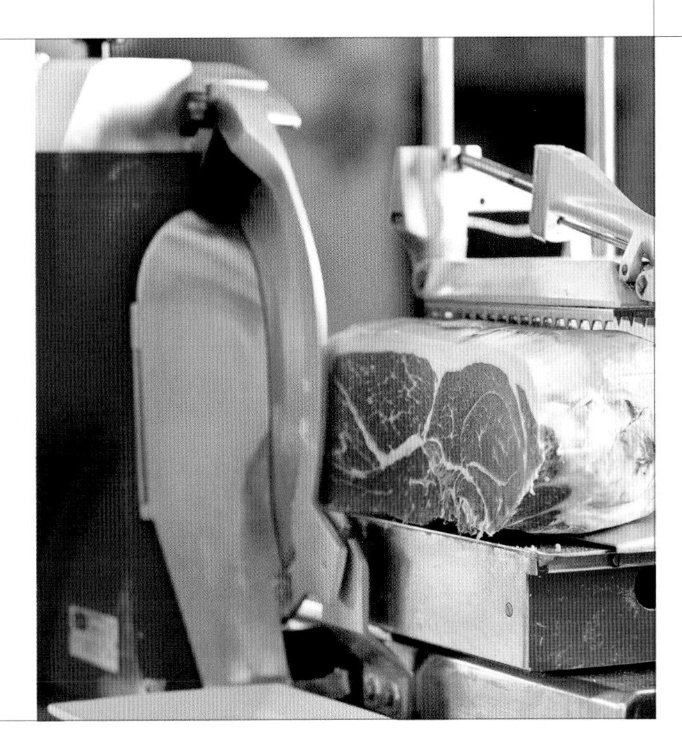

*Using a meat slicer will ensure thin, even slices of prosciutto.*

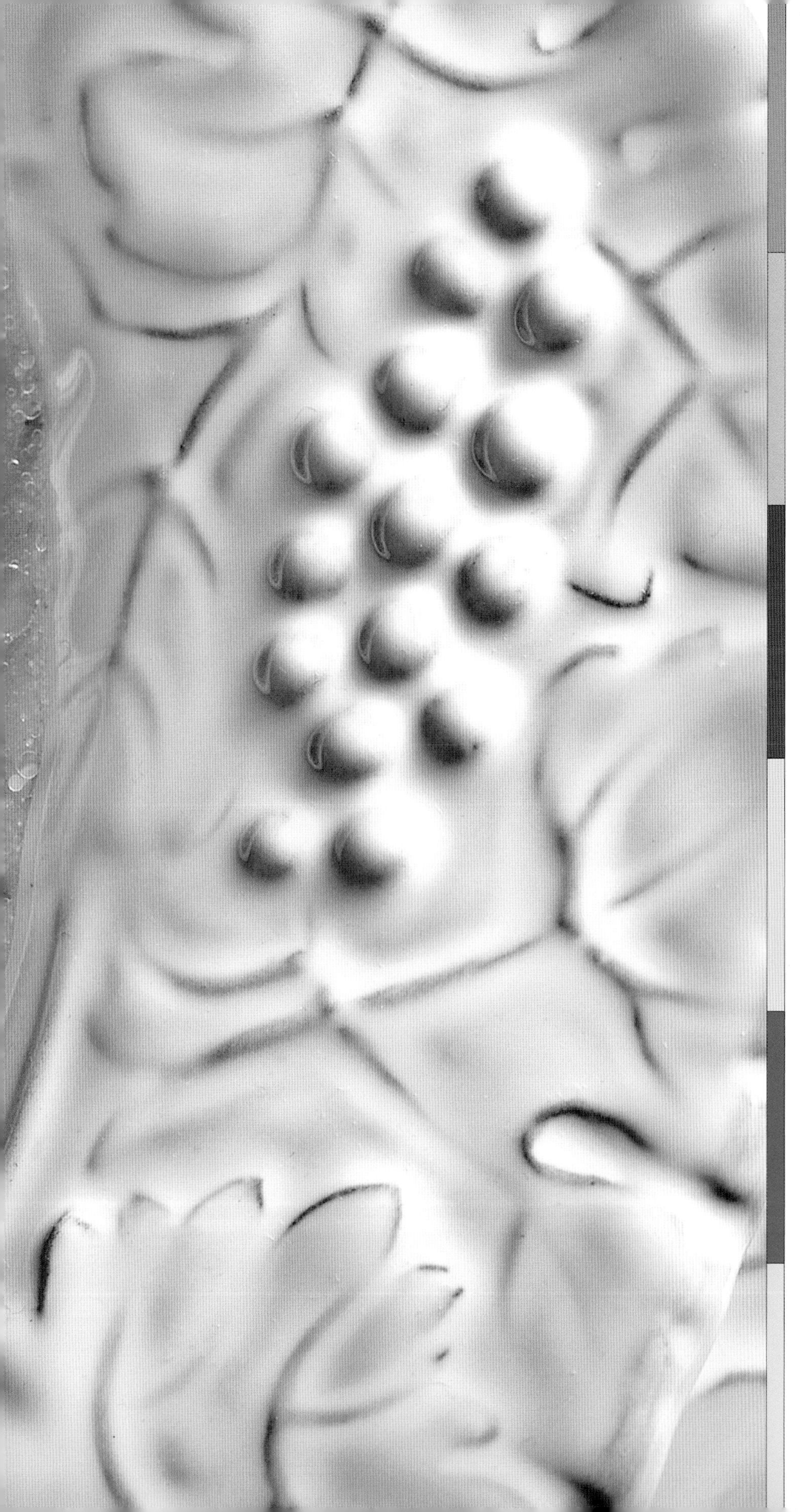

# Brodi

Making a good broth, one like our mothers and grandmothers made, takes time but only a few simple ingredients. You need to have patience and the time to devote to tending to your broth. The rewards are a rich brodo that has incomparable depth and a satisfying fullness. A brodo can be made from a combination of meats like those we include in our recipe on page 88, or you might use just a single meat. Capon, less widely used in the United States, is popular in Italy and makes a remarkable broth. You can use it to make a brodo or feature it in a boiled dinner, Cappone Ripieno (see page 100).

After the broth is strained, the Italian cook's ingenuity takes over. No one would waste the meats used to prepare the broth. The meat is shredded or minced to use in fillings for ravioli or tortellini, ground to make polpette, or used in a salad. The broth itself becomes the mainstay of some classic soups: stracciatella, tortellini in brodo, passatelli, and zuppa pavese.

# Brodo

## BROTH

A big pot of simmering brodo is a common sight. The cook visits the brodo frequently, checking that the simmer is very gentle and never approaching a boil. A skimmer is nearby to lift any debris on the surface. And a spoon is handy to check the brodo while it simmers so that the cook is ready to add a bit of seasoning when it is needed.

**MAKES 1½ GALLONS**

One 3- to 4-lb chicken

3 lb beef (top blade chuck or shank)

3 medium yellow onions

3 carrots

3 celery stalks

3 fresh or canned plum tomatoes

1 sachet containing 3 cloves, 8 black peppercorns, 2 bay leaves, 1 small bunch flat-leaf parsley, and 3 thyme sprigs

Kosher salt, as needed

1. Pull out any pockets of fat from the chicken and rinse well. Trim the beef of any visible fat. Put the chicken and beef in a large pot and add enough cold water to completely cover the meats.

2. Put the pot over medium heat, cover, and bring the water to a simmer. As soon as it comes to a simmer, remove the lid and start skimming any foam that rises to the surface. Add the onions, carrots, celery, and tomatoes.

3. Partially cover the pot by setting the lid slightly ajar to leave an opening; that way, the pot won't be as likely to boil over and you can keep an eye on it more easily. Bring it back to a simmer and cook, periodically skimming the foam that rises to the surface, for about 2 hours. Add the sachet to the pot and cook for 30 minutes longer. Remove the meats from the brodo, letting any brodo inside the chicken drain back into the pot. Reserve the meat to use in other dishes. At this point, the brodo should have a rich, deep flavor. If not, remove the sachet, but continue to simmer for 20 to 30 minutes longer. Add salt to taste.

4. Strain the broth through a wire-mesh sieve directly into a pot if you are planning to serve the brodo right away. If you plan to serve the brodo another day, cool it quickly and store in covered container in the regrigerator for up to 1 week.

1. Ingredients used to prepare broth.

2. Place the ingredients into the pot and cover with water.

3. As it cooks, impurities will float to the surface.

4. After cooking, strain the broth until it's clear and free of all solids.

# Passatelli in brodo

## PARMESAN DUMPLINGS IN MEAT BROTH

It is important to have a good broth when making this dish, so we strongly suggest you make the brodo in this book (see page 88) rather than relying on a store-bought version. Try adding some lemon or orange zest to the dumpling batter.

**SERVES 6**

**1½ cups grated Parmigiano-Reggiano (6 oz)**

**⅔ cup plain dry bread crumbs, not too coarse**

**2 large eggs**

**1 egg yolk**

**1 tbsp chopped flat-leaf parsley**

**Grated nutmeg, as needed**

**Kosher salt and freshly ground black pepper, as needed**

**5 cups Brodo (page 88)**

1. Combine the cheese, bread crumbs, eggs, egg yolk, and parsley in a large bowl. Mix until the mixture comes together in a stiff batter. Season with nutmeg and salt and pepper).
2. Bring the brodo to a simmer in a soup pot over medium-high heat.
3. Transfer the dumpling mixture to a ricer, a colander, or a pastry bag with a very small opening (less than ¼ inch). Press the dumpling batter through the ricer or colander or squeeze it out of the pastry bag into the simmering brodo. If you are using a pastry bag, cut the passatelli into 3-inch lengths as they drop into the brodo. (Note: If your first few passatelli don't hold together when they are simmering in the brodo, add a tablespoon or two more of the bread crumbs to the batter.)
4. Simmer the passatelli in the brodo for no more than 1 minute. Serve the brodo and the passatelli in heated soup plates or bowls at once.

Wine notes: **White:** Chardonnay from Sicily or Trentino-Alto Adige, Soave Classico from Veneto **Red:** Sangiovese di Romagna from Emilia-Romagna; Chianti from Tuscany

# Stracciatella

## EGG-DROP SOUP

Le Marche claims this soup, where it was traditionally served at all important meals. This broth would be served after the appetizer and before the boiled meat. Our recipe comes from Le Marche and calls for a little bit of bread crumbs, but you may omit the bread crumbs altogether to make this soup in the Roman style.

**SERVES 4**

4 large eggs

¼ cup grated Parmigiano-Reggiano (1 oz)

2 tbsp plain dry bread crumbs (optional)

½ tsp lemon zest

Pinch of salt

4 cups Brodo (made with chicken or capon; page 88)

1. Whisk together the eggs, cheese, bread crumbs, lemon zest, and salt in a medium bowl. Be sure the eggs are evenly blended into the mixture.
2. Bring the brodo to a simmer in a pot over medium-high heat. Pour in the egg mixture and whisk (straccia) well so that the eggs separate into small pieces and shreds, about 1 minute.
3. Serve the soup immediately in heated soup plates or bowls.

*It is important to whisk the eggs vigorously so that they do not turn into scrambled eggs in the hot broth.*

Wine note: **White:** Verdicchio dei Castelli di Jesi from Le Marche

# Zuppa pavese

## EGGS IN BROTH

This is a very old soup recipe made from a few simple ingredients that are usually already in the kitchen.

**SERVES 4**

- 4 cups Brodo (page 88)
- 2 tbsp unsalted butter
- 12 slices baguette
- 4 large eggs
- ¾ cup grated Grana Padano (3 oz), plus more for serving (optional)

1. Bring the brodo to a boil in a soup pot over medium-high heat.
2. Heat 1 tablespoon of the butter in a large skillet over medium heat. Add the bread slices and sauté the slices of bread until crisp and golden brown on both sides, about 2 minutes per side. (Work in batches and add more butter between batches as needed.)
3. Put 3 slices of toasted bread into each heated soup plate. Crack a fresh egg on top of the toast. Top with cheese and ladle the boiling brodo over the egg and bread.
4. Serve the soup immediately. Pass additional cheese on the side if desired.

Wine notes: **Sparkling:** Prosecco from Veneto **White:** Orvieto Classico from Umbria; Frascati Superiore from Lazio

# Panada

## BREAD CRUMB AND EGG SOUP

This soup is a dish typical of Cremona, where it is also called *Panada Cremonese*. Another name for this soup in the local dialect is *paan trit maridaa*, which means "the marriage between broth and eggs." In the 1940s and 1950s, this soup was the first food given to people who had been sick for a long time and needed to get their energy and strength back. Cremona cooks use a special bread, a hard bread that has been toasted slowly overnight at a very low heat; *paan biscutt* is the Cremonese word for it. Make sure you buy fresh bread crumbs or make your own. Stale bread crumbs will give a funny taste.

**SERVES 6**

**4 cups plain dry bread crumbs, freshly made if possible**

**8 cups Brodo (page 88)**

**¼ cup (½ stick) unsalted butter**

**3 large eggs**

**¼ cup grated Parmigiano-Reggiano (1 oz)**

**¼ tsp salt**

**Pinch of grated nutmeg**

1. Combine the bread crumbs and brodo in a soup pot and let them stand for 15 minutes.
2. Bring the brodo to a simmer over low heat. Add the butter, return to a simmer, partially cover the pot, and simmer slowly for 25 minutes, stirring every 5 minutes or so to prevent the bread crumbs from sticking to the bottom.
3. Whisk the eggs, cheese, salt, and nutmeg together in a small bowl. Pour this mixture into the simmering brodo and whisk well to break up the eggs into fine shreds. Simmer until the eggs are cooked, no more than 1 to 2 minutes. The finished soup should have the consistency of a soft polenta.
4. Remove the pot from the heat and serve the soup immediately in heated soup plates or bowls.

Wine notes: **White:** Pinot Bianco from Trentino-Alto Adige or Friuli-Venezia Giulia; Soave Classico from Veneto

# Vitello tonnato

## VEAL IN TUNA DRESSING

The veal is normally poached in a broth, although some people prefer to roast it. Veal eye round can be part of the mix of meats used to make the actual broth and then also used in the vitello tonnato preparation.

**SERVES 8**

- 6 cups Brodo (page 88)
- 1 carrot
- ½ medium yellow onion
- 1 celery stalk
- 1 bay leaf
- 1 thyme sprig
- ½ tsp peppercorns
- 2 lb veal eye round, left whole
- ¾ cup plus 2 tbsp mayonnaise
- 5 oz canned tuna (packed in oil)
- 1 tbsp salt-cured capers, soaked and chopped (page 81)
- 2 salted anchovies
- 1 tbsp dry white wine
- Kosher salt and freshly ground black pepper, as needed
- Whole capers, for garnish
- Chopped flat-leaf parsley, for garnish

1. Bring the brodo to a simmer in a soup pot over medium-high heat. Add the carrot, onion, celery, bay leaf, thyme, and peppercorns.
2. Trim the veal of any visible fat. (Optional, but a good idea: Tie the veal roast with butcher's twine to keep its shape compact and even while you poach it.)
3. Add the veal to the simmering brodo, decrease the heat to low, and gently poach the veal until it is almost completely cooked through, about 1 hour (the temperature on an instant-read thermometer should be 135 degrees F; the veal will finish cooking as it cools in the brodo).
4. Transfer the veal from the brodo to a bowl. Remove the pot from the heat and let the liquid cool to at least 120 degrees F. Pour the warm broth over the veal, cover the bowl, and let the veal chill in the refrigerator for at least 12 and up to 24 hours before you plan to serve the vitello tonnato. (Reserve the remaining broth to use in other dishes.)
5. To make the sauce, put the mayonnaise, tuna, capers, anchovies, and wine into the bowl of a food processor. Pulse the machine on and off until a thick sauce forms. It should be about the consistency of a good mayonnaise. If it is too thick, add a bit of the broth to thin it. Taste the sauce and if necessary add salt and pepper.
6. To serve the vitello tonnato, remove the veal from the cold brodo and remove the strings. Cut the veal into thin slices with a sharp knife. Arrange the slices on a platter and spoon the sauce over the top. Garnish the vitello tonnato with whole capers and some parsley. Serve at once.

Wine notes: **White:** Roero Arneis from Piedmont; Vermentino from Tuscany; Traminer (Gewürztraminer) from Trentino-Alto Adige

**Rosé:** Bardolino Chiaretto from Lugano; Montepulciano d'Abruzzo Cerasuolo from Abruzzo

**Red:** Dolcetto d'Alba from Piedmont; Valpolicella Classico from Veneto

# Bollito misto

## BOILED MEATS

Some of the earliest mentions of this dish associate it with Vittorio Emanuele II. He used to spend some time in Moncalvo (Piedmont), where his main pursuits were hunting, reading love stories, and eating great meals. The mainstay of these meals consisted of boiled meats paired with some good Barbera wine. A great bollito misto like the ones he enjoyed depends upon a selection of meats that have been well rested and left to age (*frollare*) for several days. Some cooks like to add an apple to the bollito as it cooks to give an interesting perfume to the broth and a great aroma to the kitchen while it simmers.

**SERVES 8 TO 12 (DEPENDING ON THE QUANTITY OF CUTS YOU USE)**

One 3- to 4-lb chicken, capon, or stewing hen

3 lb beef chuck (top blade) or shank

3 fresh or canned plum tomatoes

3 medium yellow onions

3 carrots

3 celery stalks

1 leek

1 sachet containing 3 cloves, 8 black peppercorns, 2 bay leaves, a small bunch of flat-leaf parsley, and 3 thyme sprigs

Salt, as needed

1. Pull out any pockets of fat from the chicken and rinse well. Trim the beef of any visible fat. Put the chicken and beef in a large pot and add enough cold water to completely cover the meats.
2. Put the pot over medium heat, cover it, and bring the water to a simmer. As soon as it comes to a simmer, remove the lid and start skimming any foam that rises to the surface. Add the tomatoes, onions, carrots, celery, and leek. Replace the cover, leaving it slightly ajar so the pot doesn't boil over.
3. Bring it back to a simmer and simmer for about 2 hours. Add the sachet and cook for 30 minutes longer. Remove the meats from the broth, letting any broth inside the chicken drain back into the pot, and set aside on a carving board. At this point, the broth should have a rich, deep flavor. If not, remove the sachet, but continue to simmer for 20 to 30 minutes longer. Add salt to taste.
4. Strain the broth through a wire-mesh sieve directly into a pot. (If you plan to serve the broth another day, cool the broth over an ice bath; it will last up to 4 days in a covered container in the refrigerator or up to 2 months in the freezer.) Return the broth to a simmer while you carve the meats.
5. Serve the carved meats on a platter (see next page for additional serving suggestions). Serve the broth separately in cups.

Wine notes: **Red:** Barbera d'Alba, Barbera d'Asti, Dolcetto d'Alba or Dolcetto di Dogliani from Piedmont

*Coarse sea salt and different mostardas and sauces are usually served with the sliced meats from a bollito misto, along with capers and freshly grated horseradish mixed with little vinegar and oil. Another traditional and simple garnish is made from white bread soaked in vinegar with a few pieces of garlic and some spices, mashed together to make a sauce. The classic verde (green) includes garlic, parsley, anchovy, bread soaked in vinegar, and oil; and rosso (red) includes red pepper, tomato, mustard, garlic, and vinegar.*

*You may also serve boiled eggs or potatoes to let each person mash into the broth with a fork, along with a little butter to make it a little thicker.*

## THE PERFECT BOLLITO

A true bollito misto includes a wide range of cuts, many of them difficult to find in the United States. But each of them adds something unique to a bollito misto, including most of these cuts: rump (capocollo), leg or shank (gamba o stinco), belly (pancia o scaramella, o biancostato o grasso magro), butt (culatta), head (testina), tongue (lingua), hoof (zampino), and oxtail (coda). Some other good and more readily available cuts for a tasty broth include beef short ribs, veal breast or shoulder blade, or any cut from the veal shoulder. Chicken feet might also used.

A few cuts (notably the head or tongue, as well as cotechino or zampone) might make the resulting broth too fatty or give it a strong flavor and smell. Simmer these meats separately and add them to the bollito after it has cooked.

# Cappone ripieno

## STUFFED CAPON

Serve pieces of the capon and stuffing on their own with Mostarda (see page 63) or in a soup plate with a ladleful of the broth in which you cooked the capon.

**SERVES 6 TO 8**

One 4-lb capon

¼ cup (½ stick) unsalted butter

4 oz pancetta, cubed

1 cup diced yellow onions

2 carrots, diced

1 lb savoy cabbage, thinly sliced

1 thyme sprig

1 bay leaf

Salt and freshly ground black pepper, as needed

8 to 9 slices day-old bread (8 oz)

1 cup warm milk

¼ cup grated Parmigiano-Reggiano (1 oz)

¼ cup chopped flat-leaf parsley

Zest of 1 lemon

6 cups Brodo (page 88)

1. To prepare the capon, pull out any pockets of fat from the interior and blot the capon well inside and out with paper towels. Remove the liver and heart to use in the stuffing; cut them into small pieces and reserve.
2. To make the stuffing for the capon, heat a large skillet over medium heat. Add the butter and pancetta. Cook, stirring to cook the pancetta evenly, until the pancetta is tender and translucent and most of the fat from the pancetta has melted into the butter. Add the onion and carrots and sauté, stirring often, until the onions are tender without any browning, about 5 minutes. Add the cabbage, thyme, and bay leaf and stir well to coat the cabbage evenly with the fat. Season with salt and pepper. Continue to cook, stirring occasionally, until the cabbage is very tender, about 20 minutes.
3. Break the bread apart into small chunks and put it in a large bowl. Add the milk to the bread and let it soak while you finish cooking the cabbage mixture.
4. Add the reserved chopped liver and heart to the cabbage mixture and cook, stirring frequently, until the liver is cooked through, about 4 minutes.
5. Remove and discard the thyme and bay leaf from the cabbage. Add the cabbage to the soaked bread along with the cheese, parsley, and lemon zest. Stir until you have a relatively even mixture. Add a bit of salt and pepper.
6. Stuff the cabbage-and-bread stuffing into the capon, filling the bird through the body and through the neck. Use butcher's twine and a needle to sew the openings closed. This is important to keep the stuffing inside the capon as the bird simmers in the broth.
7. Bring the brodo to a simmer in a soup pot over medium-high heat. Add the capon and cook gently until the capon is tender, 2 to 3 hours.
8. Transfer the capon to a carving board and carve the capon. Place on a platter and serve with the stuffing alongside. Serve the brodo either as a first course or to accompany the capon.

Wine notes: **White:** Verdicchio from Le Marche; Chardonnay from Tuscany, Piedmont, Veneto, or Trentino-Alto Adige **Red:** Rosso Conero or Rosso Piceno from Le Marche; Bardolino Classico from Veneto; Pinot Nero/Pinot Noir from Trentino-Alto Adige

# Insalata di carne

## MEAT SALAD

This is a typical preparation for any kind of leftover meat from the Bollito Misto on page 98. In this case we are using beef, but any combination may be used or mixed together (such as pot roast, roasted chicken, braised beef or veal, and so on). You may serve it on a bed of lettuce, arugula, radicchio, endive, or whatever greens you like, or just on its own. Buon appetito!

**SERVES 6 AS AN APPETIZER, 4 AS A MAIN COURSE**

1 lb cooked beef (top blade chuck or shank)

1 lb cooked skin-on potato

2 boiled whole carrots, peeled

3 oz cornichons or Giardiniera (page 52)

2 tbsp chopped flat-leaf parsley

¼ cup extra-virgin olive oil, or as needed

Red wine vinegar, as needed

Lemon juice, as needed

Kosher salt and freshly ground black pepper, as needed

2 hard-boiled eggs, for garnish (optional)

1. Dice the beef, potato, carrots, and pickles and place in a large bowl. Add the parsley.
2. Combine the olive oil, vinegar, and lemon juice to make a dressing. Pour the dressing over the meat and vegetables and toss to coat them evenly. Season the salad with salt and pepper.
3. If you wish, just before serving the salad, peel the eggs and either quarter them to garnish the platter or plate or dice them to fold them directly into the salad. Serve at room temperature.

Wine note: **Red:** Dolcetto d'Alba or Barbera d'Asti from Piedmont; Merlot from Veneto

# Polpette

## "NOT THE TYPICAL AMERICAN MEATBALL"

Most meatballs in the United States are made from raw ground meat that is seasoned and shaped and then fried or baked. Italian polpette are made from the cooked meats left over from making a big ragù, bollito misto, or brodo. You may use any variety of meat (boiled, braised, or even roasted) for this dish. Vegetables, spinach or other greens, braised artichokes, or even the cooked vegetables from making your broth may be added, as well as some grated or diced cheese, if you like.

**SERVES 4 TO 6 AS AN APPETIZER**

**1 lb cooked meat (left over from preparing Brodo or Bollito)**

**½ cup plain dry bread crumbs, or as needed**

**½ cup grated Parmigiano-Reggiano (2 oz)**

**1 large egg**

**1 tsp mixed herbs, such as marjoram, sage, flat-leaf parsley, and/or basil**

**Kosher salt and freshly ground black pepper, as needed**

**2 cups olive oil, or as needed, for frying**

BREADING

**1½ cups all-purpose flour**

**5 large eggs, beaten**

**3 cups plain, dry bread crumbs**

1. Set up a meat grinder with a bowl to catch the meat as you grind it. Cut the meat into pieces and drop them through the opening of the meat grinder while it is running. (If you have cooked vegetables on hand, grind them along with the meat.)
2. Add the bread crumbs, cheese, egg, herbs and salt and pepper. Mix gently to combine. Check to see if the mixture will hold together: take about ¼ cup of the meat mixture and shape it into a patty a little wider than it is thick. If it falls apart, add a tablespoon or two more of the bread crumbs. Shape the mixture into patties and put them on a plate. Chill them for at least 30 minutes before frying.
3. When you are ready to fry the polpette, pour enough oil into a heavy frying pan to come to a depth of about ½ inch. Heat the oil over low heat until it is hot (the surface will ripple and look hazy and should be about 350 degrees F).
4. To bread the polpette, place the flour on a plate, the eggs in a shallow bowl, and the bread crumbs on a plate. Coat the polpette first in a little flour, then dip them in the egg, and finally coat them in the bread crumbs.
5. Add the polpette to the hot oil, leaving room around them so they will brown evenly. Cook on the first side until golden brown, about 2 minutes. Turn them over and cook on the second side until golden and crisp, 2 or 3 minutes longer. Remove them from the oil with a slotted spoon and drain briefly on paper towels.
6. Serve the polpette at once, while they are very hot, or at room temperature.

Wine notes: **Red:** Chianti Classico from Tuscany; Montepulciano d'Abruzzo from Abruzzo

# Marubini

## CHRISTMAS RAVIOLI

This is a typical Christmas-dinner ravioli from Cremona.

**SERVES 6 TO 8**

FILLING

**½ beef brain (8 oz)**

**1 tbsp red wine vinegar**

**1 bay leaf**

**8 oz braised beef**

**8 oz roast veal or pork**

**8 oz fresh sausage**

**1 cup grated Grana Padano (4 oz)**

**1 large egg**

**Kosher salt and freshly ground black pepper, as needed**

**Grated nutmeg, as needed**

**2 tbsp heavy cream, or as needed**

**1½ lb Egg Pasta (page 153)**

**Egg wash made from 1 egg mixed with 1 tbsp water**

**6 cups Brodo (page 88)**

1. To make the filling, first prepare the brain by pulling away the thin membrane covering it. Bring about 4 cups of water to a boil in a saucepan with the vinegar and bay leaf. Add the brain and poach it for 2 minutes. (This is just long enough to firm up the brain so that you can cut it into small cubes more easily.) Remove the brain from the poaching liquid and let it cool. Cut the brain into small dice and set aside.
2. Set up a meat grinder with a bowl to catch the meat as you grind it. Cut the beef and veal into pieces and drop the pieces through the opening of the meat grinder while it is running.
3. Add the sausage, cheese, diced brain, egg, salt and pepper, and nutmeg. Mix these ingredients well. Add a few tablespoons of cream if the mixture seems too dry.
4. Roll the pasta dough into 2 thin sheets about 2 inches wide and the same length (see page 151). Spoon or pipe the filling in 2-tbsp mounds down the center of one of the pasta sheets, spacing the filling mounds about 2 inches apart. Brush the edges of the pasta sheet and around the filling with a little egg wash to help seal the marubini. Top with a second sheet of pasta and press the sheets together along the edges and around the filling. Use a pasta wheel or cutter to make 2-inch rounds. Repeat as necessary until all of the pasta is filled.
5. Bring the brodo to a simmer in a soup pot over medium-high heat. Add the marubini and cook until the pasta is tender, about 10 minutes.
6. Serve the soup immediately in heated soup plates or bowls.

Wine notes: **Red:** Inferno or Grumello from Lombardy; Nebbiolo d'Alba from Piedmont

# Tortellini in brodo

## TORTELLINI IN BROTH

This is a famous preparation often served during holidays. Tortellini can be enjoyed with meat sauce also, but in Italy, you will most often find them served in broth.

**SERVES 6 TO 8**

FILLING

**4 oz pork, chopped**

**3 oz boneless chicken breast, chopped**

**3 oz mortadella, chopped**

**3 oz prosciutto, chopped**

**1¾ cups grated Parmigiano-Reggiano (7 oz), plus more for garnish**

**1 large egg**

**Grated nutmeg, as needed**

**1½ lb Fresh Egg Pasta Dough (page 153)**

**6 cups Brodo (page 88)**

1. If you are using uncooked pork and chicken, sauté them in butter until they are golden on all sides and have cooked through, 6 to 7 minutes total. Let the meat cool before you grind it.
2. To make the filling, set up a meat grinder with a bowl to catch the meat as you grind it. Drop the pieces of meat through the opening of the meat grinder while it is running. Grind the mortadella and the prosciutto with the cooked meats.
3. Add the cheese, egg, and nutmeg to the ground meats. Stir to blend evenly.
4. Roll the pasta dough into thin sheets (see page 151) and cut it into 2-inch-diameter circles or 2-inch squares. Place a small amount of the filling (about 1 teaspoon) on each dough piece. Fold them in half and press the edges together to seal the tortellini. Finish shaping them by folding the two tips around your index finger and pressing the tips well to seal them together.
5. Bring the brodo to a simmer in a soup pot over medium-high heat. Add the tortellini and cook until the pasta is tender, about 10 minutes.
6. Serve the soup immediately in heated soup plates or bowls. Pass additional grated cheese on the side.

Wine notes: **White** (for the Broth): Albana di Romagna from Emilia-Romagna; Roero Arneis from Piedmont

**Red** (for the Meat Sauce): Sangiovese di Romagna from Emilia-Romagna; Chianti or Rosso di Montalcino from Tuscany

# Minestre

*Minestra* is a general term for anything served between the antipasti and the main course. In the broadest of interpretations, minestre include thick soups as well as "dry" soups such as risotto and pasta. These days, it typically refers to robust, hearty soups that include a variety of ingredients: beans, grains, pastas, vegetables, and meats.

Some of the basic ingredients found in traditional Italian minestre are the leftovers from other meals—the broth from a bollito misto, the contorni (side dishes) from the Sunday roast—or bits and pieces of ingredients that might otherwise go to waste—stale bread or cheese rind—which are used to add flavor and body to make the soup more filling. This careful attention to using all the ingredients available and wasting nothing is at the heart of the cucina povera tradition (the cuisine of the poor). Minestrone, perhaps one of the most famous Italian minestre around the world, is a perfect example of how a single culinary concept can be reinvented over and over again as you move from region to region.

Use your imagination when it comes to selecting the vegetables for your minestra, adding any type you like. Some typical vegetables include onions, leeks, carrots, celery, potatoes, zucchini, string beans, freshly shelled beans, tomatoes, and cabbage. During certain times of the year, pumpkin, chestnuts, and different types of greens may also be added. You might like to add some pasta to the soup as it simmers, such as ditalini or even broken spaghetti. Other grains have a place in our minestre too, including farro, barley, or rice, to give the soup some additional body.

Our mothers and grandmothers didn't have the time to spend pureeing a soup in a blender or food processor to an evenly smooth consistency. They simply broke it up with a fork so the mashed vegetables could thicken the broth a bit. Use the back of a wooden spoon or a potato masher to crush some of the vegetables or beans directly in the pot for a rustic, authentic presentation.

# Pasta e fagioli

## PASTA AND BEANS

Borlotti beans (similar to cranberry beans) would be our choice for this type of soup, but any beans could be used; if you substitute a white bean for the borlottis, omit the carrots for a nicer look. No matter what type of bean you are using, remember to watch the soup as it cooks, adding more broth or water if the soup is becoming very heavy. It is supposed to be quite thick but still easy to eat with a spoon, especially as it finishes. Add some garnishes to the soup if you like: Julienned fresh radicchio or escarole or cooked lobster pieces, shrimp, or octopus would all go very well with this soup.

**SERVES 8 TO 10**

- 1 lb dried borlotti beans (about 2½ cups)
- 1 sachet containing 4 sage leaves, 2 rosemary sprigs, 2 garlic cloves, crushed, one 2-inch-square piece Parmigiano-Reggiano rind, rinsed, and (optional) 2½ oz prosciutto or pancetta pieces
- 1 cup diced yellow onions
- ½ cup diced celery
- ½ cup diced carrot
- 1 cup crushed canned tomatoes including juices
- 4 qt water or Vegetable Stock
- 4 oz Maltagliati (page 160) or other little ribbon-shaped pasta
- Kosher salt and freshly ground pepper, as needed
- ¼ cup olive oil

1. The day before making the soup, sort and rinse the beans and soak them in cold water to cover for at least 8 and up to 24 hours.
2. Add the sachet to a soup pot along with the onions, celery, carrot, and tomatoes.
3. Drain the beans and add them to the pot. Add the water or stock and bring the soup to a boil over high heat. Decrease the heat to low and continue to simmer the soup until the beans are tender enough to mash easily, about 2 hours.
4. Use a slotted spoon to transfer about half of the beans to a food processor, food mill, or blender. Puree until the beans are smooth (add a ladleful of the soup's liquid to make it easier to puree the beans) and return them to the soup.
5. Add the pasta to the soup and simmer until the pasta is fully cooked, 10 to 12 minutes depending upon the shape of your pasta.
6. Remove and discard the sachet. Add salt and pepper to taste. (The soup is ready to finish and serve now, or you may cool and store the soup in the refrigerator for up to 3 days or in the freezer for up to 2 months.)
7. Serve the soup in heated soup plates or bowls, topped with a drizzle of olive oil.

Wine notes: **Red:** Valpolicella Classico Superiore or, even better, Valpolicella Ripasso from Veneto; Chianti or Rosso di Montalcino from Tuscany; Cannonau di Sardegna from Sardinia; Nero d'Avola from Sicily

# Pasta e ceci

## PASTA AND CHICKPEAS

Every town in Italy has its own recipe for the world-famous pasta e fagioli (see page 109), but you may not have heard as much about pasta and chickpeas, though the combination works just as well. In Le Marche it was traditional to make this soup on the day the fields were sown with grain, in the hopes that it would improve the harvest by encouraging the wheat kernels to grow to the size of chickpeas. If you are using fresh herbs instead of dry ones, add them at the end of cooking time. Serve this dish drizzled with your best extra-virgin olive oil.

**SERVES 4 TO 6**

- 1 lb dried chickpeas (about 2½ cups)
- ½ cup extra-virgin olive oil, plus more for drizzling
- 1 medium yellow onion, finely chopped
- 1 celery stalk, finely chopped
- 2 garlic cloves, chopped
- 1 rosemary sprig, leaves picked and chopped
- 3 cups Brodo (page 88) or Vegetable Broth or as needed
- ¾ cup ditalini (or any short dried pasta)
- Sea salt and freshly ground black pepper, as needed
- Crushed hot red pepper, as needed
- Chopped basil (optional)
- Chopped flat-leaf parsley (optional)

1. The day before making the soup, sort and rinse the chickpeas and soak in cold water to cover for at least 12 and up to 24 hours.
2. Drain the chickpeas and put them in a pot. Add enough cold water to cover them by at least 2 inches. Bring the water to a boil over high heat. Decrease the heat to low and continue to simmer the chickpeas until they are tender, at least 45 minutes, or longer depending upon how old the chickpeas are. Drain the chickpeas in a colander and reserve.
3. Heat a soup pot over medium heat. Add the olive oil, onion, celery, garlic, and rosemary. Stir to coat the vegetables in the oil. Cover the pot and cook over low heat until the vegetables are tender and have started to release some of their juices, about 10 minutes.
4. Drain the chickpeas and add them to the soup pot, along with the broth. Stir well and cook over low heat until the chickpeas are very tender, 30 to 40 minutes.
5. Transfer half of the soup to a large bowl. Use an immersion blender to puree the soup left in the pot. Return the unpureed soup to the pot, and add the pasta. Continue to simmer the soup until the pasta is cooked and tender, 10 to 12 minutes depending upon the shape of the pasta you use. Add salt, black pepper, and hot red pepper to taste. (The soup is ready to finish and serve now, or you may cool and store the soup in the refrigerator for up to 3 days or in the freezer for up to 2 months.)
6. Serve the soup in heated soup plates or bowls, topped with basil and parsley, if desired, and a drizzle of olive oil.

Wine notes: **White:** Verdicchio from Le Marche; Vernaccia di San Gimignano from Tuscany **Red (if meat is added):** Rosso Piceno from Le Marche; Montepulciano d'Abruzzo from Abruzzo; Chianti from Tuscany

# Zuppa di castagne, fagioli, e latte

## CHESTNUT, BEAN, AND MILK SOUP

This soup comes from the interior of Italy, in the Campania region. It is the perfect treat for a cold winter night, served with a few slices of grilled bread (see Bruschetta recipe, page 45). If fresh porcini are not available, try other mushrooms or substitute a few ounces of dried porcini for fresh ones. (Reconstitute dried mushrooms by letting them soak in a bowl of warm water until they soften. Reserve the soaking liquid to add to broths or soups.)

**SERVES 6 TO 8**

**8 oz fresh chestnuts**

**1 fresh bay leaf**

**2 oz smoked bacon, diced**

**½ medium yellow onion, minced**

**8 oz fresh porcini mushrooms, sliced**

**2 oz Marsala**

**1½ cups cooked cannellini beans**

**3 fresh sage leaves**

**Salt and freshly ground black pepper, as needed**

**4 cups whole milk**

**Extra-virgin olive oil, as needed**

1. Peel the chestnuts as described (see below). Put the peeled chestnuts in a pot and add enough water to cover them. Add 1 bay leaf and bring the water to a simmer over medium-high heat.
2. Heat a soup pot over medium heat. Add the bacon and cook, stirring occasionally, until the bacon renders some fat.
3. Add the onion and stir to coat with the fat. Sauté, stirring often, until the onions are tender without any browning, about 5 minutes. Add the porcini and cook until they are tender, 2 or 3 minutes longer. Add the Marsala and stir to release any drippings sticking to the pot.
4. Drain the chestnuts; remove and discard the bay leaf. Add the chestnuts to the soup pot, along with the beans. Tear the sage into small pieces and add that to the pot along with some salt and pepper. Add the milk and bring the soup to a simmer over low heat. Simmer slowly until all of the ingredients are tender and hot and the soup has a good flavor and consistency, about 15 minutes. If the soup becomes too thick as it simmers, you may want to add a bit of water or more milk to thin it a little, but it is supposed to be quite thick. (The soup is ready to finish and serve now, or you may cool and store the soup in the refrigerator for up to 3 days or in the freezer for up to 2 months.)
5. Serve the soup in heated soup plates or bowls topped with a drizzle of olive oil.

### CHESTNUTS

Chestnuts have sustained Italians over the centuries. They are a relatively starchy nut, perfect for cooking into thick creamy soups. To prepare fresh chestnuts:

1. Cut an X on the flatter of the nut's two sides. Try to keep your cut shallow so that you don't cut into the nutmeat.
2. Bring a pot of water to a rolling boil and add the chestnuts. Let them boil just long enough for the shell around the crosshatch cut to start coming loose, about 10 minutes.
3. Remove the pot from the heat and, working with a few chestnuts at a time, take them from the water and pull away the shell. The chestnuts are ready to use according to recipe instructions.

Wine notes: **White:** Greco di Tufo or Fiano di Avellino from Campania

# Zuppa di lenticchie con cotechino

## LENTIL SOUP WITH COTECHINO

This is another hearty and flavorful soup to enjoy in the winter, gathered around the fireplace. Green lentils from Castelluccio are perfect for this soup (see sidebar). If you can't find cotechino, you may replace it with pancetta, smoked bacon, prosciutto, or any type of sausage. Serve this soup with some grilled bread. If you choose a different type of lentil than we suggest, you may have to adjust the cooking time. For a vegetarian version, just omit the sausage and use vegetable stock or water instead of the brodo.

**SERVES 6**

1 lb green lentils (about 2½ cups; ideally from Castelluccio)

½ cup extra-virgin olive oil

3 oz cotechino (or see above for alternatives)

Pinch of ground toasted cumin seeds

½ medium yellow onion, diced

½ celery stalk, diced

½ carrot, diced

1 tsp chopped garlic

Pinch of crushed hot red pepper

½ cup peeled, chopped tomato

3 qt Brodo (page 88), Vegetable Broth or water

1 sachet containing 1 rosemary sprig, 1 thyme sprig, 1 flat-leaf parsley sprig, and 1 bay leaf

1 Idaho potato, peeled and diced

½ cup thinly sliced or diced fennel

Salt and freshly ground black pepper, as needed

1. Sort and rinse the lentils. (Castelluccio lentils do not need to be soaked prior to cooking.)
2. Heat a large skillet over medium heat. Add half of the olive oil and add the cotechino and cumin. Cook, stirring frequently, until the cotechino just starts to take on a bit of color. There should be 2 tablespoons of rendered fat and olive oil in the pan.
3. Add the onion, celery, carrot, garlic, and hot red pepper. Stir to coat them with the oil. Sauté, stirring often, until the onion is tender without any browning, about 8 minutes. Add the lentils and tomato. Cook over medium-high heat until the tomatoes develop a rich color and aroma, 3 minutes longer.
4. Add the broth, sachet, and potato. Simmer the soup until the lentils and potato are tender, about 20 minutes. Add the fennel and simmer until the fennel is tender, 2 or 3 minutes longer. Add salt and black pepper to taste. (The soup is ready to finish and serve now, or you may cool and store the soup in the refrigerator for up to 3 days or in the freezer for up to 2 months.)
5. Serve the soup in heated soup plates or bowls topped with the remaining olive oil.

## GREEN LENTILS FROM CASTELLUCCIO

Green lentils from Castelluccio are brownish-green, very small, and light. One thousand lentils weigh only 25 grams—about ¾ ounce. They don't need soaking and they hold their shape when they are cooked. You may find them sold with the skin still on.

The lentils are grown in Umbria in the Apennine Mountains, planted in April or May and harvested at the end of July or in early August. The harvesting must be done by hand so as not to knock lentils off the plants to the ground, and they are threshed and sorted by hand as well. These lentils have received IGP (Indicazione Geografica Protetta) status.

Wine notes: **Red:** Torgiano Rosso (such as Lungarotti's "Rubesco") from Umbria; Carmignano, Vino Nobile di Montepulciano, or Morellino di Scansano from Tuscany

# Maccu (zuppa di fave secche)

## FAVA BEAN SOUP

This typical Sicilian soup, made from dried fava beans, is served with fresh pasta and eaten warm or cold. Tradition has it that maccu is made on March 19, the feast day of San Giuseppe (Saint Joseph). Cooks clear their cupboards of all their dried beans and broken pasta to make this soup, served to celebrate the arrival of spring.

**SERVES 6 TO 8**

**1 lb dry fava beans (about 2½ cups), sorted and rinsed**

**1 bay leaf**

**Salt, as needed**

**¼ cup extra-virgin olive oil**

**1½ cups diced red onions**

**One 10-oz can diced tomatoes, well drained**

**¼ cup wild fennel leaves or ¼ tsp fennel seed**

**2 cups cooked pasta (use a small shape)**

**Crushed hot red pepper, as needed**

1. Pour the fava beans into a large pot. Add enough cold water to cover them by at least 2 inches, along with the bay leaf and 1 teaspoon of salt. Bring the water to a boil over high heat.
2. Reduce the heat to low and simmer the fava beans for about 2½ hours. Add a little water to the fava beans as they cook if necessary to keep them from drying out and scorching on the bottom of the pan.
3. While the beans are simmering, prepare the soffrito: Heat a medium skillet over medium heat. Add the olive oil and then the onions. Cook, stirring often, until the onions are tender without any browning, 10 to 12 minutes. Add the tomatoes and fennel. Continue to cook until any moisture released by the tomatoes has cooked away and they have a rich, roasted aroma, 15 to 20 minutes longer.
4. Add the soffrito to the fava beans and continue to cook until the fava beans fall apart into a puree, 1½ to 2 hours longer. Pass the soup through a food mill or a wire-mesh sieve directly into a soup pot if you plan to serve the soup right away. (The soup is ready to finish and serve now, or you may cool and store the soup in the refrigerator for up to 3 days or in the freezer for up to 2 months.)
5. Return the soup to a simmer over medium heat. Add the cooked pasta and simmer until the pasta is very hot, 5 to 6 minutes. Add salt and hot red pepper to taste. Serve the soup at once in heated bowls.

Wine notes: **White:** Chardonnay or Inzolia from Sicily

**Red:** Merlot from Sicily or Veneto; Chianti from Tuscany; Salice Salentino or Primitivo from Puglia

## FRESH FAVA BEANS

Italians consider fava beans their special province, as they have since ancient times. *Faba*, which means "bean", comes from the Fabii, a noble Roman family. The fresh bean is usually only available for a short time in the spring. The pods look like gigantic, engorged green beans with some obvious bulges where the beans can be found.

If the fava beans are very young, the beans may be about the size of a pea. As the fava beans get larger, there may be a discernible stem that holds the bean to the pod; pull that from the bean. After you shell the beans, taste one to see if you like the flavor and the texture. If the beans are large, if the skins seem very tough, or if the beans taste a little bitter or starchy, you may want to blanch or parcook the beans for the best texture and flavor. There really aren't any shortcuts when it comes to peeling and skinning fava beans (unless you have a source for very tender young beans), but the payoff is worth the effort.

1. Slice off the ends of the pods and run your thumbnail down the seam in each pod, slicing it open as you go. Once each pod is opened, pop the beans out and collect them in a bowl.
2. Bring a pot of salted water to a rolling boil over high heat. Add the shelled beans all at once and cook for 30 seconds. (Taste one of the beans; if it still seems starchy, cook for 10 to 15 seconds longer.)
3. Immediately pour the beans into a colander and rinse them with cold water to stop the cooking.
4. Use your thumbnail to slit open the outer skin of each bean and gently press the bean out of the skin or pull it away.

# Minestra di fagioli e cozze

## BEAN AND MUSSEL SOUP

Pasta e fagioli is a recipe found in almost every region of Italy. This version is typical in the Campania region, where mussels are added to the soup.

**SERVES 10 TO 12**

- 1 lb dried white beans (about 2½ cups)
- 1 lb mussels
- 1 cup extra-virgin olive oil, plus more for drizzling
- 2 garlic cloves, smashed
- 1 hot red chile
- ⅔ cup dry white wine
- 1 cup water
- 1 cup diced yellow onions
- ½ cup diced celery
- 1 cup canned or fresh chopped plum tomatoes (drained if canned)
- 2 bay leaves
- 2 cups cooked pasta (use a small shape)
- Salt and freshly ground black pepper, as needed
- Chopped flat-leaf parsley, as needed

1. The day before making the soup, sort, rinse, and soak the beans for at least 8 and no more than 24 hours.
2. The day you want to prepare the soup, first prepare the mussels as follows: Scrub the mussels well with a stiff brush under cold running water. Pull the "beard" away, if the mussels have them. (The beard is the tangle of fibers that poke out of the shell; pinch it tight between your finger and thumb and tug downward sharply to remove it.) Discard any empty shells or mussels with shells that stay open.
3. Heat half of the olive oil in a large pot over medium heat. (Choose a pot that has a lid and is large enough to hold the mussels after they open.) Add the garlic and chile and sauté, stirring constantly, until the garlic is just starting to brown, about 2 minutes. Add the cleaned mussels, the wine, and 1 cup water. Cover the pot tightly and steam the mussels until all of the shells open, 8 to 10 minutes depending upon their size. Lift the mussels out of the broth, letting any broth inside the shells drain back into the pot. When the mussels are cool enough to handle, remove the meat and set aside. Strain the broth through a wire-mesh sieve into a bowl and set aside.
4. Heat a soup pot over medium heat. Add the remaining olive oil and then the onions and celery. Cook, stirring often, until the onions are tender without any browning, 5 to 6 minutes. Add the tomatoes and continue to cook until the tomatoes have a sweet aroma, about 5 minutes. Drain the beans and add them to the pot along with the broth from the mussels and enough cold water to cover the beans by 2 inches. Add the bay leaves and simmer the soup, stirring frequently, until the beans are very tender; you may need to add additional water as the soup simmers to keep it from getting too dry.
5. Use the back of a wooden spoon or a potato masher to crush some of the beans directly in the pot. If you prefer, you may lift about half of the beans from the pot and puree them in a food mill or food processor; return the puree to the pot. (The soup is ready to finish and serve now, or you may cool and store the soup in the refrigerator for up to 3 days or in the freezer for up to 2 months.)
6. Return the soup to a simmer over low heat. Add the cooked pasta and the reserved mussels and simmer long enough to thoroughly heat the pasta and mussels, about 2 minutes. Add salt and pepper to taste, if necessary.
7. Serve the soup in heated soup plates or bowls topped with extra-virgin olive oil and parsley.

Wine notes: **White:** Falanghina from Campania; Vermentino di Gallura from Sardinia **Rosé:** Lacrymarosa from Campania; Bardolino Chiaretto from Lugano; Sangiovese Rosato from Tuscany

# Minestrone di verdure con pesto

## VEGETABLE MINESTRONE WITH PESTO

This is a very simple, basic recipe, but use your imagination. Some typical vegetables include onions, leeks, carrots, celery, potatoes, zucchini, string beans, freshly shelled beans, tomatoes, and cabbage. During certain times of the year, pumpkin, chestnuts, and different type of greens may also be added. You might like to add some pasta to the soup as it simmers, such as ditalini or even broken spaghetti.

**SERVES 6 TO 8**

- 1 garlic clove
- ½ cup packed flat-leaf parsley leaves
- ½ cup olive oil
- 1 cup diced yellow onion
- ½ cup diced carrot
- ½ cup diced celery
- ½ cup diced leeks
- 1½ cups diced potatoes
- 1½ cups shredded savoy cabbage
- 1 cup crushed canned plum tomatoes, with juices
- ½ cup fava beans (freshly shelled, or soaked if dried)
- One 2-inch-square piece Parmigiano-Reggiano rind, rinsed
- 2 qt water, or as needed
- 2 cups diced zucchini
- ½ cup green beans cut into ½-inch-long pieces
- ½ cup shelled fresh peas
- 1 cup packed chopped spinach leaves (or any type of greens you like)
- Salt and freshly ground black pepper, as needed
- ¼ cup Pesto (page 132)

1. Chop the garlic and parsley together with a chef's knife until they form a coarse paste (you could do this in a mini-food processor as well). This will give the soup a fuller flavor.
2. Heat a soup pot over medium heat and add the oil. Add the onions and stir to coat with the oil. Sauté, stirring frequently, until the onions are soft, about 5 minutes. Add the carrot, celery, leeks, and the garlic-parsley paste. Stir well and cook until the garlic loses its harsh aroma, about 5 minutes.
3. Add the potatoes, cabbage, tomatoes, beans, and the piece of cheese rind. Add the water on top of the vegetables and beans. Bring the soup to a simmer over medium heat and cook, stirring from time to time so the soup doesn't stick to the bottom of the pot. Reduce the heat if necessary as the soup simmers; it should not be at a hard boil. Simmer until the beans and potatoes are fully cooked and tender, about 30 to 35 minutes.
4. Stir in the zucchini, green beans, peas, and spinach. Return the soup to a simmer and cook just until the green beans are tender, about 8 minutes.
5. Transfer half of the soup to a large bowl and set aside. Use an immersion blender to puree the soup in the pot. Return the unpureed soup to the pot. Return the soup to a simmer. Add salt and pepper to taste. (The soup is ready to finish and serve now, or you may cool and store the soup in the refrigerator for up to 3 days or in the freezer for up to 2 months.)
6. Serve the soup in heated soup plates or bowls topped with the pesto.

## FRESH GREEN PEAS

Garden peas are one of the great treasures of springtime. When you find them in the market, feature them with fresh favas, which are in season at the same time, in Garmugia Lucchese (see page 117).

1. Look for bright green pods that are not shriveled or yellowed. Some experts say that if the peas are fresh, you will hear them squeak when you rub two pods together.
2. Hold the peapod between your thumb and forefinger so that the curved side is facing up and press the pod with your thumb to pop it open. Run your thumb down the inside of the pod to pop out the peas. Collect them in a bowl. A pound of peas in the pod will typically give you about ½ cup of shelled peas.

Wine notes: **White:** Chardonnay from Sicily, Tuscany, Veneto, or Trentino-Alto Adige

**Red:** Inferno from Lombardy; Dolcetto d'Alba from Piedmont; Chianti Classico from Tuscany; Aglianico del Vulture from Basilicata; Merlot from Sicily or Veneto

# Minestrone d'orzo

## BARLEY SOUP FROM TRIESTE

Once cooked, barley tends to be very thick, so if the soup comes out thicker than you like the first time you make it, use a bit less barley the next time. You could also try using farro instead of barley, and maybe add some seasonal vegetables like zucchini, peas, or string beans in the summer, or butternut squash, pumpkin, or different greens in the fall or winter.

**SERVES 6 TO 8**

6 oz dried beans, such as borlotti or cranberry (about 1 cup)

½ cup extra-virgin olive oil

2 oz pancetta, diced, or ham hock, if preferred

1 yellow onion, diced

1 carrot, diced

1 celery stalk, peeled and diced

2 garlic cloves, minced

6 oz barley, washed (about 1 cup)

2 tbsp chopped flat-leaf parsley

1 each rosemary, sage, and thyme sprigs, chopped together

1 fresh bay leaf

3 qt Brodo (page 88; made with chicken) or water

1 lb potatoes, peeled and chopped (about 3 cups)

½ cup sliced fresh mushrooms (any variety, but preferably porcini)

Salt and freshly ground black pepper, as needed

1. The day before making the soup, rinse, sort, and soak the beans for at least 8 and up to 24 hours.
2. Heat a soup pot over medium heat. Add 1 tablespoon olive oil and the pancetta. Cook, stirring to cook the pancetta evenly, until the pancetta is just starting to get crisp. There should be 2 tablespoons of rendered fat and olive oil in the pan.
3. Add the onion, carrot, celery, and garlic. Stir well to coat all of the vegetables, and cook until the onion is limp and tender with no browning, 5 to 6 minutes.
4. Drain the borlotti beans and add them to the pot with the vegetables, along with the barley, the chopped herbs, and the bay leaf. Stir well, then cover the pot and cook over low heat for 2 to 3 minutes to release the flavor from the herbs into the soup.
5. Add the broth or water and bring the soup to a simmer over medium heat. Simmer, stirring frequently and skimming the surface of the soup as necessary, until the beans are almost tender, about 30 minutes. If necessary, you may need to add more broth or water as the soup cooks; it should be quite thick, but not so thick that it is difficult to stir.
6. Add the potatoes to the soup and simmer until they are nearly tender, about 15 minutes. Add the mushrooms and continue to simmer until all of the ingredients are very hot and completely tender, 10 minutes longer. Add salt and pepper to taste. (The soup is ready to finish and serve now, or you may cool and store the soup in the refrigerator for up to 3 days or in the freezer for up to 2 months.)
7. Serve the soup in heated soup plates or bowls topped with the remaining olive oil.

Wine notes: **White:** Pinot Grigio from Friuli-Venezia Giulia or Trentino-Alto Adige **Red:** Valpolicella Classico, Bardolino Classico, or Merlot from Veneto

# Garmugia lucchese

## SOUP FROM LUCCA

This is a soup made with artichokes when they are at the end of their season and spring vegetables are just starting to come to the market. For this recipe we like to use the broth from making Vitello Tonnato (see page 97) and add some of the cooked veal to the broth before we serve the soup. In the original version, the veal is ground and sautéed before the vegetables are added to the pot, essentially making a veal broth during the same time the soup cooks.

**SERVES 8 TO 10**

Juice of 1 lemon

5 medium artichokes

½ cup extra-virgin olive oil

5 oz pancetta

1 cup diced green onions

8 oz asparagus, peeled

½ cup shelled fresh peas

½ cup shelled fresh fava beans, skinned

2 qt Brodo (page 88)

1 lb cooked veal, diced

1. Fill a bowl with cold water and add the lemon juice to hold the artichokes as you cut them. Working with one artichoke at a time, cut away the stem and then trim away the outer leaves. Trim the hairy "choke" away to reveal the artichoke bottom, and cut into wedges. Hold the artichokes in the lemon water until you are ready to cook them.
2. Heat a skillet over medium heat. Add the olive oil and pancetta. Cook, stirring to cook the pancetta evenly, until the pancetta is just starting to get crisp. There should be 2 tablespoons of rendered fat and olive oil in the pan.
3. Add the onions and stir to coat them with the fat. Sauté, stirring often, until the onions are tender without any browning, 5 to 6 minutes. Add the artichokes to the onions. Stir well and sauté long enough to coat the artichokes with oil and heat them slightly, about 5 minutes.
4. Add the asparagus, peas, fava beans, and broth. Simmer until all of the vegetables are tender, about 10 minutes. Add the veal and simmer 2 or 3 minutes longer to heat through.
5. Serve the soup at once in heated soup plates or bowls.

Wine notes: **White:** Vernaccia di San Gimignano or Sauvignon Blanc from Tuscany; Friulano or Traminer (Gewürztraminer) from Friuli-Venezia Giulia; Müller-Thurgau from Trentino-Alto Adige

# Minestra maritata

## "MARRIED" SOUP

This is a typical dish of the Campania region in which the meat "marries" with the vegetables.

**SERVES 4 TO 6**

- 8 oz pork ribs
- 4 oz pork skin
- 8 oz boneless beef chuck (in 1 piece)
- 3 oz pancetta
- 1 medium yellow onion
- 2 garlic cloves, peeled
- 1 bouquet garni with 1 thyme sprig, 1 flat-leaf parsley sprig, and 1 bay leaf
- 4 oz fresh Italian sausage, cooked and removed from casing
- 1 lb savoy cabbage
- 1 lb escarole
- 1 lb broccoli rabe
- 1 fresh hot red chile (remove stem and seeds if you are concerned about heat)

1. Put the pork ribs, pork skin, beef, and pancetta in a large pot and add enough cold water to completely cover the meats. Put the pot over medium heat, and bring the water to a simmer. As soon as it comes to a simmer, remove the lid and start skimming any foam that rises to the surface. Add the, onion, garlic, and bouquet garni.
2. Partially cover the pot by setting the lid slightly ajar to leave an opening; that way, the pot won't be as likely to boil over and you can keep an eye on it more easily. Bring it back to a simmer and cook, skimming periodically, for about 2 hours.
3. Remove the meats from the broth, let them cool enough to handle easily, remove the bones, and cut the meat into small pieces. Cut the sausage into small pieces and reserve the meats and sausages. (If you plan to serve the soup the next day, keep the meats in a covered container in the refrigerator; it is fine to mix them together.)
4. Strain the broth through a wire-mesh sieve directly into a soup pot if you are planning to serve the soup right away. If you plan to serve the soup another day cool it quickly and store in covered containers in the refrigerator for up to 1 week.
5. Prepare the vegetables for the soup: Separate the cabbage and escarole leaves from the base, rinse well, and cut into thin strips about 2 inches long. Trim and peel the broccoli rabe stems; discard any bruised or discolored leaves, and coarsely chop the stems and tops.
6. Return the broth to a simmer and add the vegetables. Simmer the soup over medium or low heat until the vegetables are tender, about 20 minutes. Add the meat and sausage to the broth, along with the chile. Simmer the soup until it is very flavorful and all the ingredients are tender and very hot, about 10 minutes.
7. Serve the soup at once in heated soup bowls.

Wine notes: **White:** Greco di Tufo or Fiano di Avellino from Campania **Red:** Cerasuolo di Vittoria from Sicily; Chianti Classico from Tuscany; Dolcetto d'Alba from Piedmont

# Zuppa di cavolo e fontina

## CABBAGE AND FONTINA SOUP

Italians living in the mountains of Val d'Aosta take full advantage of their native ingredients in this thick, hearty soup that includes a generous amount of the region's most famous cheese: Fontina. You can substitute green cabbage for savoy cabbage, if necessary.

**SERVES 4**

**6 oz Fontina**

**8 slices rye bread**

**6 oz savoy cabbage**

**Salt, as needed**

**¼ cup (½ stick) unsalted butter**

**2 oz pancetta**

**4 cups Brodo (page 88)**

1. Preheat the oven to 350 degrees F.
2. Slice the Fontina into very thin slices or grate it, if you prefer. Set aside. Put the bread slices on a baking sheet and toast them in the oven (you can do this while the oven preheats, if you wish). Set aside.
3. To prepare the cabbage, remove and discard any bruised or wilted outer leaves. Pull the remaining leaves away from the core, snapping them away at the base. Use a paring knife to slice out the heavy ribs from the larger leaves.
4. Fill a large pot with water and add enough salt to be able to barely taste it. Cover the pot and bring the water to a rolling boil over high heat. Add the cabbage leaves (work in batches to avoid overcrowding the pot) and stir to submerge them. Cook uncovered until tender, 3 to 4 minutes. Lift the cabbage leaves out of the water with a sieve or slotted spoon and transfer to a colander to drain. Continue, using the same pot of water, until all of the cabbage leaves are cooked. Rinse the leaves with cool water. Once cool enough to handle, blot the cabbage leaves dry and cut them crosswise into thin strips.
5. Heat a skillet over medium heat. Add the butter and pancetta. Cook, stirring to cook the pancetta evenly, until the pancetta is just starting to get crisp. There should be 2 tablespoons of rendered fat and butter in the pan. Add the cabbage and stir to coat with the fat. Sauté, stirring often, until the cabbage is heated through, about 3 minutes.
6. Place the toasted bread in the bottom of a large casserole dish (or, if you prefer, make this soup in individual bowls or crocks). Top with a layer of cabbage, then cheese. Continue layering bread, cabbage, and cheese until all are used up. Be sure to finish with a layer of cheese. Ladle the hot broth into the casserole or crocks. Cover the casserole or crocks and bake for 45 minutes. Serve the soup hot, directly from the oven.

Wine notes: **White:** Petite Arvine from the Valle d'Aosta; Pinot Bianco or Friulano from Friuli-Venezia Giulia **Red:** Pinot Noir from the Valle d'Aosta; Pinot Nero from Trentino-Alto Adige; Dolcetto from Piedmont

# Ribollita toscana

## TWICE-COOKED TUSCAN SOUP

*Ribollita* means reheated or re-boiled, which means that this soup is made from a soup that was made the day before. Since most soup pots are filled to make a big batch, recipes like this one "reinvent" the soup by cooking it a second time with additional ingredients. This Tuscan version is made with vegetables, beans, and cabbage; for the most authentic flavor, we like to use a cabbage specific to the region, often referred to simply as "Tuscan cabbage." You may see it under the name "Tuscan kale," "dinosaur kale," or "Lacinato kale."

**SERVES 10 TO 12**

1 lb dried cannellini beans (about 2½ cups)

2 garlic cloves

2 thyme sprigs

2 rosemary sprigs

6 oz lard or pancetta

½ cup extra-virgin olive oil

1 cup diced yellow onion

½ cup diced celery

½ cup diced carrot

1 cup diced canned or fresh plum tomatoes (with juices if canned)

1 lb Tuscan cabbage, chopped (about 4 cups)

Salt and freshly ground black pepper, as needed

10 to 12 slices day-old Italian bread

1. The day before making the soup, sort, rinse, and soak the beans for at least 8 and no more than 24 hours.
2. The next day, drain the beans and put them in a pot. Add enough cold water to cover them by at least 2 inches. Add the garlic, thyme, rosemary, and lard or pancetta. Bring the water to a boil over high heat. Decrease the heat to low and continue to simmer the beans until they are tender, at least 45 minutes, or longer depending upon how old the beans are.
3. Use a slotted spoon to transfer about half of the cooked beans to a bowl; mash or puree them into a thick puree. (If necessary, add a ladleful of the bean's cooking liquid to make them easier to puree.)
4. Heat a soup pot over medium heat. Add the olive oil and then the onions, celery, and carrot. Cook, stirring often, until the onions are tender without any browning, 10 to 12 minutes. Add the tomatoes and continue to cook until the tomatoes have a sweet aroma, about 5 minutes. Add about 2 cups of the cooking liquid from the beans and simmer until the carrots and celery are tender, about 15 minutes.
5. Add the beans (pureed and whole) to the pot, along with their cooking liquid, and the cabbage. Simmer the soup slowly over low heat until the cabbage is tender, about 20 minutes. Add salt and pepper to taste, if necessary. (The soup is ready to finish and serve now, or you may cool and store the soup in the refrigerator for up to 3 days or in the freezer for up to 2 months.)
6. Put a slice of bread into each heated soup bowl. Ladle the soup on top of the bread and serve at once.

Wine notes: **Red:** Chianti Classico or Rosso di Montalcino from Tuscany; Montefalco Rosso or Torgiano Rosso (such as Lungarotti's "Rubesco") from Umbria; Sangiovese di Romagna from Emilia-Romagna

# Pasta secca

A box of pasta in the pantry means you always have something to cook. Be sure to seek out high-quality pasta and remember to cook it properly. It should be al dente (meaning that it has a pleasant "chew" but not undercooked). Baked pasta dishes (al forno) are an exception to that general rule; in these dishes the pasta should be left slightly undercooked so that it completes cooking as it bakes in a sauce.

There aren't very many tricks to cooking pasta, beyond these: plenty of rapidly boiling water, enough salt to make the water taste salty, and a big colander for draining.

# Cooking the pasta

Different pasta manufacturers may produce similar shapes with the same names, but due to the differences in sizes and shapes, they all take a very slightly different amount of time to cook properly. You can usually find a cooking time on the package, and that is a good general guide. But don't rely just on the package; tasting a piece is the best way to tell when the pasta is properly cooked.

1. Bring a large pot of salted water to a boil. The general suggestion is 1 gallon of water for every 1 pound of pasta, which means you will want a pot that holds at least 5 quarts. Add enough salt to make the water taste salty. One tablespoon is about enough for a gallon of water, but you could use less or a little more. Don't skip the salt, however; pasta cooked in unsalted water has practically no flavor at all. Remember to cover the pot so that it comes to a boil more quickly.
2. Add the pasta all at once and stir until the strands or pieces are softened and submerged. Long shapes like linguine may need to be pushed down under the water with your spoon until they soften enough to stay there. Stir all pastas a few times to make sure the pieces are separated. If you don't take the time to do it at this point, you'll end up with large clumps.
3. Let the pasta cook until it is fully cooked with a good bite. The pasta should be cooked through, but it should not be so soft that you can't feel it resisting a little bit when you bite into it.
4. Once the pasta is done, scoop out a cup or so of the pasta water to finish the sauce. This is the "secret ingredient" that keeps sauces from feeling oily and slipping off the pasta and keeps the finished dish creamy.
5. Immediately drain the pasta through a colander and let as much water as possible drain away. You can shake the colander a few times, to be sure that any water trapped inside tube-shaped pasta is drained.

# Saucing the pasta

Your pasta should be freshly drained and very hot when you combine it with a sauce. The way you combine it depends upon the type of sauce.

Ragù-style sauces are thick and have a substantial body. To combine your pasta with a ragù-style sauce, drain the pasta as much as possible, and shake it well. Pour the pasta into a heated pasta bowl (or fill individual pasta plates), and then ladle the hot sauce over the pasta.

Other sauces, including pesto, carbonara-style, and raw tomato sauces are tossed together with the hot pasta. Drain the pasta and pour it into a bowl (you could use the pot you cooked the pasta in, but it is a little easier to work in a bowl). Add the prepared sauce and use a lifting motion to combine the pasta and sauce. Add enough of the pasta water you set aside to keep the sauce loose enough for an even, creamy coating on each strand.

# Trenette al pesto

## TRENETTE WITH PESTO

Trenette pasta is also known as bavette. It is a ribbon-shaped pasta, usually a little thinner than linguine, more like a flattened spaghetti. It is traditional in Genoa, where it is thought to be a perfect pairing with the region's famous pesto.

**SERVES 4 TO 6**

- Kosher salt, as needed
- 1 lb trenette, bavette, or linguine
- 1 cup diced potatoes
- 1½ cups trimmed green beans, cut into 1-inch lengths
- 1 cup Pesto (page 132), or as needed
- Toasted pine nuts, for garnish (optional)

1. Bring a large pot of salted water to a rolling boil; covering the pot will help it come to a boil more quickly.
2. Add the trenette all at once and stir a few times to separate the pasta. Add the potatoes and green beans 2 minutes after adding the pasta. Cook uncovered at a boil until the pasta and the potatoes are just tender to the bite, 10 to 12 minutes.
3. Transfer a few ladlefuls of pasta water from the pot to a bowl or cup to have ready for finishing the sauce. (You may need up to ½ cup.)
4. Drain the pasta and vegetables immediately through a colander. Shake well to remove any water clinging to the pasta. Pour the drained pasta and vegetables into a large serving bowl.
5. Add the pesto to the trenette and toss together until the pasta is evenly coated. The pesto should appear creamy, not oily. If necessary, add a bit of the reserved pasta water.
6. Garnish the dish with a few toasted pine nuts if desired. Serve at once.

Wine notes: Medium-bodied, fruit-driven whites will bring out the sweet pignoli flavors and the salty/sweet flavors of the cheese, while a light- to medium-bodied red will emphasize the herbal notes and earthy richness of the pesto.

**White:** Roero Arneis from Piedmont; Soave Classico from Veneto; Pinot Grigio or Chardonnay from Trentino-Alto Adige or Friulano or Sauvignon Blanc from Friuli-Venezia Giulia
**Red:** Barbera d'Alba or Barbera d'Asti from Piedmont; Chianti from Tuscany; Valpolicella Classico from Veneto

# Pesto

Pesto is such a classic condiment, and there are probably hundreds of different variations. A really great pesto has a good balance of flavors. This isn't always easy when you are dealing with seasonal produce, like basil. We strongly recommend that you weigh out the ingredients when you prepare basil pesto, especially if you are making a large batch. Use a digital scale for accuracy. Choose an olive oil with a mild flavor so the flavors of basil and garlic come through.

**MAKES 3 CUPS**

¼ oz garlic (about 1 small clove)

8 oz basil leaves, picked off the stems and then weighed (or about 4 cups loosely packed leaves)

1 oz pine nuts (¼ cup)

1 cup extra-virgin olive oil, as needed

Kosher salt, as needed

2 oz Pecorino Romano (½ cup)

2 oz Parmigiano-Reggiano (½ cup)

1. Slice the garlic and blanch it in a small amount of boiling water for 1 minute if necessary (see Note).
2. In a blender, combine the basil, garlic, pine nuts, and ¾ cup of the oil and blend until crushed; season with salt to taste. Add more olive oil if needed for good consistency.
3. Add both cheeses and blend to a smooth sauce. Do not run the blender at high speed or the heat of the blade will change the color of the pesto. Set aside with a little oil on top to avoid oxidation. After using the pesto, always flatten the surface and cover it with a little oil.

*Garlic is an important ingredient in pesto. However, its flavor intensifies in the pesto over time, so if you are making a large batch of pesto that you plan to store for a few days, you may wish to blanch the sliced garlic for about 1 minute in boiling water to remove any harsh or bitter flavors. If you are going to be using the pesto right way, you can skip this step.*

Trenette al Pesto

# Penne al pomodoro crudo

## PENNE WITH UNCOOKED TOMATO SAUCE

This recipe is wonderful, refreshing, and quick to prepare, perfect in the middle of the summer when tomatoes are at their best. There is plenty of room for innovation too. You might like to add a can of oil-packed tuna (an imported brand if available), olives, capers, fresh oregano, little pieces of buffalo mozzarella . . . the list could go on for a long time!

**SERVES 4**

Kosher salt, as needed

6 medium plum tomatoes, meaty and perfectly ripe

1 garlic clove, chopped (optional)

¼ cup flat-leaf parsley leaves

8 large basil leaves

½ cup extra-virgin olive oil

Freshly ground black pepper, as needed

1 lb penne

Grated ricotta salata, as needed

1. Bring a large pot of salted water to a rolling boil over high heat; covering the pot will help it come to a boil more quickly.
2. Cut an X in the bottom of the tomatoes and add them to the boiling water. Lift the tomatoes out of the water with a slotted spoon after 20 seconds and put them in a bowl of ice water. (Leave the pot on the heat to cook the pasta next.) When the tomatoes are cold, pull away the peel.
3. Cut the peeled tomatoes in half, remove the seeds, and dice them. Transfer to a large serving bowl. Add the garlic and parsley. Tear the basil leaves into small pieces and add them to the tomatoes. Add the olive oil and season with a little salt and pepper. Leave this to marinate for a few minutes at room temperature while you prepare the penne.
4. Add the penne all at once to the boiling water and stir a few times to separate the pasta. Cook uncovered at a boil until just tender to the bite, 10 to 12 minutes.
5. Drain the pasta immediately through a colander. Shake well to remove any water clinging to the pasta. Add the hot penne to the tomato mixture and toss them together until the pasta is evenly coated. Season with more pepper as needed.
6. Serve at once, passing the ricotta salata on the side.

Wine notes: With this summer classic, choose wines—white or red—that will bring out the sweet/sour tomato flavors and the herbal notes of the basil. Don't be afraid to chill the reds a bit; it will bring out their fruit and freshness.

**White:** Falanghina from Campania; Gavi from Piedmont; Soave Classico from Veneto
**Red:** Primitivo or Salice Salentino from Puglia; Dolcetto d'Alba or Barbera d'Asti from Piedmont; Chianti from Tuscany; Valpolicella or Bardolino from Veneto

# Spaghetti all'amatriciana

## SPAGHETTI WITH TOMATOES, GUANCIALE, AND RED PEPPER

Making the sauce for this pasta takes about an hour, in order to let the flavors of the guanciale meld together with the tomatoes. If guanciale is difficult to locate, just substitute pancetta.

**SERVES 6**

- 3 tbsp extra-virgin olive oil
- 8 oz guanciale (pork cheek)
- 1 cup diced or sliced yellow onion
- 4 cups canned or fresh San Marzano tomatoes, peeled and diced (see Note)
- ¼ tsp crushed hot red pepper, or as needed
- Kosher salt and freshly ground black pepper, as needed
- 1 lb spaghetti
- ½ cup grated Pecorino Romano (2 oz)

1. Heat a 4-quart pot (a Dutch oven is a good choice) over medium heat. Add 1 tablespoon olive oil and the guanciale. Cook, stirring frequently, until it is just starting to get crisp. There should be 2 tablespoons of rendered fat and olive oil in the pan. Add a bit more olive oil if necessary.
2. Add the onions and stir to coat them with the fat. Sauté over low, stirring often, until the onions are tender without any browning, about 10 minutes. Add the tomatoes, red pepper, and a little salt and pepper. Simmer the sauce, uncovered, until it is very flavorful, about 1 hour. (The sauce is ready to combine with the spaghetti now, or you could cool and store it to serve later. It will last in a covered container in the refrigerator for up to 5 days.)
3. Bring a large pot of salted water to a rolling boil over high heat; covering the pot will help it come to a boil more quickly.
4. Add the spaghetti all at once to the boiling water and stir a few times to separate the pasta. Cook uncovered at a boil until just tender to the bite, 10 to 12 minutes.
5. Drain the pasta immediately through a colander. Shake well to remove any water clinging to the pasta. Add the hot penne to the tomato mixture and toss them together until the pasta is evenly coated.
6. Serve at once, passing the cheese on the side.

*San Marzano DOP tomatoes are the best choice for this dish. If you can find them, there is no need to drain the tomatoes before adding them to a sauce. However, if you are using a generic canned tomato, let the tomatoes drain in a colander before using them.*

Wine notes: This spicy, relatively rich sauce will act as a perfect foil for a medium- to full-bodied dry white wine with fresh flavors, or for the medium-bodied earthy reds of southern Italy. If you like the dish extra spicy (more pepper), go with a white; for less spice, consider a red.

**White:** Verdicchio from Le Marche; Pinot Bianco, Pinot Grigio, or Sauvignon Blanc from Friuli-Venezia Giulia
**Red:** Cannonau di Sardegna from Sardinia; Primitivo di Manduria from Puglia; Cerasuolo di Vittoria or Etna Rosso from Sicily

# Pasta alla norma

## PASTA WITH TOMATOES, EGGPLANT, AND RICOTTA

This pasta originates from Catania, the birthplace of Vincenzo Bellini, who wrote the famous opera *Norma*. There is some debate as to whether the dish was meant to honor the opera, or whether the term *norma* had, by the time this dish was invented, slipped into the language as a word for something wonderful and extraordinary. Regardless of the story you subscribe to, this dish is the most proper dish to serve when you plan to entertain opera lovers. Sometimes cooks add a pinch of sugar to the sauce to tame any last bit of bitterness in the eggplant. The dish is finished with ricotta salata; although nontraditional, you might prefer to add some cubed fresh mozzarella at the very end instead of the ricotta salata.

**SERVES 4**

2 slender eggplants (Japanese, if available, about 1¾ lb total)

Kosher salt, as needed

3 tbsp extra-virgin olive oil

½ cup minced yellow onion

4 large tomatoes, peeled and diced (page 50)

Freshly ground black pepper, as needed

1 lb rigatoni or similar short tube-shaped pasta

½ cup torn basil leaves

½ cup grated ricotta salata (2 oz)

1. Slice the ends off the eggplants, cut them in half lengthwise, and then cut into pieces about the same dimensions as your pasta. Salt the eggplants and drain them for at least 1 hour (for more information, see sidebar at right).
2. Heat a large skillet over medium-high heat and add enough oil to liberally coat the skillet (about 2 tablespoons). Add the eggplants and fry, turning the pieces occasionally so they cook evenly. Keep frying until the eggplants are tender and golden brown, 8 to 10 minutes.
3. Heat another large skillet over medium-low heat. Add 1 tablespoon olive oil and the onions. Cook, stirring frequently, until the onion is tender without any browning, about 5 minutes. Add the tomatoes and a little salt and pepper. Decrease the heat to low and simmer just until the tomatoes are very hot.
4. Bring a large pot of salted water to a rolling boil over high heat; covering the pot will help it come to a boil more quickly.
5. Add the rigatoni all at once to the boiling water and stir a few times to separate the pasta. Cook uncovered at a boil until just tender to the bite, 10 to 12 minutes.
6. Drain the pasta immediately through a colander. Shake well to remove any water clinging to the pasta. Pour the hot rigatoni into a serving bowl and add the tomato mixture, about three-quarters of the fried eggplants, and the basil. Toss together to combine.
7. Serve at once, topped with the reserved eggplant and the ricotta salata.

Wine notes: While listening to a beautiful aria, choose a beautiful medium-bodied white for this dish, to bring out the subtle sweetness of the eggplant.

**White:** Inzolia or Chardonnay from Sicily; Roero Arneis from Piedmont; Fiano di Avellino from Campania

## EGGPLANT

According to traditional recipes, the eggplant for Pasta alla Norma is seasoned with salt, garlic, and hot pepper and then left to dry in the sun for a day. After that, it is fried and made into a sauce with fresh tomato, garlic, and basil.

Without the warm Mediterranean sun to help prepare eggplant for cooking, this salting and draining technique changes the texture of the flesh a bit, giving it more substance at the same time that it lessens any bitterness in the flesh.

1. Slice away the ends of the eggplant. Use a paring knife or a vegetable peeler to remove the skin, if your recipe calls for that step. Cut the eggplant in half or into slices or cubes and transfer it to a large colander.
2. Sprinkle kosher salt liberally over the eggplant and then put the colander in a large bowl to catch the liquid that the eggplant will release as it drains. If you wish, you may weigh the eggplant while it drains as follows: Place a plate or similar flat object on top of the eggplant and press down to make an even, compact layer. Add a weight on top of the plate (for instance, a can or two of beans or tuna fish).
3. Leave the eggplant to drain for at least 1 hour, and then rinse well under cold running water. Let the eggplant drain again; to be sure that the eggplant is well dried, press it between a few layers of paper towels. The eggplant is ready to cook at this point.

# Linguine alle vongole

## LINGUINE WITH CLAMS

This dish relies as much on your skills as a shopper as it does on your skills as a cook. Clams must be perfectly fresh and properly handled in the shop and at home. Try not to buy the clams too far ahead of preparing this dish. If you prefer, you may pull the clam meat out of the shells and discard the shells before finishing the sauce, but it is fine to leave them in their shells. It all depends upon how you want to present the dish.

**SERVES 4 TO 6**

- 2 medium leeks (optional)
- 4 to 5 tbsp extra-virgin olive oil, as needed
- 2 garlic cloves, thinly sliced
- 3 dozen Manila clams or littlenecks, scrubbed
- ½ cup dry white wine
- 1 fresh bay leaf, broken
- Kosher salt and freshly ground black pepper, as needed
- 1 lb linguine
- 4 tsp coarsely chopped flat-leaf parsley
- 2 tbsp unsalted butter (optional)

1. To prepare the leeks for this dish, if using, trim the root ends and the dark green leaves, leaving behind the white and light green parts of the leek. (You can save the leek tops to add to stocks or broths.) Cut the leeks in half lengthwise and clean them thoroughly under cold running water, making sure to remove any dirt that might be trapped in the layers. Let the leeks drain, and then cut them into thin slices that look like little half-moons. You should have about 2 cups.
2. Heat 2 tablespoons oil in a large skillet over medium-high heat. Add the leeks and cook, stirring frequently, until the leeks are tender and softened without any browning, 5 to 6 minutes. Lift the leeks out of the pan with a slotted spoon, transfer them to a plate, and set aside.
3. Return the skillet to medium-high heat. Add enough of the remaining oil to liberally coat the pan. Add the garlic and cook, stirring constantly, until the garlic is aromatic and translucent, about 1 minute. Add the clams, wine, and bay leaf. Cover the skillet and cook until the clams are completely opened, about 8 minutes. Add the leeks, if using, taste the sauce, and adjust with salt and pepper if needed.
4. Bring a large pot of salted water to a rolling boil over high heat. Add the linguine all at once and stir a few times to separate the pasta. Cook uncovered at a boil until the pasta is just tender to the bite but still al dente, 8 to 10 minutes. Transfer a few ladlefuls of pasta water from the pot to a bowl or cup to have ready for finishing the sauce. (You may need up to ½ cup.)
5. Drain the pasta immediately through a colander. Shake well to remove any water clinging to the pasta. Pour the drained pasta into a large serving bowl.
6. Add the clam sauce, the parsley, and ¼ cup of the pasta cooking water to the linguine and toss them together until the pasta is evenly coated. The sauce should cling slightly; if it does not, you may wish to stir in the butter.
7. Serve at once.

Wine notes: No surprise here; it's dry white wine with clams. Any of the subtly fruity wines here will bring out the essential brininess of the clams and the herbal notes in the dish.

**White:** Falanghina from Campania; Vermentino di Sardegna from Sardinia; Gavi from Piedmont; Orvieto Classico from Umbria; Soave Classico from Veneto; Friulano or Sauvignon Blanc from Friuli-Venezia Giulia

# Spaghetti cacio e pepe

## SPAGHETTI WITH PECORINO ROMANO AND FRESH CRACKED PEPPER

A very simple Roman dish, this is made with abundant freshly ground black pepper and plenty of grated pecorino cheese. *Cacio* is another name for cheese in Italian that you may hear used in the central and southern parts of Italy.

**SERVES 4 TO 6**

Kosher salt, as needed

1 lb spaghetti

1 cup grated Pecorino Romano (4 oz), plus more for serving

½ cup extra-virgin olive oil

1 tbsp freshly ground black pepper

1. Bring a large pot of salted water to a rolling boil over high heat; covering the pot will help it come to a boil more quickly.
2. Add the spaghetti all at once and stir a few times to separate the pasta. Cook uncovered at a boil until the pasta is just tender to the bite, 10 to 12 minutes. Transfer a few ladlefuls of pasta water from of the pot to a bowl or cup to have ready for finishing the sauce if your recipe calls for that step. (You may need up to ½ cup.)
3. Drain the spaghetti immediately through a colander. Shake well to remove any water clinging to the pasta. Pour the spaghetti back into the pot. Add the cheese, olive oil, and black pepper. Stir the pasta until the cheese and pepper are evenly distributed. Add about ¼ cup of the pasta cooking water to the spaghetti to moisten the pasta slightly. It should appear creamy, not oily. If necessary, add a bit more of the pasta water.
4. Serve at once, passing additional cheese on the side.

Wine notes: Cool down the black pepper of the dish with a medium-bodied, fruit-driven white, or ramp up the spice a bit with a fairly light, fruity red, which will become a "sauce in a glass" for the dish.

**White:** Frascati Superiore from Latium; Orvieto Classico from Umbria; Verdicchio from The Marches
**Red:** Merlot from Lazio; Sangiovese di Romagna from Emilia-Romagna; Chianti from Tuscany, Bardolino Classico from Veneto; Dolcetto from Piedmont

# Ziti con ragù alla napoletana

## ZITI WITH A NEAPOLITAN MEAT SAUCE

This ragù is part of the traditional Neapolitan cuisine. It is usually prepared on Sunday for the big family meal. Although it isn't difficult to make, it does requires time (at least 4 hours) and some of your attention while it cooks for a good result. It is typically served with ziti or any thick short pasta. The meat for this recipe can be beef, pork, lamb, or a mixture of meats. Select cuts from the leg (sometimes known as the round) and leave them in large pieces for a rich ragù.

**SERVES 6**

- 2 lb boneless beef rump or bottom round
- Kosher salt, as needed
- 3 tbsp extra-virgin olive oil, or as needed
- 1 medium yellow onion, chopped
- 1 garlic clove
- 2 basil sprigs
- 1 fresh bay leaf
- ½ cup dry white wine
- 4 cups fresh or canned peeled tomatoes, seeded and crushed, juices reserved
- ¼ cup tomato paste
- 1 fresh red chile
- 1 lb ziti

1. Season the beef with salt and place it into a 5-quart pot (a Dutch oven is a good choice) over medium heat. Add the olive oil and cover the pot. Cook over medium heat for about 10 minutes (long enough for the meat to lose its raw color). Add the onion, garlic, basil, and bay leaf, stirring to cook the onion evenly. When the onion is tender, after about 5 or 6 minutes, add the wine. Stir to release any of the drippings that are sticking to the pan. Let the wine cook down until it has nearly evaporated, about 5 minutes.
2. Add the tomatoes, tomato paste, and the chile. Stir well and bring the sauce to a very gentle simmer over low heat for 3 to 4 hours. Partially cover the pot and continue to simmer, stirring occasionally and adding the reserved tomato juices or a bit of water if the sauce seems too thick as it cooks. The finished sauce should be a deep, rich red color. (The sauce is ready to combine with the ziti now, or you could cool and store it in the refrigerator to serve up to 4 days later. The meat can be served as the second course, following the pasta, or it may be reserved to use in other dishes.)
3. Bring a large pot of salted water to a rolling boil over high heat; covering the pot will help it come to a boil more quickly.
4. Add the ziti all at once to the boiling water and stir a few times to separate the pasta. Cook uncovered at a boil until just tender to the bite, 10 to 12 minutes.
5. Drain the ziti immediately through a colander. Shake well to remove any water clinging to the pasta. Pour the ziti into a large mixing or serving bowl. Add the sauce and toss together until the ziti is evenly coated. Serve at once.

Wine notes: This dish calls for a full-bodied white, preferably from Campania, the home province of Naples, or for medium-bodied southern Italian reds. The whites will emphasize the meatiness of the sauce, and the reds will focus on the lighter qualities of the dish.

**White:** Fiano di Avellino or Greco di Tufo from Campania
**Red:** Aglianico del Vulture from Basilicata; Primitivo or Salice Salentino from Puglia; Cannonau di Sardegna from Sardinia, Cerasuolo di Vittoria or Merlot from Sicily

# Pasta con le sarde

## PASTA WITH SARDINES

This is a traditional Sicilian dish with typical ingredients, including sardines and wild fennel, from the Palermo area. The addition of raisins gives the dish a sweet flavor and is a reflection of the influences this cuisine has absorbed from the Arabic world. Wild fennel grows freely in southern and central Italy. It has a very distinct anise flavor and is a common ingredient in Sicilian cuisine. If you cannot find wild fennel, however, just use the feathery fronds of regular fennel.

**SERVES 4 TO 6**

- 1 lb sardines
- ½ cup raisins
- ½ cup pine nuts
- Kosher salt, as needed
- 1 bunch wild fennel tops
- 1 to 2 tbsp extra-virgin olive oil, as needed
- 1½ cups minced yellow onions
- 4 salted anchovies, rinsed in cool water, blotted dry, and bones removed
- ¼ cup dry white wine
- 1 tsp saffron threads
- 1 lb bucatini
- Toasted bread crumbs, for sprinkling (optional)

1. To prepare the sardines, make a slit through each fish's belly. Pull out the insides. Flatten each fish to open it (skin side down) and run your thumb down the spine, pressing along the bones as you go. Pull out the bones and cut away the head and gills (for more details, see page 50). Wipe the fish with paper towels to finish cleaning them, inside and out, but do not rinse them in water.
2. Put the raisins in a small bowl. Add enough hot water to cover the raisins. Let them rest for at least 15 minutes to soften and plump.
3. To toast the pine nuts, heat a dry skillet (cast iron is good; avoid nonstick pans, however) over medium-high heat. When the pan is hot, add the pine nuts. Swirl the pan over the heating element to keep the pine nuts moving as they toast, which will prevent scorching. As soon as the pine nuts start to turn a nice golden brown, after 2 to 3 minutes, pour them into a bowl.
4. Bring a large pot of salted water to a rolling boil over high heat; covering the pot will help it come to a boil more quickly. Add the fennel tops and cook until they are a deep green, about 10 seconds. Use a slotted spoon to lift the fennel tops from the water; reserve the water to cook the pasta and reserve the fennel fronds to add to the sauce.
5. Heat a large skillet over medium-high heat. Add enough oil to coat the pan well. When the pan and oil are very hot, add the sardines, skin side down, and cook on the first side until the fish is golden brown, about 2 minutes. Turn the fish and cook on the second side until golden, 1 to 2 minutes longer. Transfer the sardines to a plate and reserve. (The sardines should not be so close together that they touch in the pan; if necessary, cook them in batches.)

Wine notes: This dish needs a light to medium-bodied, fruit-driven wine—bianco, rosato, or spumante—to bring out the salinity of the sardines, the sweetness of the raisins, the richness of the pignoli nuts, and the earthy herbaceous qualities of the fennel.

**White:** Ansonica, Grillo, or Sauvignon Blanc from Sicily; Falanghina from Campania; Vermentino di Gallura or Vermentino di Sardegna from Sardinia

**Rosato:** Lacrymarosa from Campania; Bardolino Chiaretto from Veneto; Cerasuolo di Montepulciano d'Abruzzo from Abruzzo

**Sparkling:** Prosecco from Veneto; Franciacorta from Lombardy

6. Add additional oil to the pan if necessary and then add the onions. Cook the onions, stirring frequently, until they are tender and translucent, 5 to 6 minutes. Add the anchovies and cook, stirring constantly, until they appear to have "melted" into the sauce. Add the cooked fennel tops, the wine, and saffron. Simmer the sauce until flavorful, about 15 minutes.

7. Bring the large pot of salted water back to a full boil, and add the bucatini. After the strands have softened enough to submerge them, stir the pasta once or twice to keep the strands from sticking. Cook uncovered at a boil until just tender to the bite, 10 to 12 minutes. Transfer a few ladlefuls of the cooking water to a bowl to use in the sauce (about ½ cup).

8. Drain the bucatini immediately through a colander. Shake well to remove any water clinging to the pasta. Pour the bucatini into a large serving bowl.

9. Add half of the sautéed sardines, the raisins, and the pine nuts to the sauce and simmer just enough to heat the sardines, about 2 minutes. Pour the sauce over the bucatini, toss together until the bucatini is evenly coated, and top with the remaining sardines. Serve at once, with bread crumbs on top if desired.

# Bucatini alla carbonara

## BUCATINI WITH EGGS, CHEESE, AND GUANCIALE

Guanciale is the cheek of the pork, cured with salt and spices and air-dried. This may be hard to find, but you can substitute a good-quality pancetta. Pancetta is the pork belly rather than the cheek, but it is cured in the same way.

**SERVES 4 TO 6**

- 2 tbsp extra-virgin olive oil
- 5 oz guanciale or pancetta
- 2 large eggs
- 2 egg yolks
- ½ cup grated Pecorino Romano (2 oz), plus more for serving
- 1 tsp freshly ground black pepper
- 1 lb bucatini

1. Heat a large skillet over medium heat. Add 1 tablespoon olive oil and the guanciale. Cook, stirring to cook the guanciale evenly, until it is just starting to get crisp. There should be 2 tablespoons of rendered fat and olive oil in the pan. Reserve the guanciale in the skillet.
2. Blend together the eggs, egg yolks, cheese, and pepper in a medium bowl with a whisk or fork until well combined.
3. Bring a large pot of salted water to a rolling boil over high heat; covering the pot will help it come to a boil more quickly.
4. Add the bucatini all at once and stir a few times to separate the pasta. Cook uncovered at a boil until the pasta is just tender to the bite, 10 to 12 minutes. Reserve about ½ cup of the cooking water to adjust the sauce.
5. Drain the pasta immediately through a colander. Shake well to remove any water clinging to the pasta. Pour the drained pasta into the skillet with the guanciale.
6. Add the egg mixture and stir the bucatini together with the egg mixture and the bacon. The heat from the pasta should be enough to cook the eggs enough, but if necessary, you can "cook" the sauce very gently over low heat. Stop as soon as the sauce clings well; if you cook any longer, the eggs will scramble. The pasta should appear creamy, not oily. If necessary, add a bit of the pasta water.
7. Serve at once, passing additional cheese on the side.

Wine notes: **White:** Frascati or Est! Est!! Est!!! from Lazio; Roero Arneis from Piedmont; Riesling from Friuli-Venezia Giulia

**Sparkling:** Prosecco from Veneto; Franciacorta Brut from Lombardy

**Red:** Valpolicella from Veneto

# Sfoglia

The dishes that fall into the category of sfoglia include fresh pastas as well as crespelle (thin, savory pancakes). Whether you are preparing a classic shape like fettuccine to serve with butter, cheese (and white truffle if you are lucky), pasta sheets to layer into a classic lasagna, or paring a hearty buckwheat pasta with cabbage and Bitto cheese, a silky fresh egg pasta dough makes the dish exceptional. Filled pastas, stuffed with pumpkin, beets, or cheese make a perfect first course for a traditional Italian dinner, served with a sizzling butter and sage sauce. Thin, delicate crespelle are filled and then baked until bubbling and beautifully browned.

While you can buy fresh pasta, it is not difficult to make your own. The only tools you need are a flat work surface, your hands, a fork, and a rolling pin.

# Fresh pasta

The best flour for home-made pasta is the Italian variety known as "00." Some stores stock this flour, and you can always locate it in a good Italian deli or market. If you don't want to make a special trip to the market, remember that all-purpose flour works well for making fresh pasta at home, too. Eggs provide moisture, flavor, and structure. (Dried pasta sometimes includes eggs, but water is typically the only liquid used.) Some fresh pasta recipes also call for a small amount of water or oil to make the dough tender and pliable. Salt develops flavor in the dough. You can substitute a quantity of whole wheat, semolina, cornmeal, buckwheat, rye, or chickpea flour for all-purpose flour to give your pasta a unique flavor and texture. Ingredients such as spinach or saffron also may be added for flavor and color.

## MIXING INGREDIENTS

For small batches, pasta dough can be efficiently mixed by hand. Combine the flour and salt in a bowl and make a well in the center. Place the eggs, flavoring ingredients, and oil in the well. Using a fork and working as rapidly as possible, incorporate the flour into the liquid ingredients little by little, working from the outside toward the center, until a shaggy mass forms. As the dough is mixed, adjust the consistency with additional flour or a few drops of water to compensate

1. Place the wet ingredients into the well you created with the flour.

2. Use your hands to knock the walls of the well into the center, mixing the ingredients together.

3. Mix with your hands until the dough becomes a homogeneous, shaggy ball.

for the natural variations in ingredients, humidity, and temperature or for the addition of either dry or moist flavoring ingredients.

### KNEADING

Once the dough is mixed, turn it out onto a floured surface and knead until its texture becomes smooth and elastic. Use the heels of your hands to push the dough away from you, and then reverse the motion, folding the dough over on itself toward you. Give the dough a quarter turn periodically so that it is evenly kneaded.

Kneading by hand generally takes 10 to 12 minutes. Do not rush the kneading process or the texture of the finished pasta will suffer. Properly kneaded dough is uniform in texture and no longer tacky to the touch. Divide the dough into balls about the size of an orange, place in a bowl, and cover loosely with a cotton towel. Allow the dough to rest at room temperature for at least 30 minutes. This will relax the dough and make it easier to roll out.

### ROLLING AND CUTTING

Use a straight wooden rolling pin to roll out pasta dough. Lightly flour a work surface with just enough flour to prevent the dough from sticking. Too much flour will cause the pasta to be dry. Work with one ball of dough at a time, and keep the remaining dough covered to prevent it from drying out. Flatten the dough by pressing it into a disk, and then begin rolling. Try to keep the dough's thickness even as you work. Turn the dough to keep it from sticking and lightly flour the rolling pin and the work surface if necessary.

When the dough is as thin as you want it, you can cut it into sheets. After the dough is cut into sheets, it can be cut into long, flat, ribbon shapes like pappardelle, linguine, or fettuccine. To do this by hand, roll a sheet of pasta dough up into a cylinder and make crosswise cuts of the desired width: very wide for pappardelle to very narrow for linguini. The sheets can also be cut into squares or circles to fill and fold into tortellini or ravioli.

## Making fresh pasta by machine

Large batches of pasta dough are easier to make with a food processor or stand mixer. To mix in a food processor, fit the machine with the metal blade and combine all the ingredients in its work bowl. Process just until the dough is blended into a coarse meal that forms a ball when gathered together. Do not overprocess. Remove the dough, transfer to a lightly floured work surface, and knead by hand as described above.

To use a stand mixer, fit it with the dough hook attachment to combine all the ingredients, and then mix at low speed for 3 to 4 minutes, until the dough is just moistened. Increase the speed to medium and knead the dough for 3 minutes longer, until the dough forms a smooth ball that pulls cleanly away from the sides of the bowl.

### ROLLING THE DOUGH IN A PASTA MACHINE

Gather the dough into a ball, cover it, and let it relax at room temperature for at least 30 minutes. Letting the dough relax allows it to be rolled into thin sheets more easily. Cut off a piece of dough and flatten it. The amount will vary according to the width of your pasta machine. Cover the remaining dough to keep it from drying out. Set the rollers to the widest opening, fold the dough in thirds, and guide the flattened dough through the machine as you turn the handle. Roll the dough to form a long, wide strip. Pass the dough through the widest setting 2 or 3 times, folding the dough in thirds each time.

Lightly flour the dough strip to prevent sticking. Set the rollers to the next thinnest opening and run the dough through the rollers again, this time without folding. Repeat, lightly dusting the dough with flour each time, and passing the dough through the rollers twice on each setting, until it reaches the desired thinness—the second-to-last setting for most pastas, or the thinnest setting for lasagna or stuffed pasta such as ravioli. Cut each rolled sheet of dough into shorter lengths, 1 or 2 feet long, for easier handling.

## CUTTING THE DOUGH

For best results—cleaner cuts and no sticking—let the pasta sheets dry slightly until the surface is leathery to the touch. This is especially important for cutting shapes by hand, but cutting by machine is also easier with slightly dried pasta. Feed the dough through the desired cutting attachment.

If you are not cooking the pasta immediately, you can dry it for storage. Spread small shapes in a single layer on a clean, dry towel or baking sheet. Gather long pasta into loose nests, arrange them on a clean baking sheet with plenty of space between each one, and let the pasta dry completely in a cool, dry place before placing in an airtight container. Store in the refrigerator for up to 2 days.

Fresh pasta cut and formed into nests.

# Pasta all uovo

## FRESH EGG PASTA

We will simply make a basic recipe and explain the different preparations you can make with it. But based on your egg size, the type of flour, even the time of the year, there may be slight variations.

**MAKES 1½ POUNDS PASTA, SERVES 4 TO 6**

**3⅔ lb all-purpose or "00" flour (1 lb)**

**4 large eggs**

1. Mound the flour on a clean surface or put it in the bowl of a stand mixer fitted with a dough hook. Create a well in the center and place the eggs in the center. Using a fork, start dragging the flour into the egg mixture. Pull the flour in from the bottom of the mound, so that the wet mixture is never really in contact with the work surface before it is blended with the flour. Pull large chunks of dough away from the fork as you work.
2. Once the flour is evenly moistened, knead well by hand or a mixer until all the ingredients are well combined and the dough seems smooth and elastic (about 10 minutes if working by hand, about 5 minutes in a mixer with a dough hook). Wrap the dough in plastic wrap or place it in a covered bowl and let it rest for at least 30 minutes.
3. Using a pasta roller or by hand with a rolling pin as described on page 151, roll the pasta into very thin sheets, making sure you keep dusting your work surface with more flour at each turn to keep the pasta from sticking. Roll out the pasta to make an 8 ×12-inch rectangle, about 1⁄16 inch thick, or to the thickness suggested in your recipe.
4. At this stage, the pasta can be cut into shapes for filling, or use a knife or the pasta machine cutter to cut the pasta into ribbon shapes. Place the cut pasta on parchment paper to dry a bit before cooking the pasta. The pasta can be allowed to air-dry and then stored in plastic bags for up to 1 month.

# Fettuccine con burro, parmigiano, e tartufo

## CLASSIC PIEDMONT PASTA WITH BUTTER, PARMIGIANO-REGGIANO, AND TRUFFLE

This dish is served simply with good butter, freshly grated Parmesan cheese, and a generous shaving of truffle—preferably white, when in season.

**SERVES 6**

- 3½ cups all-purpose or "00" flour (1 lb)
- 2 large eggs
- 4 egg yolks
- 1 tbsp olive oil
- Kosher salt as needed
- 1 cup (2 sticks) unsalted butter
- 1 cup grated Parmigiano-Reggiano cheese (4 oz), or as needed
- Fresh white truffle, for shaving (optional)

1. Mound the flour on a clean surface or put it in the bowl of a stand mixer fitted with a dough hook. Create a well in the center and place the eggs, egg yolks, and oil in the center. Using a fork, whisk the eggs and slowly start dragging the flour into the egg mixture. Knead well by hand or with the mixer until all the ingredients are well combined and the dough seems smooth and elastic (about 10 minutes if working by hand, about 5 minutes in a mixer with a dough hook). Wrap the dough in plastic wrap or place it in a covered bowl and let it rest at room temperature for at least 30 minutes.
2. Set up a pasta machine and set it to the largest opening. Dust a work surface with flour. Cut off pieces of dough about the size of an egg. Working with one piece of dough at a time, roll the dough into sheets about 1/16 inch thick. (For more information about rolling dough in a pasta machine, see page 151.)
3. Cut the sheets into very thin strips with a knife or using the attachment for your pasta machine; they should be about the same width as the thickness of the dough. Wind the strips into loose "nests" and put them on a baking sheet sprinkled with some cornmeal. Reserve the noodles until ready to cook them.
4. Bring a large pot of generously salted water to a boil. Add the pasta all at once and stir a few times to separate the strands. Cook uncovered at a gentle boil until the pasta is just tender to the bite, usually 3 to 4 minutes.
5. Transfer a few ladlefuls of pasta water from the pot to a bowl or cup to have ready for finishing the sauce if necessary. (You may need up to ½ cup.)
6. Drain the pasta immediately through a colander. Shake well to remove any water clinging to the pasta. Pour the drained pasta into a large serving bowl. Add the butter and cheese. Stir until evenly blended; add some of the pasta cooking water if necessary. The pasta should look creamy, not oily.
7. Shave the white truffle over the pasta, if you are lucky enough to have one. Serve at once, passing additional cheese on the side.

**Wine notes:** This extraordinary pasta dish from Piedmont needs an extraordinary red from the same region. The more shaved tartufo bianco you add, the earthier the wine should be. If you serve the dish without truffles, go with the Barbera, but once you add that feral fungus, try a richer, deeper, more complex Nebbiolo-based wine, especially Barbaresco and the massive Barolo.

**Red:** Barbera d'Alba, Barbera d'Asti, Nebbiolo d'Alba, Barbaresco, or Barolo from Piedmont

## WHITE TRUFFLES

The white truffles from the Piedmont region of Italy are prized for their intense aroma. They grow in the roots of trees, and those growing at the base of oak trees are thought to be among the finest. Should you happen to acquire a fresh white truffle, you can make the most of it by preserving it in a glass jar filled with rice, stored in the refrigerator. When you've enjoyed the entire truffle over pastas, gnocchi, eggs, or veal, use the scented rice to make a risotto or pilaf.

# Lasagna classica

## CLASSIC LASAGNA

Many variations on lasagna may be found all over Italy. If you go toward the south of Italy, you will see cooks using ricotta instead of béchamel. This is the classic lasagna Bolognese; try this version and you won't be disappointed. If you want your pasta dough to be green (lasagna verde), replace 1 egg with 3 ounces of pureed cooked spinach, well drained. This lasagna may be frozen when uncooked and then defrosted and baked as though it were freshly made.

**SERVES 6 TO 8**

BESCIAMELLA

**¼ cup unsalted butter**

**¼ cup minced yellow onion**

**⅓ cup all-purpose or "00" flour**

**5 cups milk**

**1 bay leaf**

**Kosher salt and freshly ground black pepper, as needed**

**Pinch of grated nutmeg**

PASTA DOUGH

**3⅔ cups all-purpose or "00" flour (1 lb)**

**4 large eggs, beaten**

**1 tsp olive oil**

**4 cups Bolognese Sauce (page 174)**

**2 cups grated Parmigiano-Reggiano (8 oz)**

1. To make the besciamella, heat the butter in a saucepan over low heat. Add the onion and cook, stirring frequently, until the onion is tender but has no brown color, about 5 minutes. Add the flour and cook, stirring frequently, until the mixture is a golden brown color and it has a rich, nutty aroma, about 6 minutes.
2. Add the milk and the bay leaf and stir well with a whisk to break up any lumps and smooth the sauce. Stir the sauce constantly with a wooden spoon as it returns to a simmer.
3. Once simmering, lower the heat slightly and continue to cook until the sauce is thickened and creamy, 10 to 15 minutes. Taste the sauce and season it to taste with salt and pepper and nutmeg. Strain through a fine-mesh sieve and reserve. (You may make the sauce up to 3 days in advance. After straining it, let it cool completely, then store in a covered container in the refrigerator. Warm the sauce over very low heat or in a microwave when you are ready to assemble the dish.)
4. To make the pasta dough, mound the flour on a clean surface or put it in the bowl of a stand mixer fitted with a dough hook. Create a well in the center and place the eggs and oil in the center. Using a fork, whisk the eggs and slowly start dragging the flour into the egg mixture. Knead well by hand or with the mixer until all the ingredients are well combined and the dough seems smooth and elastic (about 10 minutes if working by hand, about 5 minutes in a mixer with a dough hook). Wrap the dough in plastic wrap or place it in a covered bowl and let it rest at room temperature for at least 30 minutes.
5. Set up a pasta machine and set it to the largest opening. Dust a work surface with flour. Cut off pieces of dough about the size of an egg. Working with one piece of dough at a time, roll the dough into sheets about ⅛ inch thick. (For more information about rolling dough in a pasta machine, see page 151.)
6. Cut the sheets into noodles that are about 5 inches wide and as long as your lasagna pan (usually about 10 inches) and reserve them on a baking sheet.
7. Bring a large pot of generously salted water to a boil. Add the noodles all at once and stir a few times to separate them. Cook uncovered at a gentle boil until the noodles are just cooked through, 3 to 4 minutes.

(continued)

8. Drain the pasta immediately through a colander. Shake well to remove any water clinging to the pasta. Immediately rinse the pasta under cold running water until the pasta feels cool. Drain in the colander, and then set the noodles flat on a clean cloth towel or several layers of paper towels to dry completely.

9. Preheat the oven to 350 degrees F. Brush a lasagna pan or baking dish (about 3-quart capacity) liberally with butter or oil. Layer the lasagna in the following order: ¾ cup besciamella spread into an even layer, topped with lasagna noodles (lay them into the pan so that they very slightly overlap each other), another ¾ cup besciamella, ¾ cup Bolognese sauce, and ⅓ cup cheese. Repeat this sequence 3 more times. Spoon the remaining besciamella over the lasagna to make a top layer. Spread it evenly to make sure that the noodles are coated. Spoon the remaining Bolognese sauce on top of the besciamella and sprinkle with the remaining cheese.

10. Bake the lasagna until it is very hot all the way through and a rich, golden crust forms, 40 to 45 minutes. Let the lasagna rest for at least 15 minutes before cutting into pieces and serving.

Wine notes: Classic lasagna is one of the richer pasta preparations, and it needs a wine that can stand up to the swirl of ingredients that create that richness. These red wines are powerful but feature a bracing acidity that will help cleanse the palate and stimulate the appetite for both food and wine.

**Red:** Sangiovese di Romagna from Emilia-Romagna; Carmignano, Vino Nobile di Montepulciano, or Chianti Classico from Tuscany; Torgiano Rosso from Umbria; Grumello from Lombardy

Lasagna Classica

# Maltagliati ai porcini

## "BADLY CUT" PASTA WITH PORCINI MUSHROOMS

Use fresh porcini mushrooms when available or any type of mushrooms you can find in the market.

**SERVES 4 TO 6**

PASTA DOUGH

**3⅔ cups all-purpose or "00" flour (1 lb)**

**2 large eggs**

**4 or 5 egg yolks**

**1 tbsp olive oil**

**¼ cup extra-virgin olive oil**

**2 garlic cloves, thinly sliced or chopped**

**1 lb mushrooms, sliced**

**½ cup chopped flat-leaf parsley**

**½ cup dry white wine**

**½ cup Brodo (page 88) (or vegetable stock for a vegetarian version)**

**Salt and freshly ground black pepper, as needed**

**¾ cup grated Parmigiano-Reggiano (3 oz)**

**2 tbsp unsalted butter or olive oil**

1. To make the pasta dough, mound the flour on a clean surface or put it in the bowl of a stand mixer fitted with a dough hook. Create a well in the center and place the eggs, egg yolks, and oil in the center. Using a fork, whisk the eggs and oil together and slowly start dragging the flour into the egg mixture. Knead well by hand or with the mixer until all the ingredients are well combined and the dough seems smooth and elastic (about 10 minutes if working by hand, about 5 minutes in a mixer with a dough hook). Wrap the dough in plastic wrap or place it in a covered bowl and let it rest at room temperature for at least 30 minutes.
2. Set up a pasta machine and set it to the largest opening. Dust a work surface with flour. Cut off pieces of dough about the size of an egg. Working with one piece of dough at a time, roll the dough into sheets about ⅛ inch thick. (For more information about rolling dough in a pasta machine, see page 151.)
3. Cut the pasta into wide ribbons (up to 1½ inches wide and 4 inches long) without making the cuts too neat or precise. As you cut out the ribbons, place them on a plate or baking sheet sprinkled with a little flour to keep them from sticking.
4. Heat a skillet over medium heat. Add ¼ cup olive oil and the garlic. Sauté, stirring often, until the garlic is aromatic, about 1 minute. Add the mushrooms and stir well. Continue to cook until the mushrooms start to release their moisture, usually about 5 minutes, but the time will vary depending upon the type of mushrooms you are using. Stir in half of the parsley, and then add the wine and stir well. Continue to cook until the wine is almost completely cooked away, about 5 minutes. Add the stock and simmer until the mushrooms are very flavorful, another 5 minutes. Season with salt and pepper if necessary. Reserve in the skillet while you prepare the pasta.
5. Bring a large pot of generously salted water to a boil. Add the pasta all at once and stir a few times to separate the strands. Cook uncovered at a gentle boil until the pasta is just tender to the bite, 10 to 12 minutes.

Wine notes: If you want to focus on the meaty quality of the mushrooms in this dish, choose a medium- to full-bodied white, which will create a canvas to draw out the earthy mushroom flavors. To create a savory "sauce" for those mushrooms, choose a dry red—not too complex—with noticeable fruit and acidity.

**White:** Chardonnay from Tuscany; Verdicchio from Le Marche

**Red:** Chianti Colli Fiorentino or Rosso di Montalcino from Tuscany; Pinot Nero (Pinot Noir) from Trentino-Alto Adige; Aglianico del Vulture from Basilicata; Cannonau di Sardegna from Sardinia

6. Transfer a few ladlefuls of pasta water from the pot to a bowl or cup to have ready for finishing the sauce if necessary. (You may need up to ½ cup.)
7. Drain the pasta immediately through a colander. Shake well to remove any water clinging to the pasta. Pour the drained pasta into the skillet with the mushrooms. Add the cheese, butter or olive oil, and the remaining parsley. Stir until evenly blended; add some of the pasta cooking water if necessary. The pasta should look creamy, not oily.
8. Serve the pasta at once from a heated serving bowl or in individual pasta plates.

## PORCINI

If you are using fresh porcini, make sure you choose mushrooms that are not very spongy or old-looking. Open them and see if there are any worms, which can be typical in these particular mushrooms. To clean them, brush them with a little brush to remove any dirt. If you wash them, they tend to become very spongy. If porcini are not available, you may use any other type of mushroom; just adjust the cooking time according to the delicacy of the mushrooms you are using.

# Ravioli di melanzane

## EGGPLANT-FILLED RAVIOLI

You can shape these summertime ravioli into rounds, ovals, triangles, or other shapes. Try adding scamorza (smoked or not) to the filling for a more complex flavor.

**SERVES 4**

### FILLING

**1 firm eggplant, partially peeled and diced (about 1½ lb)**

**Kosher salt, as needed**

**1 tbsp extra-virgin olive oil**

**1 garlic clove, lightly crushed**

**1 tbsp minced shallot**

**½ cup ricotta, preferably sheep or goat's milk**

**½ cup grated Parmigiano-Reggiano (2 oz), plus more for serving**

**1 tbsp chopped flat-leaf parsley**

**1 tsp chopped mint**

**1 tsp chopped marjoram**

**Freshly ground black pepper, as needed**

### PASTA DOUGH

**3⅔ cups all-purpose or "00" flour (1 lb)**

**3 large eggs**

**3 egg yolks**

**1 tbsp olive oil**

1. To make the filling, put the eggplant in a colander, sprinkle it generously with salt, and let it drain for about 1 hour. Taste the eggplant before cooking it; if it is very salty, you can rinse it and then blot it dry on paper towels before using it in the filling.
2. Heat a large skillet over medium heat. Add 1 tablespoon olive oil and the garlic clove. Sauté, stirring often, until the garlic has flavored the oil, about 1 minute. Remove and discard the garlic and add the shallot. Continue to cook until the shallot is soft, 2 to 3 minutes. Add the eggplant, stir well, and cook until tender, 5 to 7 minutes longer. Transfer the eggplant mixture to a bowl and let it cool completely.
3. Add the ricotta, Parmigiano-Reggiano, parsley, mint, marjoram, and salt and pepper. Reserve in the refrigerator while you prepare the pasta dough.
4. To make the dough for the ravioli, mound the flour on a clean surface or put it in the bowl of a stand mixer with a dough hook. Create a well in the center and place the eggs, egg yolks, and oil in the center. Using a fork, whisk the eggs and oil together and slowly start dragging the flour into the egg mixture. Knead well by hand or with the mixer until all the ingredients are well combined and the dough seems smooth and elastic (about 10 minutes if working by hand, about 5 minutes in a mixer with a dough hook). Wrap the dough in plastic wrap or place it in a covered bowl and let it rest at room temperature for at least 30 minutes.
5. Set up a pasta machine and set it to the largest opening. Dust a work surface with flour. Cut off pieces of dough about the size of an egg. Working with one piece of dough at a time, roll the dough into sheets about 1/16 inch thick. (For more information about rolling dough in a pasta machine, see page 151.)
6. Lay one of the sheets flat on a lightly floured work surface. Use a pastry brush to lightly wet one side of the dough. Spoon the filling in 2-teaspoon mounds onto half of the wet side of the dough. There should be about ½ inch between the mounds so that you can cut individual ravioli. Fold the sheet in half lengthwise to cover the filling. Press the pasta sheet together to seal the edges well around the filling. Use a pastry cutter or a knife to cut individual ravioli. As you cut out the ravioli, place them on a plate or baking sheet sprinkled with a little flour to keep them from sticking.
7. Bring a large pot of generously salted water to a boil. Add the ravioli all at once and stir a few times to separate them. Cook uncovered at a gentle boil until the pasta is just tender to the bite, 5 to 6 minutes.
8. Drain the ravioli immediately through a colander. Serve the pasta at once from a heated serving bowl or in individual pasta plates topped with Parmigiano-Reggiano.

**Wine notes:** If you decide to include fish or crustaceans in this pasta dish, by all means choose a medium-bodied dry white, or a dry rosato. These wines will focus on the salinity of the dish. If you choose not to include seafood, and especially if you try the ravioli with smoked scamorza,, choose a simple, lighter red wine that will honor the cheese as well as the herb-infused eggplant.

**White:** Inzolia from Sicily; Falanghina from Campania; Verdicchio from Le Marche
**Rosé:** Lacrymarosa from Campania; Montepulciano d'Abruzzo Cerasuolo from Abruzzo
**Red:** Chianti from Tuscany; Freisa or Dolcetto from Piedmont; Valpolicella or Merlot from Veneto

# Casunziei all'ampezzana

## BEET-FILLED RAVIOLI FROM THE DOLOMITES

This type of ravioli is very typical of the Belluno area, in the northern part of the Veneto region. Good melted brown butter with poppy seeds makes a dramatic presentation, and the flavor of beet combined with a hint of orange zest and cinnamon makes it all very interesting. The very colorful red filling will show nicely through the dough once cooked. You may omit the ricotta and add some cooked pancetta or even bacon to the stuffing if you like a little bit of smoked flavor.

**SERVES 4 TO 6**

FILLING

**½ cup (1 stick) unsalted butter**

**½ cup coarsely chopped flat-leaf parsley**

**1 tbsp chopped sage**

**1 tbsp minced rosemary**

**1 cup diced yellow onions**

**1½ lb beets, peeled and diced**

**1½ cups diced parsnips**

**1½ cups diced Yukon gold potatoes**

**2 cups grated Parmigiano-Reggiano (8 oz)**

**⅔ cup drained fresh ricotta (optional)**

**1 tsp finely grated orange zest**

**Pinch of ground cinnamon**

**Kosher salt and freshly ground black pepper, as needed**

**3 egg yolks**

**½ cup fine dry bread crumbs, or as needed**

**(continued)**

1. To make the filling, heat a large skillet over medium heat. Add the butter and let it melt (it should foam up but shouldn't darken in color). Add the parsley, sage, and rosemary. Sauté just long enough to heat the herbs, about 20 seconds. Add the onions and continue to cook, stirring frequently, until the onions are tender, about 4 minutes. Add the beets, parsnips, and potatoes and pour in enough water to cover the vegetables about halfway. Cover, bring the liquid to a simmer, and continue to simmer, adjusting the heat level as necessary, until all of the vegetables are tender enough to mash easily with a fork, about 45 minutes. Remove from the heat and let the vegetables cool before chopping them finely with a knife or in a food processor. They should be fairly smooth. Transfer to a large bowl.

2. Add the Parmigiano-Reggiano, ricotta (if desired), the orange zest, cinnamon, and salt and pepper and stir with a wooden spoon until blended. Stir in the egg yolks. The filling should be firm enough to mound when dropped from a spoon. If it is soft enough to run off the spoon, add some of the bread crumbs to help it hold together. Reserve in the refrigerator while you prepare the pasta dough.

3. To make the pasta dough, mound the flours on a clean surface or combine them in the bowl of a stand mixer fitted with a dough hook. Create a well in the center and place the eggs and oil in the center. Using a fork, whisk the eggs and oil together and slowly start dragging the flour into the egg mixture. If the dough is too dry, you may sprinkle it with a little cold water, about 1 tablespoon at a time, until you have a manageable dough. Knead well by hand or with the mixer until all the ingredients are well combined and the dough seems smooth and elastic (about 10 minutes if working by hand, about 5 minutes in a mixer with a dough hook). Wrap the dough in plastic wrap or place it in a covered bowl and let it rest at room temperature for at least 30 minutes.

4. Set up a pasta machine and set it to the largest opening. Dust a work surface with flour. Cut off pieces of dough about the size of an egg. Working with one piece of dough at a time, roll the dough into 4 sheets about ⅛ inch thick. (For more information about rolling dough in a pasta machine, see page 151.)

5. Lay one of the sheets flat on a lightly floured work surface. Use a pastry brush to lightly wet one side of the dough. Spoon the filling onto the wet side of the dough, mounding about 2 tablespoons of the filling for each ravioli. There should be about 2 inches between the mounds

(continued)

PASTA DOUGH

2¾ cups all-purpose or "00" flour (11 oz)

¾ cup semolina (durum) flour (5 oz)

4 large eggs

1 tbsp olive oil

3 tbsp unsalted butter

6 sage leaves

Grated Parmigiano-Reggiano, for serving

2 tbsp poppy seeds, or as needed

so that you can cut individual ravioli. Place a second pasta sheet on top of the first one. Press the dough together to seal the sheets together along the edges and around the filling, creating little pockets of filling. Use a fluted or plain biscuit cutter to cut out round ravioli. As you cut out the ravioli, place them on a plate or baking sheet sprinkled with a little flour to keep them from sticking.

6. Bring a large pot of generously salted water to a boil. Add the ravioli all at once and stir a few times to separate them. Cook uncovered at a gentle boil until the pasta is just tender to the bite, 5 to 6 minutes. While the pasta is cooking, melt the butter with the sage leaves in a small skillet over medium heat until the butter takes on a brown color.

7. Drain the ravioli immediately through a colander. Serve at once from a heated serving bowl or in individual pasta plates topped with the butter-sage sauce. Sprinkle with cheese and poppy seeds.

Wine notes: The intense root vegetable flavor of the beets calls for a dry white or bubbly that will highlight those flavors on the palate.

**White:** Soave Classico from Veneto; Friulano from Friuli-Venezia Giulia; Pinot Grigio from Trentino-Alto Adige

**Sparkling:** Prosecco di Valdobbiadene from Veneto; brut rosato from Trentino-Alto Adige; brut Franciacorta from Lombardy

# Ravioli di ricotta

## RICOTTA-FILLED RAVIOLI

You may add blanched pureed spinach (see page 23), or any type of green you like, to the filling. Be sure to drain the greens well before you mix them in.

**SERVES 4**

### FILLING

**1 lb fresh ricotta, drained**

**2 egg yolks**

**1 cup grated Parmigiano-Reggiano (4 oz), plus more for serving**

**Pinch of grated nutmeg**

**Pinch of lemon zest (optional)**

**Salt and freshly ground black pepper, as needed**

### PASTA DOUGH

**3⅔ cups all-purpose or "00" flour (1 lb)**

**2 large eggs**

**2 egg yolks**

**1 tbsp olive oil**

1. To make the filling, combine the drained ricotta, egg yolks, Parmigiano-Reggiano, nutmeg, lemon zest (if desired), and salt and pepper. Stir well and set aside.
2. To make the dough for the ravioli, mound the flour on a clean surface or put it in the bowl of a stand mixer fitted with a dough hook. Create a well in the center and place the eggs, egg yolks, and oil in the center. Using a fork, whisk the eggs and oil together and slowly start dragging the flour into the egg mixture. Knead well by hand or with the mixer until all the ingredients are well combined and the dough seems smooth and elastic (about 10 minutes if working by hand, about 5 minutes in a mixer with a dough hook). Wrap the dough in plastic wrap or place it in a covered bowl and let it rest at room temperature for at least 30 minutes.
3. Set up a pasta machine and set it to the largest opening. Dust a work surface with flour. Cut off pieces of dough about the size of an egg. Working with one piece of dough at a time, roll the dough into sheets about ⅛ inch thick. (For more information about rolling dough in a pasta machine, see page 151.)
4. Lay one of the sheets flat on a lightly floured work surface. Use a pastry brush to lightly wet one side of the dough. Spoon the filling onto half of the wet side of the dough in 2-teaspoon mounds. There should be about ½ inch between the mounds so that you can cut the pasta into individual ravioli. Fold the sheet in half lengthwise to cover the filling. Press the pasta sheet together to seal the edges well around the filling. Use a pastry cutter or a knife to cut individual ravioli. As you cut out the ravioli, place them on a plate or baking sheet sprinkled with a little flour to keep them from sticking. Repeat with the remaining pasta and filling.
5. Bring a large pot of generously salted water to a boil. Add the ravioli all at once and stir a few times to separate them. Cook uncovered at a gentle boil until the pasta is just tender to the bite, 5 to 6 minutes.
6. Drain the ravioli immediately through a colander. Serve the pasta at once from a heated serving bowl or in individual pasta plates topped with Parmigiano-Reggiano.

---

**Wine notes:** Deceptively rich, these ravioli will match well with a white that by virtue of its fruit and acid notes cuts through that richness. If you want to celebrate the richness and create a match that turns the wine into a liquid spice, choose a light- to medium-bodied red.

**White:** Roero Arneis from Piedmont; Chardonnay from Sicily; Fiano di Avellino from Campania

**Red:** Sangiovese di Romagna from Emilia-Romagna; Chianti Classico, Rosso di Montalcino, or Rosso di Montepulciano from Tuscany; Valpolicella, Bardolino, or Merlot from Veneto; Dolcetto d'Alba or Barbera d'Asti from Piedmont

# Anelli di ricotta e spinaci

## RINGS OF RICOTTA AND SPINACH

*Anelli* is Italian for "rings." This mixture of ricotta and herbs or any greens has ancient origins; the same filling could be used to fill tarts and ravioli rather than crespelle (crepes).

**SERVES 6 TO 8**

CRESPELLE

**⅔ cup all-purpose or "00" flour**

**2 large eggs**

**1 cup milk**

**Unsalted butter, as needed**

FILLING

**4 cups fresh spinach leaves (8 oz)**

**3 tbsp unsalted butter, plus as needed**

**1 tsp minced shallot**

**1 cup ricotta (8 oz)**

**½ cup grated Parmigiano-Reggiano (2 oz)**

**1 egg yolk**

**¼ cup melted unsalted butter, as needed**

**Grated Parmigiano-Reggiano, for serving**

1. To make the crespelle, sift the flour into a large bowl. Add the eggs and mix them into the flour using a whisk. Add the milk and mix until evenly blended and smooth, but do not overmix the batter. Strain it through a wire-mesh sieve into a clean bowl and let the batter rest for up to 30 minutes.
2. Heat a 10-inch nonstick sauté pan or crêpe pan. Add a little butter and let it melt. With one hand, grasp the handle of the pan so that you can lift the pan up and tilt it as you pour the batter over the surface with the other hand. Add about ¼ cup of the batter for each crespella.
3. Return the pan to the heat and let the crespella cook undisturbed for about 40 seconds. Check the underside; it should be set but not browned. Turn the crespella with a long metal spatula and let it cook on the second side until just cooked, 10 to 20 seconds longer. Transfer the finished crespella to a plate. Continue until all of the batter is used; you should have at least 8 crespelle. (If you are making the crespelle ahead of time or if you make more crespelle than you need for this recipe, they can be wrapped and kept in the refrigerator for up to 2 days.)
4. To make the filling, bring a large pot of generously salted water to a boil. Add the spinach all at once and stir to submerge the leaves. Cook uncovered until tender and a deep color, 3 to 4 minutes. Lift the greens out of the water with a sieve or slotted spoon and transfer to a bowl of ice water. After the greens are chilled, drain in a colander for several minutes and then squeeze them with your hands to remove as much water as you can. Use a chef's knife to finely chop the spinach.
5. Heat a sauté pan over medium heat. Add 3 tablespoons of butter and, when it has melted, add the shallot. Stir to coat with the oil. Cook over low heat until the shallot is tender, about 2 minutes. Add the spinach and cook, stirring occasionally, until any moisture remaining in the spinach has cooked away. Transfer the spinach to a bowl and let it cool. Add the ricotta, Parmigiano-Reggiano, and egg yolk to the cooled spinach and stir to blend evenly.

Wine notes: These crespelle will have a rich dairy taste thanks to the ricotta, Parmigiano-Reggiano, and melted butter, and it can accommodate a medium-bodied dry white to cut through that velvety texture with some green fruit acidity. The dish will also be at home with a lighter red that will provide red currant flavors and celebrate the glories of the dairy.

**White:** Albana di Romagna from Emilia-Romagna; Soave Classico from Veneto; Roero Arneis from Piedmont
**Red:** Sangiovese di Romagna from Emilia-Romagna; Chianti from Tuscany; Dolcetto d'Alba from Piedmont; Valpolicella or Bardolino from Veneto

6. Brush a baking dish or casserole with some of the melted butter. To fill the anelli, spoon or pipe about ¼ cup of the filling mixture down the center of each crespella and roll the crespella around the filling, making the rolls tight enough to hold together. Slice each filled crespella crosswise into 1-inch pieces and set them into the baking dish with a cut side facing down (it should look like a ring of crespelle around the green filling). Once all of the anelli are arranged in the baking dish, brush them lightly with the remaining melted butter and sprinkle with Parmigiano-Reggiano. (You may bake the dish now, or cover the pan and refrigerate for up to 2 days.)

7. Preheat the oven to 350 degrees F. Bake until the anelli are very hot and the cheese has formed a golden crust, 10 to 15 minutes.

# Pappardelle con ragù d'anatra

## PASTA WITH DUCK RAGÙ

For this recipe you will use only the meat from the leg. Typically the whole duck would be used, but we find the breast to be too lean for the long, slow cooking method used for the ragù.

**SERVES 6 TO 8 (MAKES 4 CUPS SAUCE)**

### DUCK RAGÙ

**4 duck legs (7 to 8 oz each)**

**Salt, as needed**

**1½ cups minced yellow onions**

**1 cup minced carrots**

**½ cup red wine**

**2 bay leaves**

**1 thyme sprig**

**2 cups canned diced tomatoes, with juice**

**Duck stock or chicken stock, as needed**

**Freshly ground black pepper, as needed**

### PASTA DOUGH

**3⅔ cups all-purpose or "00" flour (1 lb)**

**2 large eggs**

**4 or 5 egg yolks**

**1 tbsp olive oil**

1. To make the duck ragù, season the duck legs with salt and place them skin side down in a 5-quart pot (a Dutch oven is a good choice) over medium-low heat. Cook until the fat starts to render into the pan and the skin becomes crispy, about 10 minutes. Turn the duck legs over and continue to cook on the second side until the meat is golden brown. Transfer the duck legs to a plate and reserve.
2. Add the onions and carrots to the duck fat in the pot. When the onions are tender, after 5 to 6 minutes, return the duck legs to the pot and add the wine, bay leaves, and thyme. Let the wine cook down until it has nearly evaporated, about 5 minutes.
3. Add the tomatoes and enough of the stock to cover the legs by two-thirds. Bring the liquid to a gentle simmer over low heat, partially cover the pot, and continue to cook very slowly until the duck meat is very tender and easy to pull away from the bone, about 1½ hours. Transfer the legs to a plate and continue to simmer the sauce, uncovered, while you pull the duck meat from the bones, skin, and tendons. Break the duck meat into pieces with your fingers and return it to the sauce. At this point, the sauce should be thick and flavorful and ready to serve. (If you plan to serve the sauce later, you may cool it and then store in a covered dish in the refrigerator for up to 4 days.)
4. To make the pasta dough for the noodles, mound the flour on a clean surface or put it in the bowl of a stand mixer fitted with a dough hook. Create a well in the center and place the eggs, egg yolks, and oil in the center. Using a fork, whisk the eggs and oil together and slowly start dragging the flour into the egg mixture. Knead well by hand or with the mixer until all the ingredients are well combined and the dough seems smooth and elastic (about 10 minutes if working by hand, about 5 minutes in a mixer with a dough hook). Wrap the dough in plastic wrap or place it in a covered bowl and let it rest at room temperature for at least 30 minutes.

---

Wine notes: The duck sauce is infused with the red wine used in cooking, so echo those flavors in the glass. This is a hearty, rustic pasta dish that needs a red wine on the same wavelength.

**Red:** Chianti Classico Riserva, Morellino di Scansano, or Vino Nobile di Montepulciano from Tuscany; Aglianico del Vulture from Basilicata; Primitivo or Salice Salentino from Puglia; Cannonau di Sardegna from Sardinia; Rosso Conero or Rosso Piceno from Le Marche; Torgiano Rosso or Montefalco Rosso from Umbria

5. Set up a pasta machine and set it to the largest opening. Dust a work surface with flour. Cut off pieces of dough about the size of an egg. Working with one piece of dough at a time, roll the dough into sheets about 1⁄16 inch thick. (For more information about rolling dough in a pasta machine, see page 151.)

6. Cut the sheets into ¾-inch-wide strips with a knife. Wind the strips into loose "nests" and put them on a baking sheet sprinkled with cornmeal. Reserve the noodles until ready to cook them. (If made in advance, store the pasta in the refrigerator for up to 2 days. Freezing instructions for fresh pasta can be found on page 152.)

7. Bring a large pot of generously salted water to a boil. Add the pappardelle all at once to the boiling water and stir a few times to separate them. Cook uncovered at a boil until just tender to the bite, 4 to 5 minutes. Drain the pasta immediately through a colander. Shake well to remove any water clinging to the pasta. Pour the drained pasta into a large serving bowl. Add the duck ragù and toss the noodles and sauce together. Serve at once.

# Pizzoccheri alla valtellinese

## BUCKWHEAT PASTA WITH CABBAGE AND BITTO CHEESE

This pasta is typically found in the northern part of the Lombardy region, in the Valtellina area. Bitto is a typical cheese from this area, and it may be hard to find, but you could substitute Fontina. This recipe is also less commonly made with green Swiss chard instead of cabbage.

**SERVES 4 TO 6**

PASTA DOUGH

3 cups all-purpose or "00" flour (12 oz)

1 cup buckwheat flour (4 oz)

3 large eggs

4 to 6 tbsp milk

Salt, as needed

1½ cups diced potatoes

2 cups coarsely chopped Savoy cabbage (6 oz)

1 cup grated Bitto or Fontina cheese (4 oz)

¾ cup grated Parmigiano-Reggiano (3 oz)

½ cup (1 stick) unsalted butter

2 garlic cloves

6 sage leaves

1. To make the pasta dough for the noodles, mound the flours on a clean surface or combine them in the bowl of a stand mixer fitted with a dough hook. Create a well in the center and place the eggs and milk in the center. Using a fork, whisk the eggs and milk together and slowly start dragging the flour into the egg mixture. Knead well by hand or with the mixer until all the ingredients are well combined and the dough seems smooth and elastic (about 10 minutes if working by hand, about 5 minutes in a mixer with a dough hook). Wrap the dough in plastic wrap or place it in a covered bowl and let it rest at room temperature for at least 30 minutes.
2. Set up a pasta machine and set it to the largest opening. Dust a work surface with flour. Cut off pieces of dough about the size of an egg. Working with one piece of dough at a time, roll the dough into sheets about 1/16 inch thick. (For more information about rolling dough in a pasta machine, see page 151.)
3. Cut the sheets into noodles that are ½ inch wide and 4 inches long. As you finish cutting the noodles, put them on a baking sheet to dry. Reserve the noodles until ready to cook them. (If made in advance, store the noodles in the refrigerator for up to 2 days.)
4. Preheat the oven to 350 degrees F.
5. Bring a large pot of generously salted water to a boil. Add the potatoes and cabbage and cook until they are nearly tender, about 5 minutes. Add the pasta and stir once or twice to separate the pieces. Continue to cook until the pasta and vegetables are fully cooked, about 5 minutes longer.

**Wine notes:** Wines from Lombardy can be a bit of a challenge to find, but the search is worth it. In general, this pasta dish will work with either a medium-bodied white or red, depending on how much you like spinach; the whites will soften the greens and highlight the cheeses, while the reds will match the intensity of the cheeses and allow a background flavor of bittersweet spinach to emerge.

**White:** Terre di Franciacorta from Lombardy; Verdicchio from Le Marche; Sauvignon or Friulano from Friuli-Venezia Giulia

**Red:** Oltrepò Pavese Rosso, Inferno, or Grumello from Lombardy; Chianti Classico or Rosso di Montalcino from Tuscany; Nebbiolo d'Alba from Piedmont

6. Drain the pasta and vegetables immediately through a colander. Shake well to remove any water clinging to the pasta. Make a layer in a baking dish with about one-third of the pasta and vegetables, and top with one-third of the Bitto and one-third of the Parmigiano-Reggiano. Continue to make two more layers of pasta and cheese, ending with Parmigiano-Reggiano.

7. Cook the butter together with the garlic and sage in a small skillet over medium heat until the butter has a nutty aroma and a light brown color. Remove and discard the garlic and pour the melted butter and sage leaves over the casserole. Bake until the cheese is melted, 4 to 5 minutes. Serve at once directly from the casserole.

# Tagliatelle con ragù alla bolognese

## TAGLIATELLE WITH MEAT SAUCE FROM BOLOGNA

You can find thousands of variations on this classic meat ragù. Every family keeps their specific ratio of meat to vegetables a secret. In some areas of the country, cooks even like to add milk to the ragù for a richer, creamier, denser rendition.

**SERVES 6 (MAKES ABOUT 4 CUPS RAGÙ)**

RAGÙ

½ cup (1 stick) unsalted butter

1½ cups minced yellow onions

1 cup minced celery

¾ cup minced carrots

2 lb coarsely ground beef

½ cup red wine

1½ cups canned diced tomatoes, with juice

2 cups chicken stock or water, plus as needed

2 bay leaves

Salt and freshly ground black pepper, as needed

PASTA DOUGH

3¼ cups all-purpose or "00" flour (14 oz)

4 large eggs

Grated Parmigiano-Reggiano, for serving

1. To make the ragù, heat the butter in a 5-quart pot (a Dutch oven is a good choice) over medium-low heat. Add the onions, celery, and carrots and cook, stirring frequently, until the onions are tender, about 10 minutes. Add the beef and cook, stirring to break up any large clumps, until the meat loses its raw color, 6 to 7 minutes. Add the wine and let it cook down until it has nearly evaporated, about 2 minutes.
2. Add the tomatoes, the stock, and bay leaves. Bring the liquid to a gentle simmer over low heat, season with salt and pepper, partially cover the pot, and continue to cook very slowly until the sauce is very rich and has reduced, 4 to 5 hours. As the ragù cooks, stir it from time to time and add a bit more stock or water if it starts to stick to the bottom of the pan.
3. To make the pasta dough for the noodles, mound the flour on a clean surface or put it in the bowl of a stand mixer fitted with a dough hook. Create a well in the center and place the eggs in the center. Using a fork, whisk the eggs and oil together and slowly start dragging the flour into the egg mixture. Knead well by hand or with the mixer until all the ingredients are well combined and the dough seems smooth and elastic (about 10 minutes if working by hand, about 5 minutes in a mixer with a dough hook). Wrap the dough in plastic wrap or place it in a covered bowl and let it rest at room temperature for at least 30 minutes.
4. Set up a pasta machine and set it to the largest opening. Dust a work surface with flour. Cut off pieces of dough about the size of an egg. Working with one piece of dough at a time, roll the dough into sheets about 1⁄16 inch thick and 12 inches long. (For more information about rolling dough in a pasta machine, see page 151.)

Wine notes: The red wine infusion during cooking dictates that a hearty red should be served with this beef sauce, creating a bridge between the flavors on the plate and the flavors in the glass.

**Red:** Sangiovese di Romagna from Emilia-Romagna; Montepulciano d'Abruzzo from Abruzzo; Aglianico del Vulture from Basilicata; Primitivo or Salice Salentino from Puglia; Cannonau di Sardegna from Sardinia; Rosso Conero or Rosso Piceno from Le Marche; Torgiano Rosso or Montefalco Rosso from Umbria

5. Cut the sheets into ⅜-inch-wide strips with a knife or using the attachment for your pasta machine. Wind the strips into loose "nests" and put them on a baking sheet. Reserve the noodles until ready to cook them. (If made in advance, store the noodles in the refrigerator for up to 2 days.)

6. Bring a large pot of generously salted water to a boil. Add the noodles all at once to the boiling water and stir a few times to separate them. Cook uncovered at a boil until just tender to the bite, 4 to 5 minutes. Drain the pasta immediately through a colander. Shake well to remove any water clinging to the pasta. Pour the drained pasta into a large serving bowl. Add the ragù and toss the noodles and sauce together. Serve at once, passing Parmigiano-Reggiano on the side.

# Maccheroni alla chitarra con sugo d'agnello

## MACARONI CUT WITH A "GUITAR" IN A LAMB SAUCE

In the region of Abruzzo in the middle of Italy, the use of lamb is very common. In this recipe it takes the form of a sauce used to dress pasta typical to the region, like the maccheroni alla chitarra. The chitarra is a tool used to cut this pasta; it is usually a wooden box with metal strings wrapped around its length. The sheets of pasta are pressed against the metal strings to cut them into long strands, as shown on the following page. The meat can be prepared in larger pieces and shredded after cooking, if you prefer, but here the meat is ground before cooking.

**SERVES 6 (MAKES ABOUT 4 CUPS SUGO)**

SUGO

½ cup (1 stick) unsalted butter

2 cups minced yellow onions

1 garlic clove

2 lb lamb, coarsely ground

½ cup white wine

4 cups canned diced tomatoes, with juice

2 cups chicken stock, plus as needed

2 bay leaves

Kosher salt and freshly ground black pepper, as needed

1 red bell pepper, quartered and seeded

1 red chile

PASTA DOUGH

1 cup semolina flour (7 oz)

1¾ cups all-purpose or "00" flour (7 oz)

4 large eggs

1. To make the sugo, heat the butter in a 5-quart pot (a Dutch oven is a good choice) over medium-low heat. Add the onions and garlic and cook, stirring frequently, until the onions are tender, about 10 minutes. Add the lamb and cook, stirring to break up any large clumps, until the meat loses its raw color, 6 to 7 minutes. Add the wine and let it cook down until it has nearly evaporated, about 2 minutes.

2. Add the tomatoes, stock, and bay leaves. Bring the liquid to a gentle simmer over low heat, season with salt and pepper, partially cover the pot, and continue to cook very slowly until the sauce is half done, about 2 hours. At this point, add the bell pepper and the chile. Continue to cook until the sauce has thickened and reduced and has a rich flavor, another 2 hours. As the sugo cooks, stir it from time to time and add a bit more stock or water if it starts to stick to the bottom of the pan. Remove and discard the peppers.

3. To make the pasta dough for the noodles, mound the flours on a clean surface or combine them in the bowl of a stand mixer fitted with a dough hook. Create a well in the center and place the eggs in the center. Using a fork, whisk the eggs and slowly start dragging the flour into the eggs. Knead well by hand or with the mixer until all the ingredients are well combined and the dough seems smooth and elastic (about 10 minutes if working by hand, about 5 minutes in a mixer with a dough hook). Wrap the dough in plastic wrap or place it in a covered bowl and let it rest at room temperature for at least 30 minutes.

4. Set up a pasta machine and set it to the largest opening. Dust a work surface with flour. Cut off pieces of dough about the size of an egg. Working with one piece of dough at a time, roll the dough into sheets about ⅛ inch thick and as long as your chitarra.

5. Lay the sheets onto the chitarra and run a rolling pin over the pasta to cut it into long, thin strips. Wind the strips into loose "nests" and put them on a baking sheet sprinkled with some cornmeal. Reserve the noodles until ready to cook them. (If made in advance, store the noodles in the refrigerator for up to 2 days.)

(continued)

6. Bring a large pot of generously salted water to a boil. Add the noodles all at once to the boiling water and stir a few times to separate them. Cook uncovered at a boil until just tender to the bite, 12 to 15 minutes. Drain the pasta immediately through a colander. Shake well to remove any water clinging to the pasta. Pour the drained pasta into a large serving or mixing bowl. Add the sugo and toss the noodles and sauce together. Serve at once.

Wine notes: The flavors of lamb are earthy and savory, and this sauce needs a wine that can challenge those flavors with equal power and almost jammy black fruits, making the relationship between the plate and the glass more complex and long lasting.

**Red:** Montepulciano d'Abruzzo from Abruzzo; Sangiovese di Romagna from Emilia-Romagna; Aglianico del Vulture from Basilicata; Primitivo di Manduria or Salice Salentino from Puglia; Cannonau di Sardegna from Sardinia; Rosso Conero or Rosso Piceno from Le Marche; Torgiano Rosso or Montefalco Rosso from Umbria; Carmignano or Morellino di Scansano from Tuscany; Merlot from Veneto or Sicily

# Making Ravioli

1. Use a machine to roll the pasta into thin sheets.

2. When you've rolled to the appropriate thickness, cut the pasta off the machine and into manageable lengths.

3. Working with one sheet of pasta at a time, brush the pasta with egg wash. Use a piping bag or spoon to place even mounds of the filling along the length of the strip of pasta and then fold the sheet over the filling.

4. Press the pasta around the filling to form a sealed pocket around each mound. Use a pasta cutter to cut the individual ravioli.

# Tortelli di zucca alla mantovana

## PUMPKIN-FILLED TORTELLI FROM MANTUA

This pumpkin ravioli has an unusual flavor because it combines sweetness from the amaretti cookies, saltiness from the Parmesan, and the unique flavor of a fruit mostarda.

**SERVES 4 TO 6**

FILLING

1 small pumpkin (around 2½ lb)

¾ cup Mostarda (page 63)

24 amaretti cookies (3 oz)

1¾ cups grated Parmigiano-Reggiano (7 oz)

2 egg yolks

Salt and freshly ground black pepper, as needed

PASTA DOUGH

3⅔ cups all-purpose or "00" flour, plus as needed

4 large eggs

1 large egg blended with 1 tbsp water, for egg wash

6 to 8 tbsp (¾ to 1 stick) unsalted butter

6 sage leaves

4 to 6 tbsp grated Parmigiano-Reggiano

6 amaretti cookies, crumbled

1. Preheat the oven to 350 degrees F.
2. Pierce the pumpkin in two or three places and roast on a baking sheet until very tender, about 1 hour. Cut it in half, scoop out and discard the seeds, and scoop the flesh away from the skin. Push through a wire-mesh sieve.
3. Finely chop the mostarda and amaretti in a food processor. Add to the pumpkin along with the cheese, egg yolks, and salt and pepper and combine well.
4. To make the pasta dough for the tortelli, mound the flour on a clean surface or put it in the bowl of a stand mixer fitted with a dough hook. Create a well in the center and place the eggs in the center. Using a fork, whisk the eggs and slowly start dragging the flour into the eggs. Knead well by hand or with the mixer until all the ingredients are well combined and the dough seems smooth and elastic (about 10 minutes if working by hand, about 5 minutes in a mixer with a dough hook). Wrap the dough in plastic wrap or place it in a covered bowl and let it rest at room temperature for at least 30 minutes.
5. Set up a pasta machine and set it to the largest opening. Dust a work surface with flour. Cut off pieces of dough about the size of an egg. Working with one piece of dough at a time, roll the dough into sheets about 1/16 inch thick.
6. Working with one sheet of pasta at a time, brush the pasta with egg wash and spoon about 2 tablespoons of filling every 2 inches in the middle of the sheet of dough. Use a pastry cutter or a knife to trim away the excess dough and then cut individual tortello with a 2-inch square or round cutter. As you cut out the tortelli, place them on a plate or baking sheet sprinkled with a little flour to keep them from sticking.
7. Bring a large pot of generously salted water to a boil. Add the tortelli all at once and stir a few times to separate them. Cook uncovered at a gentle boil until the pasta is just tender to the bite, 5 to 6 minutes. Drain the tortelli immediately through a colander.
8. Melt the butter with the sage in a large skillet over medium heat. Add the drained tortelli, and toss until coated. Transfer to a heated serving bowl or pasta plates, sprinkle Parmigiano-Reggiano on top, and finish the dish by sprinkling the crumbled amaretti cookies on top.

Wine notes: This dish borders on the sweet because of the pumpkin, the mostarda, and the amaretti. The flavors are intense and focused, and an off-dry white or sparkling wine will help bring out the savory aspects of the dish.

**White:** Riesling or Traminer (Gewürztraminer) from Trentino-Alto Adige or Friuli-Venezia Giulia

**Sparkling:** Extra-dry Prosecco from Veneto; Franciacorta from Lombardy

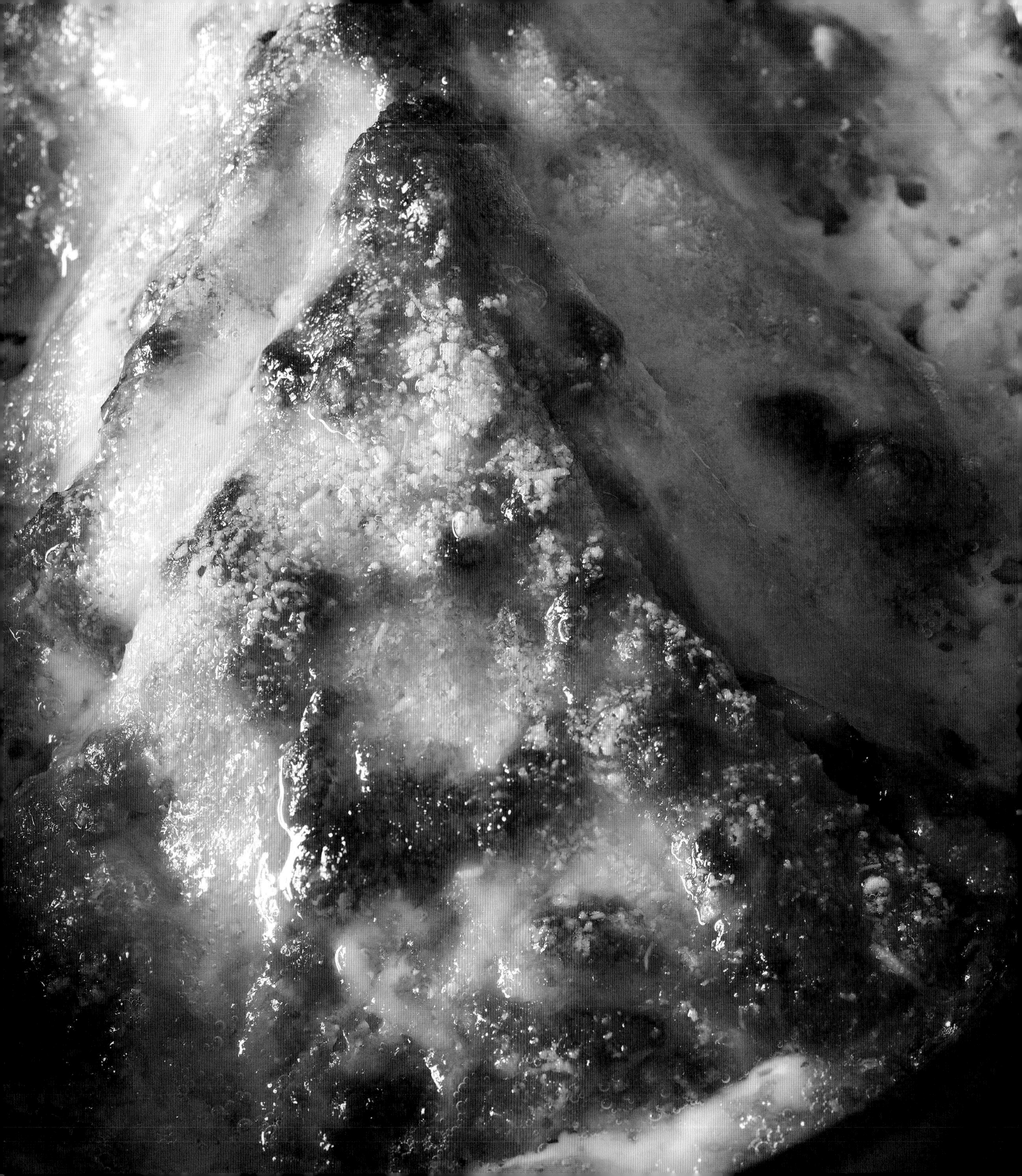

# Crespelle alla valdostana

## CRÊPES WITH FONTINA AND HAM

For this recipe of crespelle filled with Fontina cheese and ham, we added a small amount of besciamella to give the crespelle more moisture during the baking time.

**SERVES 6 TO 8**

CRESPELLE

**2/3 cup all-purpose or "00" flour**

**2 large eggs**

**1 cup milk**

**Unsalted butter as needed**

FILLING

**2 tbsp unsalted butter**

**1/4 cup all-purpose or "00" flour**

**2 cups milk**

**2 egg yolks**

**6 oz Fontina, sliced**

**6 oz ham, sliced**

**Melted unsalted butter**

**Grated Fontina**

**Grated Parmigiano-Reggiano**

**Heavy cream**

1. To make the crespelle, whisk the flour with the eggs in a medium bowl. Add the milk and mix to combine, but do not whisk too much. Strain into another bowl.
2. Butter a 10-inch sauté pan, and heat it over medium heat. Ladle about 1/4 cup of batter into it. By lightly tilting in a rotating motion, spread the batter in a thin layer over the entire surface of the pan. Cook for about 40 seconds, until the batter is set, and then flip the crespella and cook for 10 seconds longer. Transfer to a plate and repeat until all the batter is used.
3. To make the filling, melt the butter in a small saucepan over medium-low heat and add the flour. Cook for a few minutes, and then add the milk. Stir until the milk thickens, and cook the besciamella for 10 minutes over low heat, stirring frequently and being careful to not scorch it. Blend the egg yolks with some of the hot besciamella and then return the mixture to the saucepan. Simmer an additional 2 or 3 minutes and then remove from the heat.
4. Preheat the oven to 350 degrees F.
5. Lay a crespella on a work surface, and with a small spatula spread some of the besciamella on top in a thin layer about 1/4 inch thick. Do this step while the sauce is still hot or it will be too hard to spread. Top with some of the Fontina and then some of the ham.
6. Cut the crespella in half, and working with each half-moon, fold one of the corners in to the original center, and then do the same with the other corner, so that the half-moon becomes a triangle. Do this step with the rest of the crespelle, and place them in a buttered baking dish, overlapping the tips of the crespelle over each other.
7. Brush the filled crespelle with melted butter. Cover with more Fontina and sprinkle a small amount of Parmigiano-Reggiano over the top. Pour enough heavy cream in the dish to just cover the bottom, and bake for 10 to 15 minutes, until browned. Serve at once.

Wine notes: With cheese, cream, butter, and ham in this dish, you want to choose a wine that will match the richness but at the same time provide enough fruit and acidity to cut through that silky, creamy texture, all without the interference of oak in a white wine or too much tannins in a red. A fruity, off-dry rosato will work wonders in bringing all the flavors of the dish together and creating a cranberry-raspberry counterpoint for the dairy products and the ham.

**White:** Pinot Grigio from Friuli-Venezia Giulia or Trentino-Alto Adige; Chardonnay from Veneto, Trentino-Alto Adige, or Sicily

**Rosé:** Bardolino Chiaretto from Veneto

**Red:** Valpolicella, Bardolino, or Merlot from Veneto; Chianti from Tuscany

# Gnocchi

Gnocchi may have a longer history than pasta in Italy. A cookbook from the 1300s includes a recipe for gnocchi made by mashing together cheese and egg and mixing it with flour to make a dumpling. Since that time, gnocchi have remained popular. Today, you can find gnocchi made from potatoes, semolina, polenta, squash, ricotta, and bread. There are savory gnocchi for a primi piatti, gnocchi served as an accompaniment to the main course, and even sweet gnocchi for dessert.

There are gnocchi made as you would a ravioli filling, except that there is no pasta involved; these are known as gnudi (or naked). Gnocchi, like pasta, can be enhanced by a number of different sauces, and there are stuffed and filled gnocchi, too.

# Potato gnocchi

It seems that you can find thousands of recipes for potato gnocchi. That doesn't mean that gnocchi are difficult to make, however. In fact, it shows just how adaptable a simple gnocchi recipe can be when it travels from one cook to another. Some cooks may want to use whole eggs; some yolks only; others no eggs at all.

What is true about gnocchi is that it is one of those recipes that you have to make a couple of times to get the feel for it. There is a famous story from one of Italy's most renowned cookbook authors, Pellegrino Artusi (*La Scienza in Cucina e L'Arte di Mangiar Bene, The Science of Cookery and the Art of Eating Well*). Apparently, a woman trying to prepare the little dumplings failed to use enough flour. When she stirred the pot, the gnocchi disappeared.

"'Where'd they go?' asked another lady, to whom I told the story, wondering if a fairy had spirited them away. 'Don't raise your eyebrows, madam,' replied I. 'Though unexpected, it's perfectly normal. The gnocchi were made with too little flour, and dissolved upon coming into contact with the boiling water.'"

Choosing the right potatoes, cooking them properly, and mixing in just the right amount of flour is the key to success. While you are just learning to make these dumplings, we strongly suggest that you prepare a couple of test gnocchi at first, so that yours won't disappear as they cook.

## PREPARING POTATOES FOR GNOCCHI

You can make gnocchi with any type of potato. Some are starchier (russet, baking, and Idaho), while others have a waxy texture (red, new, and Yukon gold). If you use starchy potatoes, you may need a bit less flour; if you use waxy potatoes, you may need a bit more. Some recipes call for eggs or egg yolks to help hold the dumplings together, but there are a few recipes that don't. It is just a little more difficult to keep the gnocchi from falling apart as they cook if you don't use eggs.

Some of our recipes call for the potatoes to be cooked in their skins; others call for the potatoes to be peeled and cut into quarters before cooking.

1. Put the potatoes into a pot with enough salted water to cover, and simmer long enough for the potatoes to become tender. Test them by piercing them with a wooden skewer or a table fork.
2. Drain the potatoes right away through a colander. There will still be some moisture left in the potatoes; you can let it cook away by returning the potatoes to the pot and letting them dry over very low heat for a few minutes.
3. If you want a light, tasty gnocchi, the potatoes need to be peeled and pureed while they are still hot. Use a kitchen towel to protect your hands as you peel off the skin. Use a potato ricer or a food mill to puree the potatoes. These tools give the potatoes a lighter texture, but if you don't have one of these tools you can use a handheld potato masher instead.
4. We puree the potatoes directly onto a floured work surface, mounding them and making a well in the center. The potatoes should still be warm as you mix the gnocchi. Pour about half of the flour called for in the recipe around the outside of the potato mound. Add the eggs to the well and use the fingertips of one hand to mix in the egg.
5. Use your other hand to hold up the potato wall and to pull in the flour until you've got a light dough. You may need to add more of the flour if the dough seems very wet or soft; the amount you need to add depends on the way you cooked the potatoes and the amount of water they absorbed during cooking. Before going on to shape the gnocchi, test a few pieces to be sure they have the right taste and texture.

# Testing gnocchi

Since you want to add enough flour to bind the gnocchi but not so much that they become heavy or dense, you need to test them to see if they are holding together. Bring a small pot of salted water to a gentle boil over medium-high heat. Pull off a couple of pieces of the dough that are about the size you want your finished gnocchi to be. Add them to the water and simmer over medium heat until the gnocchi rise to the surface and float there for 2 or 3 minutes.

If the gnocchi fall apart as they cook or when you try to lift them from the water, you should add a bit more of the reserved flour to the dough and test again. Repeat, if necessary, until the test gnocchi hold together. Pay attention to the way the dough feels when the gnocchi hold together so that you can reproduce the texture next time. You should add more seasoning now as well, if the gnocchi didn't have as much flavor as you wanted.

## SHAPING POTATO GNOCCHI

Cut the dough into pieces about the size of an egg and roll each piece out on a floured surface into a long coil or rope about 1 inch thick. Cut the ropes into pieces about 1 inch long. You can simply cook them like that, if you like, or you can roll them over the tines of a fork or a grooved surface (there are specific tools for shaping gnocchi available). Once they are shaped, you can keep the gnocchi on a lightly floured tray or baking sheet for a little while, but if you plan to serve them later, it is best to cook them right away and then, when ready to serve, bake them in a sauce until they are very hot.

## COOKING GNOCCHI

For most gnocchi, you need a generous amount of boiling salted water. Use the same pot that you would use to cook your pasta—tall and deep. The water should be at a gentle boil, with just a few lazy bubbles rising to the surface.

When you add the gnocchi to the water, they'll drop to the bottom of the pot. As they cook, they will rise to the surface and float. After they have risen, let them cook for 2 or 3 minutes longer. Use a slotted spoon or a skimmer to lift the cooked gnocchi from the water; pouring them through a colander might smash them.

## SERVING GNOCCHI

Gnocchi are delicious served very simply, with just a bit of butter or some grated Parmigiano-Reggiano. We like the flavor of brown butter and fried sage leaves for something a little more interesting. There are other sauces that are perfect for gnocchi as well. A simple tomato sauce is good, as is a more elaborate ragù made with rabbit. Cream sauces are also a good accompaniment. A classic sauce is fonduto, a cheese sauce made with Fontina, eggs, and milk. You might also serve them with sautéed mushrooms or other vegetables.

# Gnocchi di patate alla bava

## POTATO GNOCCHI WITH A QUICK FONDUE

Any type of cheese may be used for the "fondue" of cheeses as long as it isn't extremely salty.

SERVES 4

1½ lb Idaho or other starchy potatoes

Kosher salt, as needed

1 cup all-purpose or "00" flour, or as needed

1 large egg

1 egg yolk

½ cup grated Parmigiano-Reggiano (2 oz), plus more for serving

Pinch of grated nutmeg

1 cup heavy cream

1 oz Fontina

1 oz Gruyère

1 oz Gorgonzola dolce (not too strong)

1. Put the potatoes in a pot and add enough cold water to cover them by about 2 inches. Add enough salt to make the water taste salty, and bring it to a gentle boil over medium-high heat. Cook until the potatoes are easy to pierce with a wooden skewer (the time will depend on the size of the potatoes). Drain the potatoes and dry them in the pot over low heat, about 3 minutes. Remove the skin and puree though a food mill or potato ricer onto a lightly floured work surface.
2. Gather the potatoes into a mound and make a well in the center. Surround the well with half of the flour. Add the egg, egg yolk, Parmigiano-Reggiano, ½ teaspoon salt, and nutmeg to the well.
3. Mix the ingredients by hand to form a soft dough. If necessary, add more of the flour, a little at a time, until the dough has the correct consistency. Shape and cook a few test gnocchi and adjust the dough if necessary with additional flour or seasoning.
4. Roll the dough into 1-inch-thick ropes, and cut them into 1-inch-long pieces. (Flour your work surface as needed while you roll and cut the gnocchi.) Roll the gnocchi over a fork to shape them, if desired. Once shaped, the gnocchi can be reserved on a floured baking sheet, loosely covered, in the refrigerator for up to 8 hours.
5. Heat the cream in a small saucepot over very low heat. When it reaches a bare simmer (you should see wisps of steam, but no big bubbles), add the cheeses. Stir over low heat until the cheeses are melted, about 3 minutes; keep warm while cooking the gnocchi.
6. To cook the gnocchi, fill a deep pot two-thirds full with cold water and place over high heat. Add salt to taste and bring the water to a boil.
7. Add the gnocchi and cook uncovered at a gentle boil until they rise to the surface and are cooked through, 2 to 4 minutes depending on their size. (To be certain, taste one of the gnocchi.) Use a slotted spoon to lift the cooked gnocchi out of the water.
8. Serve the gnocchi in a heated serving bowl or individual pasta plates topped with the sauce, passing additional Parmigiano-Reggiano on the side.

Wine notes: **White:** Roero Arneis or Chardonnay from Piedmont

**Red:** Dolcetto d'Alba, Barbera d'Alba, or Barbera d'Asti from Piedmont; Grumello or Inferno from Lombardy; Sangiovese di Romagna from Emilia-Romagna

1. Use a chef's knife to cut the strands of dough into uniform pieces.

2. Make sure that the pieces are well floured before shaping.

3. Use a rolling motion to shape each piece of dough against the tines of a fork.

Gnocchi di Patate

# Gnocchi di ricotta e ortiche

## RICOTTA-NETTLE DUMPLINGS

Nettles may be a bit difficult to find, but you can replace them with other greens, such as dandelion, chicory, spinach, or a combination. Good-quality ricotta is the secret of this dish; if your ricotta seems wet or loose, remember to let it drain for at least 4 hours before you prepare these gnocchi.

**SERVES 4 TO 6**

**1 cup fresh ricotta, well drained (8 oz)**

**½ cup goat cheese, not too wet (4 oz)**

**¼ cup grated Pecorino Romano or Parmigiano-Reggiano (1 oz), plus more for serving**

**½ cup blanched and chopped baby nettles or other greens (page 23)**

**1 large egg, beaten**

**1 egg yolk**

**Salt and freshly ground black pepper, as needed**

**½ cup all-purpose or "00" flour, or as needed**

1. In a large bowl, combine the ricotta, goat cheese, and pecorino; mix well to incorporate the three cheeses together, then fold in the greens (make sure you drained them well or else they will make the dough very wet and difficult to work).
2. Add the egg, egg yolk, and salt and pepper and fold together.
3. Slowly add the flour and mix the dough until combined, but take care not to overwork it. Refrigerate until the dough has firmed up, about 1 hour.
4. Turn the dough out onto a well-floured surface, as it may be a little sticky, and roll into cylinders approximately ¾ inch thick. Place the cylinders on a floured baking sheet and refrigerate for 1 hour.
5. Remove the cylinders from the fridge one at a time and cut them into ½-inch lengths, forming them into little balls. You may flatten them gently with the tines of a fork, or leave them as is.
6. To cook the gnocchi, fill a deep pot two-thirds full with cold water and place over high heat. Add salt to taste and bring the water to a boil.
7. Add the gnocchi and cook uncovered at a gentle boil until they rise to the surface and are cooked through, 2 to 4 minutes depending upon their size. (To be certain, taste one of the gnocchi.) Use a slotted spoon to lift the cooked gnocchi out of the water.
8. Serve the gnocchi in a heated serving bowl or individual plates with additional pecorino on the side.

Wine notes: **White:** Sauvignon Blanc from Friuli-Venezia Giulia; Vernaccia di San Gimignano from Tuscany; Falanghina from Campania; Gavi from Piedmont **Sparkling:** Prosecco from Veneto

# Gnocchi al Taleggio

## POTATO GNOCCHI WITH TALEGGIO

Here, we've stuffed a potato gnocchi with cheese. Taleggio is a soft, creamy cheese with a rich flavor. Other cheeses you might try include Gorgonzola or other blue cheese, Brie, or even a soft pecorino. We've suggested two different ways to finish these gnocchi: a simple tomato fondue or bubbling hot butter with sage leaves, toasted walnuts, and shaved pecorino or Parmesan. See the notes following the recipe.

**SERVES 4**

- 1½ lb Idaho or other starchy potatoes
- Kosher salt, as needed
- 1 cup all-purpose or "00" flour, or as needed
- 1 large egg
- 1 egg yolk
- ½ cup grated Parmigiano-Reggiano (2 oz), plus more for serving
- Pinch of grated nutmeg
- 8 oz Taleggio, cut into strips

1. Put the potatoes in a pot and add enough cold water to cover them by about 2 inches. Add enough salt to make the water taste salty and bring it to a gentle boil over medium-high heat. Cook until the potatoes are easy to pierce with a wooden skewer (the time will depend on the size of the potatoes). Drain the potatoes and dry them in the pot over low heat, about 3 minutes. Remove the skins and puree though a food mill or potato ricer onto a lightly floured work surface.
2. Gather the potatoes into a mound and make a well in the center. Surround the well with half of the flour. Add the egg, egg yolk, Parmigiano-Reggiano, ½ teaspoon salt, and nutmeg to the well.
3. Mix the ingredients by hand to form a soft dough. If necessary, add more of the flour, a little at a time, until the dough has the correct consistency. Make a few test gnocchi, and adjust the dough if necessary with additional flour or seasoning.
4. Roll the dough into 2-inch-thick ropes and make a slit down center of each log to hold the strips of Taleggio. Place the cheese in the center and pinch the dough so that the cheese will not escape once in the water simmering. Cut 1-inch-long gnocchi and pinch the ends of the gnocchi closed around the cheese. Once shaped, the gnocchi can be reserved on a floured baking sheet, loosely covered, in the refrigerator for up to 8 hours.

(continued)

*Create a canal in the log of dough to hold the filling of cheese. Completely close the dough around the filling and slice the dough into pieces.*

5. To cook the gnocchi, fill a deep pot two-thirds full with cold water and place over high heat. Add salt to taste and bring the water to a boil.
6. Add the gnocchi and cook uncovered at a gentle boil until they rise to the surface and are cooked through, 2 to 4 minutes depending upon their size. (To be certain, taste one of the gnocchi.) Use a slotted spoon to lift the cooked gnocchi out of the water.
7. Serve the gnocchi in a heated serving bowl or individual pasta plates topped with a sauce (see Note), passing additional Parmigiano-Reggiano on the side.

*After the gnocchi are drained, you can either coat them with a little tomato fondue (see below), or try this sauce:*

*Heat about 4 tablespoons unsalted butter in a sauté pan over medium heat until it is melted, foamy, and has a nutty aroma, about 2 minutes. Add 12 small sage leaves and ½ cup chopped toasted walnuts. When the sage leaves are crisp, after about 1 minute, pour this mixture over the gnocchi and garnish with shaved Parmigiano-Reggiano or pecorino.*

# Tomato fondue

Here is a quick fresh tomato sauce, perfect to pair with gnocchi or pasta.

**MAKES ABOUT 6 CUPS**

- ½ cup olive oil
- 2 cups minced yellow onions
- 2 tsp chopped garlic
- 3 qt canned plum tomatoes, whole, drained
- 2 fresh bay leaves
- 2 cups chopped basil
- Salt and freshly ground black pepper, as needed

1. Heat the olive oil in a large saucepan over medium-high heat. Add the onions and garlic and sauté until the onions are tender but not browned, 4 to 5 minutes.
2. Use your hands to crush and break up the tomatoes. Add them to the onions, along with the bay leaves. Simmer the sauce over low heat until thickened and flavorful, about 30 minutes.
3. Puree the tomatoes through a food mill into a clean pot. Add the basil and season with salt and pepper if necessary. You may reheat the sauce over low heat before serving it.

Wine notes: **White:** Roero Arneis or Chardonnay from Piedmont

**Red:** Dolcetto d'Alba, Barbera d'Alba, or Barbera d'Asti from Piedmont; Grumello or Inferno from Lombardy; Sangiovese di Romagna from Emilia-Romagna; Merlot from Veneto

# Chicche ai spinaci e funghi

## SMALL POTATO DUMPLINGS WITH SPINACH AND MUSHROOMS

To prepare the potatoes for this version of gnocchi, peel and quarter them before boiling. Blanched and chopped spinach gives the gnocchi a beautiful green color. Serve them with Mushroom Sauce (page 196), or enjoy them with a simple tomato sauce and a spoonful of the freshest, creamiest ricotta right on top.

**SERVES 4 TO 6**

- 10 oz fresh spinach, blanched and chopped (page 23)
- 1 large egg
- 1 egg yolk
- 1½ lb Idaho or other starchy potatoes
- Kosher salt, as needed
- 1¾ cups all-purpose or "00" flour, or as needed
- ¾ cup grated Parmigiano-Reggiano (3 oz), plus more for serving
- Pinch of grated nutmeg
- Mushroom Sauce (recipe follows)

1. Mix the spinach, egg, and egg yolk together in a food processor or blender until smooth. Set aside.
2. Peel and quarter the potatoes. Put them in a pot and add enough cold water to cover them by about 2 inches. Add enough salt to make the water taste salty and bring it to a gentle boil over medium-high heat. Cook until the potatoes are easy to pierce with a wooden skewer, about 15 minutes. Drain the potatoes and dry them in the pot over low heat, about 3 minutes. Puree though a food mill or potato ricer onto a lightly floured work surface.
3. Gather the potatoes into a mound and make a well in the center. Surround the well with half of the flour, and sprinkle with the Parmigiano-Reggiano, nutmeg, and ½ teaspoon salt. Add the egg-spinach mixture to the well.
4. Mix the ingredients by hand to form a soft dough. If necessary add more of the flour, a little at a time, until the dough has the correct consistency. Make a few test gnocchi and adjust the dough if necessary with additional flour or seasoning.
5. Roll the dough into ¾-inch-thick ropes, and cut them into ¾-inch-long pieces. (Flour your work surface as needed while you roll and cut the gnocchi.) Roll the gnocchi over a fork to shape them, if desired. Once shaped, the gnocchi can be reserved on a floured baking sheet, loosely covered, in the refrigerator for up to 8 hours.
6. To cook the gnocchi, fill a deep pot two-thirds full with cold water and place over high heat. Add salt to taste and bring the water to a boil.
7. Add the gnocchi and cook uncovered at a gentle boil until they rise to the surface and are cooked through, 2 to 4 minutes depending upon their size. (To be certain, taste one of the gnocchi.) Use a slotted spoon to lift the cooked gnocchi out of the water.
8. Toss the gnocchi together with the mushroom sauce over low heat until evenly coated and very hot. Serve in a heated serving bowl or individual pasta plates, passing additional Parmigiano-Reggiano on the side.

# Mushroom sauce

**SERVES 4 TO 6**

- 1 tbsp extra-virgin olive oil
- 3 garlic cloves, lightly crushed
- 1½ lb white or cremini mushrooms, diced
- ½ cup dry white wine
- 1 cup Brodo (page 88)
- ¾ cup chopped flat-leaf parsley
- ¼ cup (½ stick) unsalted butter
- Salt and freshly ground black pepper, as needed

1. Combine the olive oil with the garlic in a large sauté pan over medium heat. Once the garlic is lightly browned, lift the garlic from the oil with a slotted spoon and discard it.
2. Add the mushrooms and toss them over medium-high heat until they begin to release some of their juices, about 2 minutes. Add the wine and continue to cook until it has nearly cooked away, 2 to 3 minutes.
3. Add the brodo and the parsley and simmer until the sauce is hot and flavorful, about 3 minutes. Whisk in the butter over low heat until it is blended into the sauce. Season with salt and pepper. Keep the sauce warm until ready to serve.

Wine notes: **White:** Roero Arneis from Piedmont; Chardonnay from Sicily or Piedmont; Pinot Grigio or Pinot Bianco from Friuli-Venezia Giulia or Trentino-Alto Adige **Red:** Valpolicella from Veneto; Grignolino or Barbera d'Alba from Piedmont; Chianti from Tuscany; Torgiano Rosso from Umbria; Montepulciano d'Abruzzo from Abruzzo

# Gnocchi soffiati alla parigina

## PUFFED GNOCCHI (PARISIENNE)

These very light puffed or "soufflé" dumplings are poached, not boiled, and then they are cooled in a bowl of ice-cold water. As soon as they are cool, lift them from the water and put them on a baking sheet or tray. When ready to serve, combine them with a sauce and bake them until very hot. They puff up as they bake.

**SERVES 6 TO 8**

1 cup water

½ tsp salt

¼ tsp grated nutmeg

2 tbsp unsalted butter, plus 1 tbsp melted

1 cup all-purpose or "00" flour

¾ cup grated Parmigiano-Reggiano (3 oz)

3 large eggs

1. Put the water, salt, nutmeg, and 2 tbsp butter in a medium saucepan and bring to a boil. As soon as it boils, drop the flour into the mixture at once and mix quickly with a wooden spoon. Stir until the mixture forms a smooth mass that separates easily from the sides of the saucepan. Cook and stir for about 40 seconds longer to dry the mixture further.
2. Transfer the dough to the bowl of a stand mixer fitted with a dough hook, or you may want to use a regular bowl and mix with your hands. Let the mixture cool slightly, and then add half of the Parmigiano-Reggiano and 1 of the eggs. Mix at low speed (or by hand) until the egg is incorporated. Add another egg and mix again, and then repeat with the third egg. At first the mixture will seem to separate, but keep mixing and eventually it will tighten up. Cover and let cool.
3. Place 3 inches of salted water in a large saucepan and heat it over medium heat until there are several small bubbles rising around the edges (180 degrees F). It shouldn't boil completely; if the water is too hot the dumplings will cook too fast, which will cause them to expand and eventually (once baked) deflate. They should just poach and expand later in the oven when baked.
4. Using 2 spoons to shape the dough or a pastry bag with a plain 1-inch tip, drop dumplings into the water; they should be 1 to 1½ inches long. Work close to the surface of the water so you don't get splashed.
5. Poach the gnocchi until they rise to the surface, about 3 minutes. Lift the gnocchi out with a slotted spoon and put them in a bowl of ice water to cool. They will sink to the bottom of the bowl when cool. Drain and use them right away, or refrigerate for later use.
6. Preheat the oven to 350 degrees F. Butter two 9-inch baking dishes and arrange the gnocchi in them so that they have enough space to expand in the oven (they will almost double in size).
7. Sprinkle with the remaining Parmigiano-Reggiano, drizzle 1 tablespoon of melted butter on top, and bake until doubled in size and golden brown, 20 to 25 minutes. Serve the gnocchi right away, before they begin to deflate.

Wine notes: **White:** Trebbiano d'Abruzzo from Abruzzo; Vernaccia di San Gimignano from Tuscany; Soave Classico from Veneto

**Red:** Chianti from Tuscany; Montepulciano d'Abruzzo from Abruzzo

**Sparkling:** Prosecco from Veneto

# Cavatelli con cozze, patate, e pecorino

## SEMOLINA DUMPLINGS WITH MUSSELS, POTATOES, AND PECORINO

This is another little dumpling typical of Puglia and other southern regions.

**SERVES 4**

½ cup plus 2 tbsp extra-virgin olive oil

3 garlic cloves, lightly crushed

1 lb mussels, scrubbed and debearded

½ cup dry white wine

1 cup water

1 teaspoon sea salt

1 red chile

2 or 3 fresh or canned plum tomatoes, peeled, seeded, and drained

1 medium yellow potato, sliced (8 oz)

Salt, as needed

1 lb cavatelli

½ cup grated Pecorino Romano (2 oz)

3 tbsp coarsely chopped flat-leaf parsley

1. Heat ¼ cup of the oil and 2 of the garlic cloves in a wide pan over medium heat. As soon as the garlic starts to turn a light golden color, add the mussels, wine, water, and salt. Cover the pot tightly and let the mussels steam until they are all open, 5 to 6 minutes. Lift the mussels from the cooking liquid. Reserve the cooking liquid to use in step 2. Pick the meat from the shells and set aside.
2. In a clean large pan, heat the remaining olive oil over medium heat. Add the remaining garlic clove and the chile. As soon as the garlic gets some color, after about 1 minute, add the tomatoes, the cooking liquid from the mussels, and the potato. Simmer slowly over low heat until the potato is tender, 25 to 30 minutes.
3. Fill a large pot about two-thirds full with cold water and add enough salt to make the water taste salty. Bring the water to a boil over high heat. Add the cavatelli and stir once or twice to keep them separate. Cook until al dente. Drain the cavatelli in a colander, shaking off any excess water, and then add the cavatelli to the sauce. Keep stirring over low heat until the sauce coats the pasta, about 2 minutes. Add the reserved mussels, the cheese, and the parsley. Serve at once.

Wine notes: **White:** Inzolia from Sicily; Vermentino di Sardegna or Vermentino di Gallura from Sardinia; Salice Salentino Bianco from Puglia; Falanghina from Campania

# Strangolapreti

## BREAD GNOCCHI

When you have very little to work with, as the peasants living in Italy did throughout most of their history, you learn to get the most out of every single thing you have. Just because the bread is dry and stale is no reason not to eat it. This dish comes from the cucina povera tradition. According to legend, these gnocchi are so delicious that a priest practically choked trying to stuff them into his mouth (*strangolapreti* translates as "priest stranglers").

**SERVES 6**

- 2 lb day-old peasant bread, torn into chunks
- 4 cups milk, warm
- 1 lb Swiss chard
- 1 large egg
- 2 egg yolks
- ½ cup all-purpose or "00" flour
- Kosher salt and freshly ground black pepper, as needed
- Pinch of grated nutmeg
- 6 tbsp (¾ stick) unsalted butter
- 6 sage leaves
- ½ cup grated Parmigiano-Reggiano (2 oz)

1. Soak the bread in the milk for about 1 hour. Meanwhile cook the Swiss chard stems and leaves (see page 23).
2. Squeeze the bread to remove any excess milk. Grind the bread and the cooked Swiss chard in a meat grinder, catching the mixture in a bowl as it falls from the grinder.
3. Add the egg, egg yolks, flour, salt and pepper, and nutmeg and stir them into the bread-chard mixture until smooth.
4. To cook the strangolapreti, fill a deep pot two-thirds full with cold water and put it over high heat. Add salt to taste and bring the water to a boil.
5. Use 2 spoons to shape the strangolapreti by scooping up the batter with one spoon, then smoothing and pushing it off into the water with a second spoon. Cook uncovered at a gentle boil until they rise to the surface and are cooked through, 2 to 4 minutes depending upon their size. (To be certain, taste one of them.) Use a slotted spoon to lift the cooked strangolapreti out of the water.
6. To dress them, cook the butter in a small pot over medium-high heat until very hot and foamy, with a nutty aroma. Add the sage leaves and fry until they are crisp, about 1 minute. Pour the sizzling hot butter and sage leaves over the dumplings and sprinkle with the cheese. Serve at once.

Wine notes: **White:** Soave Classico from Veneto; Friulano from Friuli-Venezia Giulia; Roero Arneis from Piedmont; Vernaccia di San Gimignano from Tuscany; Falanghina from Campania

**Red:** Dolcetto d'Alba or Dolcetto d'Asti from Piedmont; Chianti from Tuscany; Sangiovese di Romagna from Emilia-Romagna

# Gnocchi di polenta

## POLENTA GNOCCHI

These gnocchi can be created by just making a regular polenta and then shaping it with a spoon right on the plate. In this recipe we are using leftover polenta and kneading it with other common gnocchi ingredients to improve the flavor and texture. These can be simply dressed with Parmigiano-Reggiano and butter; in this case, go with one of the white wines. If you would like to serve the gnocchi with a meat sauce, select one of the red wines.

**SERVES 4**

4 tbsp (½ stick) unsalted butter

12 small sage leaves

1 lb cooked Polenta (page 261)

1 cup all-purpose or "00" flour

2 large eggs

½ cup grated Parmigiano-Reggiano (2 oz)

Salt, as needed

1. Heat the butter in a small pan over medium-high heat until the butter is completely melted but still foaming. Add the sage leaves and continue to cook until the sage leaves are crisped and the butter has a deep brown color and a nutty aroma, about 1 minute. Remove from the heat and reserve.
2. Push the polenta through a fine-mesh sieve to break it up into tiny pieces about the size of a grain of rice.
3. Spread the flour on a counter and place the polenta in the center with the eggs, cheese, and the butter that you have previously browned with a few sage leaves. Knead all the ingredients together to a compact mass.
4. Divide the dough into smaller pieces and roll the pieces into small cylinders. Cut into pieces about 1½ inches long.
5. Fill a deep pot two-thirds full with cold water and place over high heat. Add salt to taste and bring the water to a boil. Add the gnocchi to the water. When the gnocchi are floating, let them cook for 2 to 3 minutes longer, and then use a slotted spoon to transfer them to a serving bowl. Dress with the desired sauce and serve at once.

Wine notes: **White:** Gavi or Roero Arneis from Piedmont; Soave from Veneto; Friulano from Friuli-Venezia Giulia; Orvieto Classico from Umbria

**Red:** Valpolicella Classico from Veneto; Chianti from Tuscany; Sangiovese di Romagna from Emilia-Romagna; Montepulciano d'Abruzzo from Abruzzo; Cerasuolo di Vittoria from Sicily; Cannonau di Sardegna from Sardinia

# Gnocchi di semolina

## SEMOLINA DUMPLINGS

Also called gnocchi alla romana, this is a typical dish from Rome.

**SERVES 4 TO 6**

4 cups milk

¼ cup (½ stick) unsalted butter, plus 2 tbsp melted butter for drizzling

1 tsp salt

2 cups semolina flour (also known as durum flour)

2 egg yolks

½ cup grated Parmigiano-Reggiano (2 oz), plus more for sprinkling

Pinch of grated nutmeg

1. Bring the milk to a boil in a large saucepan with ¼ cup butter and the salt. Add the semolina slowly, whisking constantly. As soon as the mixture becomes thick, reduce the heat to low and switch to a wooden spoon. Cook, stirring frequently, until the mixture pulls away from the sides of the pan, about 30 minutes. Remove from the heat and add the egg yolks, cheese, and nutmeg.
2. Pour the semolina mixture onto a lightly oiled surface. Using a rolling pin, press the dough to a thickness of about ½ inch. Let the dough cool slightly and then, with a 2½-inch round cookie cutter, cut out the gnocchi.
3. Preheat the oven to 375 degrees F. Butter a baking dish, place the gnocchi in the dish, sprinkle the top with more cheese, and drizzle some melted butter on top.
4. Bake until hot and golden-brown on top, about 20 minutes. Serve at once.

Wine notes: **White:** Frascati Superiore or Est! Est!! Est!!! from Lazio; Orvieto Classico from Umbria

# Gnocchi di zucca con fonduta piemontese

## PUMPKIN DUMPLINGS WITH PIEDMONT-STYLE FONDUE

This is a delicate gnocchi preparation: The right proportion of flour to squash is important for the consistency and flavor. Choose a hard, heavy squash, and allow the squash to lose some moisture overnight. Butternut, Hubbard, and kabocha squash are all good for this preparation, but any hard, heavy squash will work fine.

**SERVES 4 TO 6**

### GNOCCHI

**14 oz drained fresh pumpkin puree (page 23)**

**1¼ cups all-purpose or "00" flour**

**½ cup grated Parmigiano-Reggiano (2 oz)**

**2 large eggs**

**Salt and freshly ground black pepper, as needed**

**Pinch of grated nutmeg**

### FONDUTA

**9 oz Fontina**

**½ cup plus 2 tbsp milk**

**2 tbsp unsalted butter**

**1 tbsp all-purpose flour**

**3 egg yolks**

**2 tbsp minced chives**

1. To make the gnocchi, combine the squash, flour, cheese, eggs, ½ teaspoon salt, ¼ teaspoon pepper, and nutmeg in a bowl and stir together with a spoon. (Note: These gnocchi will not be like regular potato gnocchi. They are so soft that you will need to shape them with a spoon and use the spoon to lower them into the boiling water.)
2. To cook the gnocchi, fill a wide, shallow pan with water. Bring to a boil and season with salt. Dip a tablespoon in the water and then scoop up a small amount of gnocchi dough and lower it (still on the spoon) into the boiling water; it will fall off the spoon. Repeat this step for the rest of the dough. Cook the dough in small batches to allow for a more uniform cooking time between the first and the last spooned gnocchi. The gnocchi will take 3 to 5 minutes to cook; use a slotted spoon to lift the cooked gnocchi out of the water and spread each batch on a baking sheet to cool.
3. To make the fonduta, cut the Fontina into thin strips, place the strips in a bowl, pour the milk over, and macerate the cheese in the milk in the refrigerator for 2 to 3 hours.
4. Melt the butter in a saucepan over low heat, add the flour, and stir to combine. Add the cheese and milk and stir until the cheese melts, but do not allow the mixture to boil.
5. When the cheese is melted, add the egg yolks and stir to combine. At this point the fondue will look runny. Cook over very low heat, stirring constantly, until the mixture starts to thicken and has a creamy consistency. Do not allow the temperature to go over 185 degrees F or else the eggs will scramble.
6. When all the gnocchi are cooked, reheat them all at once in boiling water for 30 seconds. Combine them in a serving dish with the fonduta, or put them on individual plates and pour the fonduta on top. Garnish with the minced chives.

---

Wine notes: **White:** Roero Arneis from Piedmont; Pinot Grigio from Trentino-Alto Adige or Friuli-Venezia Giulia

**Red:** Dolcetto d'Alba or Dolcetto d'Asti from Piedmont; Bardolino Classico from Veneto; Rosso di Montalcino or Chianti from Tuscany

# Gnocchi con le prugne secche

## GNOCCHI STUFFED WITH PRUNES

These typically are made with prunes, but any dried fruit may be used.

**SERVES 6 TO 8**

25 prunes

2 lb Idaho or other starchy potatoes

Salt, as needed

1½ to 2 cups all-purpose or "00" flour, or as needed

¼ tsp grated nutmeg

2 large eggs

½ cup (1 stick) unsalted butter

½ cup plain dry bread crumbs

¼ cup sugar

1 tbsp ground cinnamon

1. Soak the prunes in a bowl with warm water to soften for about 30 minutes and then drain away the excess water.
2. Peel and quarter the potatoes. Put them in a pot and add enough cold water to cover them by about 2 inches. Add enough salt to make the water taste salty and bring it to a gentle boil over medium-high heat. Cook until the potatoes are easy to pierce with a wooden skewer, about 15 minutes. Drain the potatoes and dry them in the pot over low heat, about 3 minutes. Puree though a food mill or potato ricer onto a lightly floured work surface. Let the potatoes cool to room temperature.
3. Gather the potatoes into a mound and make a well in the center. Surround the well with half of the flour, and sprinkle with the nutmeg. Add the eggs to the well.
4. Mix the ingredients by hand to form a soft dough. If necessary add more of the flour, a little at a time, until the dough has the correct consistency.
5. Roll the dough to a thickness of ¼ inch and, using a 3-inch round cookie cutter, cut out gnocchi. Place a prune half in the center of each circle and wrap the dough around it to form a ball. Continue in the same way with the rest of the dough.
6. Melt the butter in a large sauté pan and toss the bread crumbs, sugar, and cinnamon in the butter, constantly tossing until the bread crumbs start to get some color. Keep this mixture warm while you cook the gnocchi.
7. Fill a deep pot two-thirds full with cold water and place over high heat. Add salt to taste and bring the water to a boil.
8. Add the gnocchi and cook uncovered at a gentle boil until they rise to the surface and are cooked through, 2 to 4 minutes depending upon their size. (To be certain, taste one of the gnocchi.) Use a slotted spoon to lift the cooked gnocchi out of the water. Immediately roll the gnocchi in the bread crumb mixture and serve at once.

Wine notes: **White:** Moscato d'Asti from Piedmont (*frizzantino*: just a bit of sparkle) **Sparkling:** Extra-dry Prosecco from Veneto; Asti or Brachetto d'Acqui from Piedmont

# Gnocchetti con ragù

## QUILL-SHAPED GNOCCHI WITH SAUSAGE SAUCE

Gnocchetti are a classic dish from Sardinian cuisine and are especially associated with the Campidano area. The dough is white but it is often prepared with an addition of saffron, a signature product in this region, to give them a vibrant yellow color.

**SERVES 4 TO 6**

### GNOCCHETTI

**2⅓ cups semolina (durum) flour (14 oz)**

**Scant 1 cup warm water**

**1 tbsp extra-virgin olive oil**

### RAGÙ

**½ cup chicken stock, plus as needed**

**½ tsp saffron threads**

**2 tbsp olive oil**

**¾ cup minced yellow onion**

**12 oz mild or hot Italian sausage, removed from its casings**

**6 tbsp dry white wine**

**1 tbsp all-purpose flour**

**2 cups coarsely chopped plum tomatoes, peeled and seeded**

**Salt, as needed**

**Grated Pecorino Sardo, for serving**

1. To make the gnocchetti, work all the ingredients together to form a pasta dough. Knead the dough for about 15 minutes. The dough should be smooth and elastic. Wrap the dough in plastic wrap and let it rest at room temperature for 30 minutes.
2. To shape the gnocchetti, pinch off a small piece of dough (about the size of a large marble) and roll it into a rope about ¼ inch thick. Cut ½-inch-long pieces and roll them with your thumb on a grooved gnocchi board or the tines of a fork. Repeat with the rest of the dough. Once shaped, the gnocchetti can be reserved on a floured baking sheet, loosely covered, in the refrigerator for up to 8 hours.
3. To make the ragù, combine the stock and saffron and let the saffron steep for about 15 minutes. Heat the oil in a deep skillet over medium-high heat, add the onion and cook, stirring frequently, until the onion is tender and barely golden, about 5 minutes. Add the sausage and stir to break the sausage up; cook until it looses its raw look, about 5 minutes. Add the wine and simmer until the wine reduces, another 2 or 3 minutes. Sprinkle the flour over the mixture and stir it in. Add the stock and saffron and stir until combined. Add the tomatoes and simmer until flavorful and thickened, 30 to 40 minutes. If the sauce is getting too thick, add a bit of stock to loosen it as it simmers. Reserve the sauce.
4. To cook the gnocchetti, fill a deep pot two-thirds full with cold water and place over high heat. Add salt to taste and bring the water to a boil. Add the gnocchetti and cook uncovered at a gentle boil until they rise to the surface and are cooked through, about 2 minutes. Use a slotted spoon to lift the cooked gnocchi out of the water.
5. Combine the gnocchetti with the sausage sauce over low heat until the gnocchi are coated and very hot, about 2 minutes. Serve at once in a heated serving bowl or individual plates. Pass the cheese on the side.

Wine notes: **White:** Greco di Tufo from Campania; Pinot Grigio from Trentino-Alto Adige or Tuscany

**Red:** Cannonau di Sardegna from Sardinia; Nero d'Avola from Sicily; Aglianico del Vulture from Basilicata; Salice Salentino from Puglia; Cirò from Calabria

# Risi

Italy's most famous rice dish is most likely risotto, but there are lots of other rice dishes, from refreshing rice salads to enjoy in warm weather to delicious, soul-warming rice puddings. And despite risotto's nearly universal popularity, there are some occasions when you might prefer to simply steam the rice.

There are also differences in the cooking qualities of different types of rice, and the results you get from a recipe will vary depending upon the rice you use. Once you find a good-quality brand of rice that you like, stick with it for the most consistent results.

# Risotto

In Italy they say *e' un peccato mortale* ("it's a mortal sin or a blasphemy") to use the wrong pot to cook risotto. You need a deep saucepan (choose a 2-quart size for about 1½ cups of rice, which will give you about 4 cups of risotto, including the garnish). Absolutely avoid using a sauté pan or skillet—you will find that the liquid evaporates too quickly before the rice has a chance to absorb it.

## COOKING RISOTTO

There are many myths about stirring the rice. Our opinion is that you don't need to stir the rice constantly, especially during the first 10 minutes. Just make sure to keep the rice wet at all times during the first stage of cooking, and gently stir it every few minutes during the simmering stage to make sure that the rice doesn't stick to the bottom of the pan and that it stays uniformly wet at all times. You do need to have a good saucepan and a good wooden spoon for stirring.

Make sure you keep the rice quite dry toward the end; you can always adjust the consistency by adding more brodo. The risotto is supposed to be all'onda (wave-like).

Once the risotto has absorbed the brodo and the grains are tender, you should stir the risotto vigorously to develop the surface starches and give the dish a creamy texture. This last step is called mantecatura, and it is crucial to a good risotto.

## SERVING RISOTTO

There is also strong sentiment regarding the proper way to serve (and eat) risotto. Serving risotto in a bowl instead of on a flat plate is another peccato mortale. You are supposed to eat your risotto from the outside edge of the plate inward, so that the rice has time to cool slightly as you eat it, enabling you to really enjoy the flavor.

A good broth is one of the keys to a successful risotto, and for the best results, it should be boiling hot when you add it to the rice in the pan.

## TYPES OF ITALIAN RICE

All varieties of rice can be divided into short-, medium-, and long-grain varieties. All Italian rice varieties are strains of a thick, short-grained rice called "japonica" (*Oryza sativa japonica*). They may not taste different from one another, but they do behave differently when cooked. There are four grades of rice:

**COMUNE or ORIGINARIO:** This is the cheapest, most basic rice, typically short and round, used for soups and desserts but never risotto.

**SEMIFINO:** This grade, of medium length, maintains some firmness when cooked. Risotto can be made with a semifino grade, although semifino is better used in soups. Types of rice graded semifino include Vialone Nano and Baldo.

**FINO:** The grains are relatively long and large and taper at the tips. Fino-grade rice remains firm when cooked. Several varieties are commonly graded fino, including Razza 77 and San Andrea.

**SUPERFINO:** This grade represents the fattest, largest grains. They take the longest to cook, and they can absorb more liquid than any of the others while still remaining firm. Superfino rices include Arborio and Carnaroli.

# Risotto ai fegatini di pollo

## RISOTTO WITH CHICKEN LIVERS

A classic risotto from the northern part of Italy where everything gets used (in this case, chicken livers) for making the risotto.

**SERVES 6**

- 6 cups Brodo (page 88), or as needed
- ¼ cup olive oil
- 5 tbsp unsalted butter
- ½ cup minced yellow onion
- 2 oz chopped soppressata
- 1 tbsp chopped sage
- 2¼ cups Carnaroli or Vialone Nano rice
- 8 oz chicken livers (see Note), cut into small cubes
- ¾ cup chopped flat-leaf parsley
- ½ cup dry white wine
- ½ cup Marsala
- ¾ cup grated Parmigiano-Reggiano (3 oz)
- 1 tsp finely grated lemon zest
- Salt and freshly ground black pepper, as needed

1. Heat the brodo over low heat; keep it warm.
2. Heat the oil and 1 tablespoon of the butter in a large pot over low heat. Add the onion and cook, stirring frequently, until tender but with no color, about 4 minutes. Add the soppressata and render it so that it becomes completely cooked and almost dry, about 2 minutes.
3. Add the sage and rice and toast lightly, about 2 minutes. Add the chicken livers and half of the parsley and mix until well combined. Add the wine and Marsala and cook until the wine is cooked away by one-quarter.
4. Add some of the warm brodo a little at a time, enough to come ½ inch above the rice, and cook, stirring frequently to be sure the rice doesn't stick to the bottom. As the rice absorbs the broth, keep adding more.
5. Once the rice has absorbed almost all the broth, and it is still al dente, about 20 minutes total cooking time, remove from the heat. Add the remaining butter, the Parmigiano-Reggiano, and the rest of the parsley and stir vigorously to develop the surface starches.
6. Just before serving the risotto, stir in the lemon zest. Season with salt and pepper to taste. Serve the risotto on flat plates.

*Look for organic chicken livers; not only for their better flavor, but also because it is a healthier option, as the liver is one of the organs that filters out toxins. This is one case where moderation is important, but still, try it as a treat. It is very delicious, believe us.*

Wine notes: To match the wine with rice flavors and also feature the intense flavors of the liver, pair with a medium-bodied, fruit-driven white. To match the intensity of the liver and create another spice, in effect another sauce, try a light- to medium-bodied red with good acidity.

**White:** Pinot Grigio from Veneto, Trentino-Alto Adige, or Friuli-Venezia Giulia

**Red:** Valpolicella Classico, Bardolino Classico, or Merlot from Veneto; Dolcetto d'Alba or Barbera d'Asti from Piedmont; Chianti Classico, Rosso di Montalcino, or Pomino Rosso from Tuscany

# Risotto alla parmigiana

## CLASSIC RISOTTO PARMIGIANA

This is the classic risotto, and the perfect showcase for creamy superfino rices.

**SERVES 6**

- 6 cups Brodo (page 88), or as needed
- ¼ cup olive oil
- 5 tbsp unsalted butter
- ½ cup minced yellow onion
- 2¼ cups Carnaroli or Vialone Nano rice
- ¾ cup dry white wine
- 1 cup grated Parmigiano-Reggiano (4 oz)
- Salt and freshly ground black pepper, as needed

1. Heat the brodo over low heat; keep warm.
2. Heat the oil and 1 tablespoon of the butter in a large pot over low heat. Add the onion and cook, stirring frequently, until tender but with no color, about 4 minutes. Add the rice and toast lightly, stirring frequently, about 2 minutes.
3. Add the wine and cook until almost dry. Add some of the brodo a little at a time, enough to come ½ inch above the rice, and cook, stirring frequently to be sure the rice doesn't stick to the bottom. As the rice absorbs the broth, keep adding more.
4. Once the rice has absorbed almost all the broth, and the grains are still al dente, about 20 minutes total cooking time, remove the pot from the heat. Add the remaining butter and the cheese and stir vigorously.
5. Taste, season with salt and pepper if necessary, and serve on flat plates.

1. Sprinkle the Parmigiano-Reggiano cheese into the cooking risotto.

2. Continue to stir as the rice absorbs the brodo.

3. Properly prepared risotto is creamy, not at all gummy or sticky.

Wine notes: This risotto is quite flavorful and quite flexible with wine. If you want to bring out the sweet flavors of the rice, pair the dish with a medium-bodied white. If you want to create a "sauce" for the rice, and emphasize the richness of the butter and Parmigiano-Reggiano, choose a light red. Finally, if you want to invigorate the palate and balance the flavors, try a crisp sparkling wine.

**White:** Albana di Romagna from Emilia-Romagna; Soave Classico from Veneto; Roero Arneis from Piedmont; Falanghina from Campania

**Red:** Sangiovese di Romagna from Emilia-Romagna; Chianti from Tuscany; Valpolicella Classico or Bardolino from Veneto; Dolcetto or Barbera from Piedmont

**Sparkling:** Prosecco from Veneto; Franciacorta from Lombardy

# Risi e bisi

## SOUPY RICE AND PEAS

This "soupy" risotto makes the most of fresh peas. If your fresh peas are large, you may want to cook them in a generous amount of butter with some minced onion and parsley until tender; otherwise they might not cook to the correct creamy consistency in the same time as the rice. The peas should be cooked almost to the point of breaking down to give a nice green color to the risotto.

**SERVES 6 TO 8**

- 2 qt plus 1 cup Brodo (page 88)
- ½ cup olive oil
- ⅔ cup minced yellow onion
- 2¼ cups Vialone Nano or Carnaroli rice
- 2 cups shelled fresh small peas
- 6 tbsp dry white wine
- 6 tbsp unsalted butter
- ½ cup grated Parmigiano-Reggiano (2 oz)
- 2 tbsp chopped flat-leaf parsley
- Kosher salt, as needed

1. Bring the brodo to a boil and keep warm.
2. Heat the oil in a large pan over low heat. Add the onion and cook, stirring frequently, until tender but with no color, about 4 minutes. Add the rice and lightly toast it, stirring constantly until each grain is translucent and hot, about 2 minutes. Be careful to not burn the onions or scorch the rice. Add the peas and combine well with the rice.
3. Add the wine and let it evaporate. Add some of the brodo a little at a time, enough to come ½ inch above the rice, and cook, stirring frequently to be sure the rice doesn't stick to the bottom. As the rice absorbs the broth, keep adding more.
4. When the risotto is done, after 15 to 18 minutes, remove the pan from the stove. At this point, you should have a creamy and quite soupy risotto. This particular dish does not have to be too dry toward the end, unlike other risotto dishes.
5. Add the butter, cheese, and parsley, and stir vigorously. Season to taste with salt and serve on flat plates.

Wine notes: Choose a fruity white or light sparkling wine to create a crisp, refreshing counterpoint to the smooth texture of the rice and peas.

**White:** Soave or Breganze from Veneto; Falanghina from Campania; Pinot Bianco from Trentino-Alto Adige; Friulano from Friuli-Venezia Giulia
**Sparkling:** Prosecco from Veneto

# Risotto con funghi

## RICE WITH MUSHROOMS

Depending on the quality and type of mushrooms, this recipe may vary. Clean fresh mushrooms carefully, making sure you remove any impurities. During the cooking procedure, add the firmest mushrooms first, then add the softer ones toward the end. Chanterelle, morel, fresh porcini, oyster, shimeji, and many other mushrooms may be available at your local specialty store. We personally like just dried porcini, especially when they are soft and still in large pieces. Avoid any crumbled or very dry ones; they won't be very flavorful or tender.

**SERVES 6**

- 2 oz dried porcini mushrooms
- 6 cups Brodo (page 88), or as needed
- ¼ cup olive oil
- 5 tbsp unsalted butter
- ½ cup minced yellow onion
- 1 garlic clove, chopped
- ½ cup chopped flat-leaf parsley
- 2¼ cups Carnaroli or Vialone Nano rice
- ¾ cup dry white wine
- 1 lb mixed fresh mushrooms
- 1 cup grated Parmigiano-Reggiano (4 oz)
- Salt and freshly ground black pepper, as needed

1. Put the porcini mushrooms in a bowl with warm water to cover for about 30 minutes, until very soft.
2. Heat the brodo over low heat; keep warm.
3. Heat the oil and 1 tablespoon of the butter in a large pot over low heat. Add the onion, garlic, and parsley and sweat until tender, about 5 minutes. Add the rice and toast lightly without letting the rice or onion take on any color.
4. Add the wine and cook until almost dry. Strain the porcini mushrooms, strain their liquid, and add both to the pot. Add some of the brodo a little at a time, enough to come ½ inch above the rice, and cook, stirring frequently to be sure the rice doesn't stick to the bottom. As the rice absorbs the broth, keep adding more. During the last half of the cooking time (after about 10 minutes), add the fresh mushrooms.
5. Once the rice has absorbed almost all the broth, and it is still al dente, about 20 minutes total cooking time, remove from the heat. Add the remaining butter and the cheese, and stir vigorously to develop the surface starches.
6. Taste, season if necessary with salt and pepper, and serve on flat plates.

Wine notes: The mushrooms take on a meaty flavor in this dish, so you can pair it with a medium-bodied red, just as if you're matching the wine to a lean red meat. If you prefer to focus on the rice, pair with a medium-bodied, somewhat fruity unoaked white.

**White:** Roero Arneis from Piedmont; Pinot Grigio or Traminer (Gewürztraminer) from Trentino-Alto Adige; Fiano di Avellino from Campania

**Red:** Grumello from Lombardy; Pinot Nero/Pinot Noir from Trentino-Alto Adige or Valle d'Aosta; Barbera d'Alba from Piedmont; Bardolino Classico or Merlot from Veneto; Chianti Classico or Carmignano from Tuscany; Torgiano Rosso from Umbria

# Risotto con zucca

## PUMPKIN RISOTTO

This classic autumn dish requires a great pumpkin, so make sure you have a good source or a great-quality squash when preparing this risotto. Other flavors can be layered in this dish. You may sprinkle some crumbled amaretti cookies on top or combine the risotto with seafood, such as lobster, shrimp, or scallops. Or serve with some stewed boar or even rabbit. You may make this dish vegetarian by using a vegetable broth instead of chicken brodo.

**SERVES 4**

- 3 cups chicken Brodo (page 88), or as needed
- 4 cups peeled and chopped sugar pumpkin, butternut, or kabocha squash
- ¼ cup olive oil
- 3 tbsp unsalted butter, room temperature
- ½ cup minced yellow onion
- 1⅓ cups Carnaroli or Vialone Nano rice
- ½ cup dry white wine
- 3 tbsp heavy cream
- ½ tsp orange zest
- ½ cup grated Parmigiano-Reggiano (2 oz), plus shavings, for garnish
- Salt and freshly ground black pepper, as needed

1. Heat the brodo over low heat; keep warm.
2. In a separate pot, simmer 3 cups of the pumpkin with enough water to almost cover until tender, about 15 minutes. Transfer to a food processor and puree. Set the puree aside.
3. Heat the olive oil and 1 tablespoon of the butter in a large saucepan over low heat, and sweat the onion until tender, about 5 minutes. Add the rice and toast lightly without letting the rice or onion take on any color, about 2 minutes. Add the remaining 1 cup pumpkin and the wine and cook until the wine is almost completely cooked away. Add about one-third of the brodo and stir constantly while the rice absorbs the brodo, making sure the rice doesn't stick to the bottom. Add another cup of the broth and continue simmering as for the first addition.
4. Once the rice has absorbed the brodo (after about 10 minutes), add the pumpkin puree and cook for 7 minutes longer, adding some of the remaining brodo as needed if the mixture gets too dry.
5. When the risotto is al dente, remove from the heat. Add the cream, the remaining 2 tablespoons butter, the orange zest, and cheese, and stir vigorously to make the risotto creamy. Taste, season with salt and pepper if necessary, and serve on flat plates with shavings of Parmigiano-Reggiano on top.

Wine notes: If you decide to include only the pumpkin with the rice or to add seafood, go for a medium-bodied white or a refreshing sparkler; both will bring out the earthy spiciness of the pumpkin. If you decide to add meats (including game), try the dish with light- to medium-bodied reds.

**White:** Lugana or Terre di Franciacorta from Lombardy; Vernaccia di San Gimignano from Tuscany; Verdicchio from Le Marche; Orvieto Classico from Umbria
**Red:** Grumello or Sasella from Lombardy; Chianti from Tuscany; Grignolino from Piedmont; Valpolicella from Veneto
**Sparkling:** Franciacorta from Lombardy

# Risotto alla milanese

## RISOTTO MILANESE-STYLE

This is one of the most classic risottos; it's from Milan and can be served with a variety of dishes, the most traditional one being osso buco. It is also called risotto allo zafferano (with saffron) because saffron is an indispensible ingredient for this risotto. Serve it on its own, or, if you can find it, top each plate with a piece of fresh marrow.

**SERVES 6**

- 6 cups Chicken Brodo (page 88), or as needed
- ¼ cup olive oil
- 5 tbsp unsalted butter
- ½ cup minced yellow onion
- 2¼ cups Carnaroli or Vialone Nano rice
- ¾ tbsp saffron threads, crumbled
- ¾ cup dry white wine
- ¾ cup grated Parmigiano-Reggiano (3 oz)
- Salt and freshly ground black pepper, as needed
- Beef marrow, for garnish (optional)

1. Heat the brodo over low heat; keep warm.
2. Heat the olive oil and 1 tablespoon of the butter in a large pot over low heat. Add the onion and sweat until tender (there should be no color in the onion), about 5 minutes. Add the rice and toast lightly without letting the rice or onion take on any color. Add the saffron and combine well. Add the wine and cook until almost dry.
3. Add some of the brodo a little at a time, enough to come ½ inch above the rice, and cook, stirring frequently to be sure the rice doesn't stick to the bottom. As the rice absorbs the broth, keep adding more.
4. Once rice has absorbed almost all the broth, and it is still al dente, about 20 minutes total cooking time, remove from the heat. Add the remaining 4 tablespoons butter and the cheese, and stir vigorously to develop the surface starches. Taste, season with salt and pepper if necessary.
5. Serve the risotto on flat plates and spoon or place a piece of the meat marrow in the center, if desired.

Wine notes: The wine you choose for this dish will depend on what you serve with the rice: select medium-bodied whites for the rice without accompaniments and medium-bodied reds for serving with the classic osso buco.

**White:** Lugana or Terre di Franciacorta from Lombardy; Vernaccia di San Gimignano from Tuscany; Verdicchio dei Castelli di Jesi from Le Marche; Orvieto Classico from Umbria
**Red:** Grumello or Inferno from Lombardy; Vino Nobile di Montepulciano or Carmignano from Tuscany; Barbera d'Alba or Barbaresco from Piedmont; Taurasi from Campania

# Arancini di riso

## RICE BALLS

Arancini, or plini, are made from leftover rice made the previous day, which is why we mention in the instructions that you should cook the rice a little longer than usual. That means the rice will be sticky enough to stay together and hold the filling once it is deep-fried. You may use any type of filling; in this case we use a beef ragù, not too wet, but alternatively you may sauté some chicken livers, deglaze the pan with Marsala, and chop them for a filling. Or, you can keep it very simple and just fill the rice balls with a good creamy cheese like mozzarella, and that's it.

**SERVES 12**

**Mild olive oil as needed, for frying**

**7 cups Chicken Brodo (page 88), or as needed**

**¼ cup olive oil**

**1 tbsp unsalted butter**

**½ cup minced yellow onion**

**2¼ cups Carnaroli or Vialone Nano rice**

**¾ cup dry white wine**

**1 cup grated Parmigiano-Reggiano (4 oz)**

**Salt and freshly ground black pepper, as needed**

**1 egg yolk**

BREADING

**2 cups all-purpose or "00" flour**

**4 large eggs**

**2 tbsp water**

**4 cups plain dry bread crumbs**

FILLING

**12 oz mozzarella, small dice**

**1 cup Meat Ragù (page 143), drained of excess liquid, or chicken livers (see headnote above)**

1. Preheat the olive oil in a deep-fryer to 375 degrees F.
2. Heat the brodo over low heat; keep warm.
3. Heat the oil and butter in a large pot over low heat. Add the onion and sweat until tender (there should be no color in the onion), about 5 minutes. Add the rice and toast lightly without letting the rice or onion take on any color. Add the wine and cook until almost dry. Add some of the brodo a little at a time, enough to come ½ inch above rice, making sure the rice doesn't stick to the bottom. Add more broth as it is absorbed. Cook the rice a little longer than usual so that it is thick and quite sticky, about 25 minutes.
4. Once the rice has absorbed almost all the broth and it is well cooked and quite dry, remove from the heat. Add the Parmigiano-Reggiano and stir vigorously. Let it cool slightly, then taste, season with salt and pepper, and incorporate the egg yolk, combining it well.
5. Set up the breading ingredients: Put about 1 cup of flour in a shallow bowl. Beat 2 of the eggs together with the 2 tablespoons water in a second bowl. Put 1 cup of the bread crumbs in a third bowl. You may need to add more to each of the bowls in order to bread all of the arancini.
6. Form little balls of rice (about 1 inch in diameter for snacks or 2 inches to serve as an appetizer). Using your finger, poke a hole in the center of each ball and insert 1 piece of mozzarella and some of the meat. Pinch the rice back into shape to enclose the filling in the ball. Dip the rice balls into the flour, then the egg wash, and finally the bread crumbs.
7. Fry the risotto balls until they are golden and crisp on the outside and heated through, about 4 minutes. Drain on paper towels and serve hot.

Wine notes: The rice ball holds the beef, livers, lamb, duck, and so forth together. Pair the wine with the flavors of the meat and the rice will happily go along for the ride.

**Red:** Nero d'Avola from Sicily; Cannonau di Sardegna from Sardinia; Aglianico del Vulture from Basilicata; Salice Salentino from Puglia; Dolcetta d'Alba or Barbera d'Asti from Piedmont; Chianti Classico or Rosso di Montalcino from Tuscany

# Risotto ai frutti di mare

## SEAFOOD RISOTTO

This is an easy way to make a very flavorful seafood risotto at home. This particular combination of seafood is easy to come by at most markets, and most of the fish can be cleaned by the fishmonger, saving you the work and mess. You might also try lobster or just about any type of fish you can think of, except for fatty or strongly flavored fish like salmon or bluefish. The touch of brandy at the end really brings out the full flavor of the seafood. For this risotto only, we like to add some chopped raw garlic at the last minute.

SERVES 4

- 2½ cups seafood or vegetable broth, or as needed
- ⅓ cup olive oil
- 3 tbsp unsalted butter
- ½ cup minced shallots or onion
- 1⅓ cups Carnaroli or Vialone Nano rice
- ½ cup dry white wine
- 8 medium shrimp, peeled and deveined
- 4 medium-large sea scallops
- 4 oz squid, cleaned and cut into thin rings
- 8 mussels, scrubbed and debearded
- 8 small clams, such as Manila
- ½ cup peeled, seeded plum tomatoes, crushed
- ½ cup chopped flat-leaf parsley
- ½ tsp chopped garlic
- 1 tbsp brandy
- 1 tbsp extra-virgin olive oil
- Salt and freshly ground black pepper, as needed
- ½ cup grated Parmigiano-Reggiano (2 oz; optional)

1. Heat the broth over low heat; keep warm.
2. Heat the olive oil and 1 tablespoon of the butter in a large saucepan over low heat, and sweat the shallots or onion until tender but with no color, about 5 minutes. Add the rice and toast lightly. Add the wine and cook until almost dry. Add some of the broth a little at a time, enough to come ½ inch above the rice, making sure the rice doesn't stick to the bottom. Add more broth as it is absorbed.
3. Once the rice has absorbed some of the liquid (after about 8 minutes), start adding the seafood in stages: first the shrimp; then after 2 to 3 minutes the scallops; then after 2 minutes longer the squid; then after 2 minutes longer the mussels, clams, and tomtaoes. That way, the seafood will be properly cooked at the same time the rice is, without overcooking anything. Once you start adding the seafood, it will take another 7 minutes for the rice to be ready. Keep adding broth as needed, remembering that the seafood will release their own juices. If the mussels and clams are very small and super-fresh, add them at the very end with just enough time for them to open, about 2 minutes.
4. Once the seafood is cooked and the risotto is al dente, remove from the heat. Add the parsley, garlic, brandy, the remaining butter, and the extra-virgin olive oil, and stir well to release the starches and make it creamy.
5. Taste, season with salt and pepper if necessary, and serve on flat plates. Leave the shells in the risotto and let diners remove the clams and mussels from them. If you wish, you may garnish with some cheese.

Wine notes: For this ideal dry white wine dish, choose a wine that is medium-bodied and that will bring out the sweet flavors of the rice and the seafood. The risotto is also a lovely pairing with sparkling wine that will enhance the briny qualities of the dish and then erase the saltiness from the palate.

**White:** Soave Classico from Veneto; Pinot Grigio from Trentino-Alto Adige; Gavi from Piedmont; Orvieto Classico from Umbria; Falanghina from Campania; Vermentino di Sardegna or Vermentino di Gallura from Sardinia
**Sparkling:** Prosecco from Veneto; Franciacorta from Lombardy

# Risotto all'astice

## LOBSTER RISOTTO

In Italy, this is made with European lobsters, which are a little smaller than American lobsters.

**SERVES 6 TO 8**

Three 1-lb lobsters

LOBSTER BROTH

6 tbsp unsalted butter

1 medium yellow onion, finely chopped

1 leek, finely chopped

¼ cup brandy

5 or 6 fresh or canned plum tomatoes

2 qt Brodo (page 88)

2 thyme sprigs

1 bay leaf

4 tbsp extra-virgin olive oil, as needed

½ cup minced shallots

4 garlic cloves, minced

2¼ cups Carnaroli rice

¾ cup dry white wine

Salt and freshly ground black pepper, as needed

2 tbsp chopped chives

1. Halve the lobsters lengthwise. Twist away the tail pieces and set aside. Twist off the legs and hit the claws lightly with a mallet to crack the shells. Remove and discard the sandy bag from underneath the mouth opening. Chop the head into small pieces.
2. To make the lobster broth, heat 2 tablespoons of the butter in a large saucepan over low heat and sweat the onion and leek over medium-low heat, stirring frequently, until tender, about 3 minutes. Add the reserved lobster head and legs. Increase the heat to medium-high and cook for 3 to 4 minutes, until the shells turn bright red and the onion and leek start to caramelize.
3. Add the brandy and let it cook away completely, and then add the tomatoes. Cook for a few more minutes. Remove the legs and set aside to cool slightly. Add the brodo. Bring to a simmer and add the thyme and bay leaf.
4. Remove the meat from the claws and reserve; return the shells to the broth. Continue to simmer gently over low heat until fully flavored, another 30 minutes, and then strain. Keep the broth warm (or, if you are making the broth ahead of time, it can be cooled and then stored in the refrigerator for up to 3 days).
5. Heat 2 tablespoons of the olive oil in a large pot over low heat, add the shallots and garlic and sweat, stirring occasionally, until tender, about 4 minutes. Add the rice, raise the heat to medium-high, and parch the rice for a few minutes. Add the wine, let it evaporate, and then add enough brodo to cover the rice. Cook for 15 to 18 minutes, stirring frequently and adding the brodo gradually as the rice absorbs it. Add the chopped claw meat.
6. Pull the tail meat from the shell, slice it into 1-inch-thick pieces, and season with salt and pepper. Heat about 2 tablespoons olive oil in a sauté pan over medium-high heat and place the tail pieces in the pan. Sauté for about 2 minutes, turning to cook on both sides, and remove the pan from the heat.
7. When the risotto is al dente, remove from the heat and vigorously stir in 4 tablespoons of butter to give the risotto its creamy characteristic. Serve on flat plates, garnished with slices of lobster tail and chives.

Wine notes: As with the previous dish—risotto with seafood—you want to bring out the sweet and saline flavors of the lobster in this dish. A fruity white or a refreshing sparkler is the obvious choice.

**White:** Vernaccia di San Gimignano or Sauvignon Blanc from Tuscany; Albana di Romagna from Emilia-Romagna; Sauvignon from Friuli-Venezia Giulia; Gavi from Piedmont; Vermentino di Gallura from Sardinia; Falanghina from Campania

**Sparkling:** Trento Brut from Trentino-Alto Adige; Franciacorta from Lombardy

# Sartù di riso

## MOLDED RICE TIMBALE

This is an antique preparation of a rice timbale from Naples; today the specific ingredients may vary from family to family, but the dish is a magnificent regional classic regardless of the exact filling.

**SERVES 8**

- ½ oz dried porcini mushrooms
- 1 tbsp olive oil, plus more as needed for frying meatballs
- 1 cup minced yellow onion
- 2 cups canned plum tomatoes, passed through a food mill
- 2 whole sausages (mildly spicy, about 8 oz)
- ½ cup peas, blanched if fresh, thawed if frozen
- 5 tbsp unsalted butter
- 4 oz chicken livers
- 8 oz ground beef
- 2 slices Italian bread, torn into pieces and soaked in 2 tbsp milk
- 2 large eggs
- ¼ cup plus 2 tbsp grated Parmigiano-Reggiano
- ¼ cup chopped flat-leaf parsley
- 1 garlic clove, minced
- Salt and freshly ground black pepper, as needed
- Pinch of grated nutmeg
- Flour, as needed for dusting
- 2¼ cups medium-grain rice
- 2 qt Chicken Brodo (page 88)
- 1 cup plain dry bread crumbs, or as needed
- 8 oz mozzarella, sliced

1. Preheat the oven to 325 degrees F.
2. Soak the mushrooms in warm water for 30 minutes to soften. Strain them, then strain their liquid and reserve. Chop the mushrooms into small pieces. Reserve the mushrooms and their soaking liquid separately.
3. Heat 2 tablespoons olive oil in a large skillet over medium heat. Add half of the onion and cook, stirring frequently, until tender and translucent, 4 to 5 minutes. Add the chopped mushrooms and tomatoes and stir to combine.
4. Add the whole sausages and cook until the sausages are cooked through and very hot, 10 to 15 minutes. Add the peas for the last 3 or 4 minutes of cooking time. Remove the sausages and slice them into rounds. Reserve the sauce and sausage separately.
5. Clean the skillet and heat 1 tablespoon of the butter in the skillet over medium heat. When the butter stops foaming, add the livers and sauté on all sides until cooked through but still pink inside, turning as necessary to cook evenly, 8 to 10 minutes total. Remove the livers from the pan and, when cool enough to handle, dice and set aside.
6. Blend the beef, bread soaked in milk, eggs, the ¼ cup of Parmigiano-Reggiano, the parsley, and garlic in a bowl until combined. Season with salt and pepper and nutmeg. Shape into meatballs about 1 inch in diameter.
7. Heat about ¼ inch of oil in a deep skillet over medium heat. Coat the meatballs with flour and immediately put them into the hot oil (you will need to work in batches or use 2 pans). Fry them, turning as necessary, until they are browned on all sides and just cooked through, 6 to 8 minutes. Set aside.
8. Heat 2 tablespoons olive oil in a large saucepan over medium heat. Add the remaining onion and cook, stirring frequently, until tender and translucent, 4 to 5 minutes. Add the rice and stir until the rice is coated with the oil and has a nutty aroma, about 2 minutes.
9. Add enough of the brodo to cover the rice by about ½ inch. Simmer, stirring frequently, until the rice absorbs most of the brodo. Continue to add the broth, a bit at a time, letting the rice absorb each addition. Continue to cook, stirring to make sure the rice doesn't stick, until all the brodo is added and the rice is tender and creamy, about 20 minutes total. Remove the pot from the heat and add the remaining 4 tablespoons butter and the remaining 2 tablespoons Parmigiano-Reggiano, stirring vigorously to incorporate.

10. In a large round baking dish or 3-quart soufflé dish, brush butter all over the sides and sprinkle with bread crumbs. Add about three-quarters of the rice to the dish and press it into a layer on the bottom and sides, leaving room to fill the middle.

11. Fill the hole in layers: first a few spoonfuls of sauce, followed by slices of sausage, meatballs, livers, and mozzarella. Continue in this manner until all the ingredients are layered in the dish. Cover the top with the remaining rice and level the top. Sprinkle more bread crumbs on top.

12. Dot the surface with the remaining butter. Bake until heated through and golden brown on top, about 30 minutes. Let the timbale rest for 5 minutes after you take it out of the oven, then unmold it onto a platter as follows: Hold the casserole (with a protective mitt) on the palm of one hand. Put the platter over the top of the casserole and hold it in place by putting your hand flat on top of the platter. Flip the casserole and platter over in one motion. The timbale will drop out onto the platter. Serve immediately.

Wine notes: This dish, filled with hearty red meats, sausages, organ meats, and mushrooms, calls for a hearty, full-bodied red wine, preferably from southern Italy. The local powerhouse, Taurasi, is a very special wine that will stand up to the strong, meaty flavors.

**Red:** Taurasi from Campania; Nero d'Avola from Sicily; Cannonau di Sardegna from Sardinia; Aglianico del Vulture from Basilicata; Salice Salentino or Primitivo di Manduria from Puglia; Barbera d'Asti or Barbera d'Alba from Piedmont; Grumello or Inferno from Lombardy; Merlot from Veneto

# Risotto al salto

## SAUTÉED RISOTTO

This is a way to use a leftover risotto, and it is especially delicious (and attractive) made from Risotto alla Milanese, the saffron-colored risotto on page 215. The risotto is sautéed in a pan until crispy, making a tasty, crusty cake with a soft center.

**SERVES 4 TO 6**

½ cup (1 stick) unsalted butter

4 cups Risotto (page 215), chilled

1. Melt the butter in a cast-iron skillet over medium heat.

2. Add the risotto and press it into an even layer, about ½ inch thick. Sauté the risotto patty until crispy and golden in color, about 2 minutes. Flip the patty over and cook on the other side until golden, about 2 minutes longer.

3. Serve hot.

# Risotto al nero di seppia

## BLACK RISOTTO

This risotto is an inky black color because of the ink found in the head of the cuttlefish (known in Italian as *seppia* and related to the squid and octopus). Used for centuries to write documents and for ink drawings, the ink is also a culinary ingredient and here creates a briny risotto.

**SERVES 6 TO 8**

- 1 lb cuttlefish
- 2 qt Chicken Brodo (page 88)
- Salt, as needed
- ¾ cup (1½ sticks) unsalted butter
- 1 cup chopped shallots
- 2¼ cups Carnaroli rice
- 6 tbsp dry white wine
- 6 tbsp olive oil
- ½ cup minced yellow onion
- 2 tsp minced garlic
- 2 tbsp chopped flat-leaf parsley
- Grated Parmigiano-Reggiano, for serving

1. To prepare the cuttlefish, cut off the head and the backbone. Peel the skin from the body and remove the inner organs. Look for the ink bag (it is located at one end of the body); remove it and set it aside on a plate. Cut the head in half and remove the mouth and the eye. Wash and dry all the fish, cut into thin strips, and set aside.
2. Bring the brodo to a boil and season it with salt; keep warm.
3. Over low heat in a large wide pan, melt half of the butter and sweat the shallots until very tender but not colored, about 2 minutes. Add the rice and cook, stirring constantly, until each grain is translucent and hot. Be careful not to burn the shallots or scorch the rice.
4. Add the wine and cook until the wine is nearly cooked away, about 5 minutes. Add enough brodo to cover the rice by about ½ inch and cook, stirring occasionally, until all the brodo is absorbed. Add the brodo as needed and stir occasionally just to make sure the rice is not sticking on the bottom of the pan. The rice will take 10 to 12 minutes to cook to the point at which you will add the cuttlefish and ink.
5. While the risotto is cooking, heat the oil in a skillet over medium heat and sweat the onion, garlic, and parsley for 3 minutes. Add the cuttlefish and toss it in the pan over high heat until it is just barely cooked, about 1 minute. Add the squid ink and about ½ cup of brodo. Gently simmer for 2 minutes. Add this mixture to the risotto after the risotto has been cooking for about 12 minutes.
6. Continue to cook the risotto until the rice is tender to the bite, another 7 or 8 minutes. When the risotto is done, remove the pan from the stove. Add the rest of the butter. Stir vigorously to create the characteristic creamy consistency. Serve at once, passing additional Parmigiano-Reggiano to add if desired.

Wine notes: Rice with cuttlefish creates a light dish, but one with intense flavors. Choose a medium-bodied white with character that will match that intensity without overwhelming the subtle background flavors of the dish.

**White:** Soave or Chardonnay from Veneto; Friulano or Sauvignon Blanc from Friuli-Venezia Giulia; Vernaccia di San Gimignano from Tuscany; Vermentino di Sardegna or Vermentino di Gallura from Sardinia

# Risotto alla paesana

## PEASANT-STYLE RISOTTO

In some places, you may find this vegetable risotto made with cooked dried beans in place of the peas.

**SERVES 6 TO 8**

- ½ cup olive oil
- 2 oz pancetta, cut into thin strips
- ¾ cup finely chopped yellow onion
- 1 cup diced carrot
- 2 celery stalks, cut into small cubes
- 1 garlic clove, minced
- 2¼ cups Arborio rice
- Salt, as needed
- 2 qt Chicken Brodo (page 88)
- 2 bay leaves
- 2 small fresh or canned plum tomatoes, peeled and seeded
- 1½ cups peas, blanched if fresh, thawed if frozen
- 1½ cups cubed zucchini
- 6 tbsp (¾ stick) unsalted butter
- ½ cup grated Parmigiano-Reggiano (2 oz)
- 2 tbsp chopped flat-leaf parsley

1. Heat the olive oil in a large saucepan over medium heat and add the pancetta, onion, carrot, and celery. Sauté for a few minutes, then add the garlic and sauté for another minute. Add the rice and cook, stirring constantly, until the rice is coated with oil and toasted, about 2 minutes. Season with salt. Add the enough of the brodo to cover the rice by about ½ inch. Add the bay leaves and tomatoes and cook, stirring frequently, until the rice absorbs the brodo. Keep adding brodo as needed and stir occasionally just to make sure the rice is not sticking to the bottom of the pan. It will take 15 to 18 minutes total to cook the risotto.
2. While the risotto is cooking, sauté the peas and zucchini in 2 teaspoons of the butter in a skillet. The zucchini should be tender and the peas bright green. Set aside; stir them into the risotto when the last of the brodo has been added.
3. Remove the saucepan from the stove. Add the remaining butter, the cheese, and parsley to the risotto. Stir vigorously to create the characteristic creamy consistency. Serve at once.

Wine notes: The rice, peas, and squash conspire to create a light, garden-infused dish that will pair comfortably with a medium-bodied dry white or rosé. The dry white wine will emphasize the flavors of the veggies, and the rosé will highlight the creaminess of the rice.

**White:** Vernaccia di San Gimignano or Chardonnay from Tuscany; Pinot Grigio from Friuli-Venezia Giulia or Trentino-Alto Adige; Soave Classico from Veneto; Arneis from Piedmont
**Rosé:** Montepulciano d'Abruzzo Cerasuolo from Abruzzo; Lacrymarosa from Campania

# Risotto ai carciofi

## ARTICHOKE RISOTTO

When selecting artichokes, make sure they are healthy, heavy, and firm.

**SERVES 6 TO 8**

8 to 10 small artichokes

Juice of ½ lemon

2 qt Chicken Brodo (page 88)

Salt, as needed

½ cup (1 stick) unsalted butter

½ cup finely minced yellow onion

2¼ cups Carnaroli rice

6 tbsp dry white wine

6 tbsp olive oil

3 garlic cloves, peeled

1 rosemary sprig

½ cup grated Parmigiano-Reggiano (2 oz)

2 tbsp chopped flat-leaf parsley

1. Clean the artichokes by removing the first few layers of leaves. When you reach the tender leaves, cut off the tops of the leaves and peel the stems. Cut them in half and then slice them thinly. Reserve in water mixed with the lemon juice.
2. Bring the brodo to a boil and season it with salt; keep warm.
3. Over low heat in a large wide pan, melt half of the butter and sweat the onion until very tender but not colored. Add the rice and cook, stirring constantly until each grain is translucent and hot, about 2 minutes. Add the wine and cook, stirring occasionally, until it almost completely absorbed, about 5 minutes.
4. Add enough of the brodo to cover the rice by about ½ inch. Continue to cook, stirring from time to time and adding more broth until it has all been absorbed into the rice. Add the brodo as needed and stir occasionally to make sure the rice is not sticking to the bottom of the pan. Continue to cook for about 15 minutes.
5. While the risotto is cooking, heat the oil in a large sauté pan or casserole over very low heat. Add the whole garlic cloves and rosemary. When the garlic starts to take on a golden color, turn the heat to high and add the artichokes. Sauté them, tossing or stirring so they cook evenly, until tender, about 6 minutes. Season with salt. Remove and discard the garlic and rosemary.
6. Add the artichokes to the risotto and simmer, stirring constantly, until the rice is fully cooked, another 5 minutes. When the risotto is done, remove the pan from the stove. Add the remaining butter, the cheese, and parsley. Stir vigorously to create the characteristic creamy consistency. Serve at once.

Wine notes: Artichokes can be tricky to pair with wine. Choose a fruity white or sparkler—Prosecco is ideal—that literally will be made a touch sweeter when you taste the wine with the earthy artichokes. Avoid complex, oaky wines with this dish.

**White:** Vermentino or Pigato from Liguria; Gewürztraminer (also known as Traminer), Riesling, or Müller-Thurgau from Trentino-Alto Adige; Frascati Superiore or Est! Est!! Est!!! from Lazio

**Sparkling:** Prosecco from Veneto

# Risotto con melanzane e scamorza

## RISOTTO WITH EGGPLANT AND SCAMORZA

Serve this dish on a big platter so that you can see the layers of risotto and eggplant. The heat from the risotto will start to melt the scamorza, a cheese typical of the central and south of Italy; it is produced by the same method as mozzarella, and then it is typically smoked and aged for 7 days. You could substitute a locally made smoked mozzarella.

**SERVES 6 TO 8**

**2 or 3 eggplants, sliced into 18 to 24 slices ½ inch thick (about 3 lb total)**

**2 qt Chicken Brodo (page 88)**

**Salt, as needed**

**10 tbsp extra-virgin olive oil**

**½ cup finely minced yellow onion**

**2 tsp minced garlic**

**2¼ cups Carnaroli rice**

**½ cup Tomato Sauce (page 194)**

**4 fresh plum tomatoes, peeled, seeded, and diced**

**6 tbsp dry white wine**

**10 tbsp unsalted butter**

**½ cup grated Parmigiano-Reggiano (2 oz)**

**2 tbsp chopped basil**

**10 oz scamorza, thinly sliced**

1. Season the eggplant slices with salt and let them sit for at least an hour to drain off excess liquid. Rinse away the excess salt and blot dry with paper towels.
2. Bring the brodo to a boil and season it with salt; keep warm.
3. Over low heat in a large wide pan, heat the olive oil and sweat the onion until very tender but not colored, about 3 minutes. Add the garlic and cook for another minute. Add the rice and cook, stirring constantly, until each grain is translucent and hot. Be careful not to burn the onions or scorch the rice. Add the tomato sauce, tomatoes, and wine, stir to mix.
4. Add enough of the brodo to cover the rice by about ½ inch. Continue to cook, stirring from time to time and adding more broth until it has all been absorbed into the rice. Add the brodo as needed and stir occasionally to make sure the rice is not sticking to the bottom of the pan. Continue to cook for about 15 minutes.
5. While the risotto is cooking, prepare the eggplant: Heat about ¼ cup olive oil in a sauté pan over medium-high heat. Add the eggplant in batches and fry until golden brown on both sides, about 4 minutes total. Blot the fried eggplant on several layers of paper towels.
6. When the risotto is done, remove the pan from the stove. Add the butter, Parmigiano-Reggiano, and basil. Stir vigorously to create the characteristic creamy consistency.
7. Chop one-third of the eggplant and mix it in to the risotto. Make a layer of the risotto on a serving plate, topped with a layer of the eggplant slices, and then the scamorza. Continue until all the risotto, eggplant, and scamorza are used up. Serve at once.

**Wine notes:** The eggplant and scamorza make for a pliable pairing with wine. Fairly full-bodied whites and medium-bodied rosés and reds will match beautifully with this dish. The whites will make the food taste richer, and the rosés will add a fruity note to the dish. The reds will bring out the sweetness of the eggplant as the richness of the cheese tames the reds, emphasizing red and black fruit at the expense of complexity.

**White:** Greco di Tufo or Fiano di Avellino from Campania; Chardonnay from Sicily, Tuscany, Veneto, or Trentino-Alto Adige; Verdicchio from Le Marche

**Rosé:** Montepulciano d'Abruzzo Cerasuolo from Abruzzo

**Red:** Salice Salentino or Primitivo from Puglia; Cerasuolo di Vittoria or Merlot from Sicily; Montepulciano d'Abruzzo from Abruzzo; Valpolicella, Bardolino, or Merlot from Veneto; Lagrein or Teroldego Rotaliano, from Trentino; Pinot Nero/ Pinot Noir from Trentino-Alto Adige; Chianti from Tuscany; Sangiovese di Romagna from Emilia-Romagna

# Pesci

Italy offers cooks an abundance of different types of fish: trout from the mountains, swordfish from the sea, along with tuna, mackerel, pike, mullet, and more. Squid, octopus, and cuttlefish are enjoyed all along the coasts. One of the most anticipated meals of the year is the famous feast of seven fishes, traditionally served on Christmas Eve. Fish fillets are easy to find, but many of our recipes call for whole fish. The added "challenge" of eating fish from the bones is more than paid back in flavor and succulence.

Combinations of fish and seafood coordinate with the seasons and the region in classic soups and stews like brodetto di pesce. Dried and salted fish are an important ingredient in Italy, whether made into a savory stew, whipped in to a creamy spread, or turned into crispy fritters.

# Choosing fish and seafood for Italian dishes

Some types of fish familiar in Italy are difficult to find in this country, but if you know the appropriate quality of the fish—lean and delicate, meaty and firm, or rich and flaky—your fishmonger can help you find a suitable replacement. The flavors might differ a little from what you'd enjoy in Italy, but the dish will still be delicious.

### LEAN WHITE FISH

Catfish
Pickerel
Pike
Alaskan pollock
Cod
Flounder
Haddock
Sole

### FIRM, MODERATELY FATTY FISH

Trout
Salmon
Smelt
Anchovy
Sardine
Mackerel (kingfish)
Mullet
Red mullet
Snapper

### FIRM, FLAKY FISH

Walleye pike
Shad
Fluke
Perch
Orange roughy

### FIRM, MEATY FISH

Whitefish
Tuna
Swordfish
Grouper
Mahi-mahi
Shark
Monkfish
Skate
Tilefish

### PREPARING FINFISH

In some recipes, we suggest cooking the fish whole. The trade-off for having to pick out the bones as you eat is the enhanced flavor in the dish. You can almost always ask the fishmonger in your market to help with filleting, gutting, scaling, or trimming your fish.

Having said that, the basic techniques you need to know are not very difficult to master. Whole fish, sold with the head and fins in place, may need to be scaled. This is done by running a serving spoon against the grain. You can tell which way the scales lie by running your fingertips over the skin. This can be messy, so, if possible, work directly in a (very clean) kitchen sink.

Use a sharp knife or kitchen scissors to cut off the tail and fins, if you wish. To cut off the head, if you want to remove it, make a cut right behind the gills. A standard chef's knife is sturdy enough to cut through the bones of most fish.

# Pesce al forno in sale marino

## FISH BAKED IN SEA SALT

This is an unusual way to bake a fish, but if done correctly it will keep the whole fish moist and tasty. When the fish is done and you are ready to serve, crack open the salt layer, lift and discard that salt layer, and pull the skin from the top of the fish. Carefully lift the top fillet from the bones and transfer it to a plate; discard the bones. Gently lift the second fillet from the bones and transfer to a plate. You may serve this dish with salsa verde, lemon and olive oil, or any other condiment you prefer. Serve with salad or roasted potatoes or other roasted vegetables. Red snapper, striped bass, grouper, and dourade are some of the fish we suggest for this preparation.

**SERVES 4**

- 10 egg whites
- 6 cups sea salt or kosher salt, for crust
- One 4-lb whole fish, gutted and scales left on
- 1 cup fennel fronds
- 6 garlic cloves, crushed
- 10 flat-leaf parsley stems
- 4 thyme sprigs
- 2 rosemary sprigs
- ½ cup lemon zest

1. Preheat the oven to 400 degrees F.
2. Lightly whip the egg whites and fold them into the salt, mixing well until combined. It is supposed to be grainy, so if necessary add a little water.
3. Press a ¼-inch layer of the salt mixture onto a large baking sheet or in a casserole.
4. Stuff the cavity of each whole fish with the fennel, garlic, parsley, thyme, and rosemary. Cover the fish with the lemon zest.
5. Lay the fish on top of the salt and pack the remaining salt mixture over the fish to enclose it completely.
6. Roast for about 30 minutes, or until the internal temperature reaches 135 degrees F. There will be some carryover cooking once you remove the fish from the oven. Let stand for 5 to 10 minutes and serve.

Wine notes: This a wonderfully aromatic baked fish dish, but one with a delicate taste profile. Pair the wine to the flavor of the herbs, condiments, and accompaniments—such as roasted potatoes—which will help enhance the texture and flavor of the fish.

**White:** Gavi from Piedmont; Soave Classico from Veneto; Sauvignon or Friulano from Friuli-Venezia Giulia; Pinot Bianco or Pinot Grigio from Trentino-Alto Adige; Vermentino di Gallura from Sardinia; Falanghina, Greco di Tufo, or Fiano di Avellino from Campania; Verdicchio from Le Marche

# Fritto misto di pesce

## MIXED FRIED FISH

There are different variations of this recipe used to fry fish or any other items, such as vegetables. This is a version using a light batter. Depending on the amount of shrimp and fish you will be serving, adjust the amount of flour and water. Serve with any mayonnaise-based dipping sauce or a spicy tomato sauce.

**SERVES 4**

- 1 lb squid, cleaned, tentacles and bodies separated
- 12 medium shrimp (20/25 count), peeled and deveined
- 1 lb any type of fish, cleaned and skinned
- 2 cups warm water
- 2 tsp sea salt, plus more for sprinkling
- ¾ cup all-purpose flour, or as needed
- 2 qt mild olive oil or any frying oil
- 4 lemons, cut into wedges, for garnish

1. The squid tubes may be left whole or cut into rings. Leave the shrimp whole. Cut the fish into large pieces and set aside.
2. Mix the warm water and salt in a bowl until the salt is dissolved.
3. Place the flour in a flour sifter and gradually sift the flour over the salted water while you stir it with a whisk or fork. Keep on stirring, adding the flour until you have a batter that resembles heavy cream. Make sure no lumps are formed; this is why you want to take the time to sift the flour. Based on the quality and brand it might slightly vary, so adjust accordingly.
4. Heat the oil in a deep fryer or large deep pot to 370 degrees F. Dip seafood pieces one piece at the time into the batter and drop into the hot oil. Fry only a small amount at a time so that the oil always stays hot, resulting in perfectly cooked fried food.
5. Remove with a slotted spoon and transfer to a tray covered with paper towels. Sprinkle with salt and serve immediately with lemon wedges.

Wine notes: When pairing wine with fritto misto, go for a medium-bodied, dry, fruity white that will bring out the sweetness in the battered fish.

**White:** Vermentino di Gallura from Sardinia; Inzolia from Sicily; Falanghina from Campania; Sauvignon or Pinot Bianco from Friuli-Venezia Giulia; Pinot Grigio from Trentino-Alto Adige; Gavi or Roero Arneis from Piedmont; Orvieto from Umbria; Frascati from Lazio; Soave Classico from Veneto

# Branzino all'acqua pazza

## SEA BASS IN CRAZY WATER

This dish is typically from the south of Italy, but it is popular all over in many different variations. Use a little imagination and add your favorite ingredients to make it your own. You may cook the whole fish or just fillets. Meaty white fish works well, but stay away from very flaky fish to avoid breakage during cooking. (For suggestions, see page 230.)

**SERVES 4**

¼ cup extra-virgin olive oil

1 celery stalk, peeled and chopped

1 carrot, peeled, quartered, and chopped

2 garlic cloves, crushed

1½ cups dry white wine

1 cup water

½ cup basil, torn in small pieces

3 tbsp coarsely chopped flat-leaf parsley

2 thyme sprigs

1 rosemary sprig

1 bay leaf

3 cups peeled, seeded, and quartered tomatoes

Salt and freshly ground black pepper, as needed

Pinch crushed hot red pepper

One 5-lb whole branzino, cleaned, or four 6-oz fillets

1. Preheat the oven to 375 degrees F if you are preparing a whole fish.
2. In a heavy ovenproof pan, heat half of the oil over medium heat. Add the celery and carrot with the garlic and cook gently until tender, about 6 minutes.
3. Add the wine, water, half of the basil, and half of the parsley. Add all of the thyme and rosemary, the bay leaf, and tomatoes, and bring the mixture to a gentle simmer. Lightly season with salt and pepper and add the pepper flakes.
4. Season the fish with salt and pepper and place the fish on top of the vegetables. Spoon some of the vegetables and liquid over the fish. Cover the pan and finish the whole fish in the oven until cooked through, about 10 minutes. For fillets, cover the pan and cook over very low heat for another 4 minutes, then turn off the heat and let the residual heat in the liquid finish cooking the fillets.
5. Sprinkle the rest of the basil and parsley over the fish, and drizzle the rest of the olive oil over the top. Serve the fish in a large serving bowl with the liquid from the pan.
6. If you prefer a thicker consistency for the liquid, remove the fish from the pan and reduce the liquid on the stovetop to your taste, making sure to adjust seasoning as needed.

Wine notes: Branzino is a relatively hearty and very flavorful fish dish that needs a "background" of a medium- to full-bodied dry white wine to bring out its character.
**White:** Vernaccia di San Gimignano or Sauvignon Blanc from Tuscany; Falanghina or Fiano di Avellino from Campania; Pinot Grigio or Pinot Bianco from Trentino-Alto Adige; Friulano from Friuli-Venezia Giulia; Gavi from Piedmont; Soave Classico from Veneto; Verdicchio from Le Marche

# Brodetto di pesce

## FISH SOUP

Serve this soup with a thick slice of bread grilled and rubbed with garlic and some good extra-virgin olive oil. You may add some vegetables during the process of making the fish soup, but make sure you cook them first and add them at the end.

**SERVES 4 TO 6**

- 2 tbsp extra-virgin olive oil
- 3 garlic cloves, minced
- 2 lb red snapper fillet or other firm white fish
- ¼ cup chopped parsley
- ¼ cup chopped basil
- 1 tsp crushed hot red pepper
- ¼ tsp crushed saffron threads
- ½ lb scallops, muscle tabs removed
- 2 dozen mussels, scrubbed and debearded
- 2 dozen littleneck clams, scrubbed
- 1 cup dry white wine
- 1 cup chopped tomato (peeled and seeded)
- 4 cups Fish Broth (page 238)
- ½ lb shrimp or 1½ lb langoustines (heads on)
- Kosher salt and freshly ground black pepper as needed

1. In a large casserole, heat the oil with the garlic over medium heat. Add the fish and half of the parsley, basil, hot red pepper, and saffron. Don't move the fish around too much; some types are fragile and might break apart easily. Add the scallops, mussels, and clams and gently mix. Add the wine, and 2 minutes later, add the tomato and broth.
2. Bring to a simmer, add the shrimp, turn off the heat, cover, and let rest for few minutes to cook the seafood. The brodetto will be ready once the clams and mussels are completely open. Discard any that do not open. Add the rest of the parsley, basil, hot red pepper, and saffron. Season with salt and pepper. Serve at once.

Wine notes: Fish soup is a wonderfully bracing and satisfying dish, both tasty and aromatic. Almost any dry white wine in the medium-bodied range will work beautifully to bring out the fragrance and taste of the vegetables and the salinity of the fish and broth.

**White:** Trebbiano d'Abruzzo from Abruzzo; Vermentino di Sardegna from Sardinia; Falanghina from Campania; Inzolia from Sicily; Vermentino from Tuscany; Soave Classico from Veneto; Gavi from Piedmont; Pinot Bianco from Trentino-Alto Adige

# Fish broth

This broth can be stored in the refrigerator for up to 3 days. For longer storage, keep it in the freezer. It will last there for up to 5 weeks.

**MAKES 2 QUARTS**

- 1 medium yellow onion, minced
- 2 tbsp olive oil, as needed
- 1 celery stalk, finely chopped
- ½ cup sliced leek
- 1½ lb fish heads (gills removed) and fish bones
- ⅓ cup tomato paste
- 1 cup white wine
- 1 garlic clove, crushed
- 1½ cups minced white mushrooms (4 oz)
- 1 tbsp Sambuca or pastis (anise-flavored liqueur)
- Peel from ¼ orange (optional)
- 2 bay leaves
- ½ cup herbs, such as thyme, fennel fronds, and/or flat-leaf parsley stems
- Salt and freshly ground black pepper, as needed
- 3 qt boiling water

1. In a large pot, sweat the onion with the olive oil over low heat until translucent. Add the celery and leek. Cut the fish heads into pieces and add them, along with the fish bones, and mix well. After 2 minutes, add the tomato paste and blend.
2. Add the wine and stir well. Add the garlic, mushrooms, Sambuca or pastis, orange peel (if desired), bay leaves, herbs, and salt and pepper. Let everything cook down well, about 10 minutes, then add the boiling water and bring to a gentle simmer over low heat for about 20 minutes.
3. Strain the broth, discarding the solids. Before using, remove any fat that may have accumulated on top.

*A wide variety of seafood gives Brodetto di Pesce its full-bodied flavor.*

# Calamari ripieni

## STUFFED SQUID

For the stuffing, you may use your own imagination and personal tastes to create something new. One of our favorite variations is to replace the raisins with olives. You could also braise the stuffed squid in a tomato or red wine sauce instead of white wine. Serve with polenta or a small salad.

**SERVES 4 TO 6**

- 2 lb squid, cleaned, tentacles and bodies separated
- ¼ cup extra-virgin olive oil
- ½ cup minced yellow onion
- 1 garlic clove, chopped
- ½ cup chopped flat-leaf parsley
- 1 cup packed spinach, blanched and chopped (page 23)
- ½ cup grated Pecorino Romano or Parmigiano-Reggiano (2 oz)
- 2 salted anchovy fillets, rinsed well, cleaned, and chopped
- 1 tsp chopped oregano
- 1 tbsp raisins, softened in warm water and squeezed well
- 1 tbsp salted capers, rinsed and squeezed
- 2 tbsp pine nuts, toasted
- ½ cup fresh bread crumbs, toasted
- Kosher salt and freshly ground black pepper, as needed
- 4 bay leaves
- ½ cup dry white wine

1. Preheat the oven to 350 degrees F. Chop the squid tentacles coarsely.
2. In a medium sauté pan over medium-high heat, add half of the oil and sauté the onion and garlic until soft. Add the parsley. Mix in the tentacles and as soon as they change color, add the spinach and cook for 2 minutes. Remove the pan from the heat and add the cheese, anchovy fillets, oregano, raisins, capers, and pine nuts. Based on the wetness of the stuffing, add enough of the bread crumbs to hold everything together. Taste and season with salt and pepper.
3. Stuff each squid tube loosely with the stuffing, about 2 tablespoons per tube depending on the size of the squid, making sure you do not overstuff them as the stuffing will expand during cooking and might burst the squid body. Close the end of each squid body with a toothpick.
4. Add the rest of the olive oil to a large casserole, and arrange the bay leaves on the bottom. Arrange the squid in an even layer in the dish, and pour the white wine over the top. Bake for 25 to 30 minutes, until tender and lightly browned on top. Serve at once.

Wine notes: Medium-bodied southern Italian whites are ideal for this earthy squid preparation, but dry whites from other Italian wine regions will help bring out the amalgam of flavors and textures.

**White:** Inzolia from Sicily; Vermentino di Sardegna or Vermentino di Gallura from Sardinia; Falanghina from Campania; Orvieto Classico from Umbria; Vernaccia di San Gimignano from Tuscany; Soave Classico from Veneto; Pinot Grigio or Friulano from Friuli-Venezia Giulia; Pinot Bianco from Trentino-Alto Adige

# Stoccafisso in umido

## STEWED DRIED COD

There are many variations on and many different interpretations of this simple but delicious dish. You may add a variety of different ingredients and levels of seasoning. This is a very simple version that can be adjusted as you like. You may add a variety of ingredients, from peas to olives, but make sure you don't add too many ingredients or the flavors will get confusing. At times we think less is better and prefer to let the fish "talk." If you are not using potatoes, serve with polenta or couscous or any other hearty side dishes.

**SERVES 4**

- ½ cup extra-virgin olive oil
- 2 medium yellow onions, thinly sliced
- 3 garlic cloves, thinly sliced
- 2 tbsp chopped flat-leaf parsley leaves
- ½ tsp chopped thyme leaves
- 2 bay leaves
- 2 lb dried cod, reconstituted (page 241)
- ¾ cup white wine
- 1½ lb potatoes, peeled and sliced ¼ inch thick
- 2 cups peeled crushed tomatoes
- Sea salt and freshly ground black pepper, as needed
- 4 oz unpitted black olives

1. Preheat the oven to 350 degrees F.
2. Heat the oil in a large ovenproof skillet over medium-low heat with the onions, garlic, parsley, thyme, and bay leaves and cook for about 5 minutes.
3. Place the fish on top of the mixture in the skillet. Add the wine, potatoes, and crushed tomatoes. Season with salt and pepper, cover, and bake in the oven for about 7 minutes.
4. Remove the cover, add the olives, and continue to bake, covered, until the potatoes are fork-tender but not mushy, about 8 minutes longer.
5. Serve immediately with the potatoes as the bed for the fish and the tomato-olive sauce on top.

Wine notes: Let's let the fish do the talking, communicating clearly and simply with the wine. Medium-bodied dry whites, dry rosés, or sparkling Prosecco will provide an interesting and focused counterpoint to the blended flavors of fish, sauce, and potatoes.

**White:** Gavi from Piedmont; Soave Classico from Veneto; Pinot Grigio from Trentino-Alto Adige; Vernaccia di San Gimignano from Tuscany; Falanghina from Campania; Vermentino di Sardegna or Vermentino di Gallura from Sardinia

**Rosé:** Rosato from Valle d'Aosta; Lacrymarosa from Campania; Montepulciano d'Abruzzo Cerasuolo from Abruzzo

**Sparkling:** Prosecco from Veneto

## DRIED AND SALTED COD

Dried fish has been part of Italian culinary traditions for many generations. The fish keeps for a long time, making it ideal for the seasons or regions without a good supply of fresh fish. Also, the fact that Italy has a large Catholic population who traditionally abstained from meat on Fridays and throughout Lent also means that inventive Italian cooks have for centuries been at work devising delicious ways to serve fish.

Stoccafisso (or baccalà) is simply air-dried. Salt cod is salted and then dried. Both types of cod require some specific handling before you can cook them. Salt cod is the easier of the two to find in the United States, and it can be substituted in recipes that call for stoccafisso.

Stoccafisso needs to soak for a long time to soften the fish. Pound the stoccafisso with the flat side of a cleaver or a meat pounder to break it up. It will look stringy. Place the cod in a bowl and add enough cold water to cover it completely. Let it soak in the refrigerator for 48 to 72 hours, changing the water every 12 hours. When the stoccafisso has nearly doubled in volume, it is ready to drain and use.

Salt cod may be purchased in large pieces or chunks. You will find wooden boxes packed with salt cod in many Italian food shops. The salt cod must be soaked in cool water for at least 12 hours, or longer, depending upon how salty the cod you purchased is. You may need to let it soak for 2 or 3 days, so plan accordingly!

Place the salt cod in a bowl and add enough cold water to cover the fish completely. Let it soak in the refrigerator for 12 to 72 hours, changing the water every 8 to 10 hours until a piece of the salt cod tastes the way you want it: salty, but not unbearably so. Remove the fish from the water, and check the pieces for cartilage or skin and pull it away. Break the remaining cod into flakes and shreds.

# Baccalà mantecato

## WHIPPED SALT COD

Since it is difficult to find genuine stoccafisso in the United States, we recommend making this simple recipe using salt cod. Choose thick pieces when buying salted cod, as thinner pieces tend to be very salty and removing the salt from them might be a challenge. Grilled bread or polenta is the perfect accompaniment to this dish.

**SERVES 6 AS AN APPETIZER**

**1½ lb salt cod, thick pieces if possible, soaked (page 241)**

**2 garlic cloves, crushed**

**1 lb baking potatoes, peeled and quartered**

**4 cups milk**

**½ cup mild extra-virgin olive oil, or ¼ cup extra-virgin olive oil and ¼ cup canola oil**

**½ cup flat-leaf parsley leaves**

**¼ cup grated Parmigiano-Reggiano (1 oz)**

**Freshly ground black pepper, as needed**

1. In a large pot over medium-high heat, place the cod, 1 garlic clove, the potatoes, and milk and bring to a gentle simmer.
2. Once the potatoes are tender, drain the mixture, saving some of the liquid, unless it is very salty.
3. Place the drained potatoes, cod, and garlic in a food processor and, with the machine running, add the olive oil.
4. Chop the parsley leaves with the other clove of garlic and fold into the cod mixture.
5. If the whipped cod at this point is too thick, adjust with a little milk left over from the cooking, or if that liquid is too salty, you may add a little bit of cream or water.
6. Add the cheese and blend, season with black pepper, and serve.

Wine notes: This dish is really not complete until you pair it with a dry, medium-bodied white or sparkling wine. The wine will serve as a light "sauce" for the dish and create an almost unimaginable balance of flavors and textures. Get ready for a really spectacular food and wine pairing, deceptive in its simplicity.

**White:** Soave Classico or Chardonnay from Veneto; Gavi from Piedmont; Friulano or Sauvignon from Friuli-Venezia Giulia; Pinot Bianco or Pinot Grigio from Trentino-Alto Adige

**Sparkling:** Trentino or Trento from Trentino-Alto Adige; Prosecco from Veneto

# Frittelle di baccalà

## FRIED SALT COD FRITTERS

Remember to allow enough time for the salt cod to soak; it takes at least two days. If you like, serve these with a spicy tomato sauce or even a tartar sauce.

**SERVES 6 TO 8**

1½ lb salt cod, soaked (page 241)

BATTER

1½ cups all-purpose flour

2 tsp baking powder

1 cup cold bottled sparkling water

¼ bunch chives, thinly sliced

1 green onion, green part only, thinly sliced

Freshly ground black pepper, as needed

1 tsp chopped garlic

1 tbsp chopped flat-leaf parsley

½ red bell pepper, minced

3 qt olive or peanut oil, for frying

Lemon wedges, for serving

1. Break the cod apart with your fingertips into small pieces about 1 inch in size, and set aside.
2. To make the batter, sift the flour and baking powder together twice. Place the flour mixture in a medium bowl and slowly add the water. Mix well with a spoon until a smooth batter forms that coats the spoon evenly. Mix in the chives, green onion, black pepper, garlic, parsley, and bell pepper.
3. Heat the oil in a deep fryer or large deep pot to 375 degrees F. Combine the cod with enough batter to coat and bind the cod. Make a sample piece to test before you proceed with the rest as follows: Scoop up about 2 tablespoons of the cod mixture in a serving spoon and lower the mixture, still on the spoon, into the hot oil. Fry until the fritter rises to the surface and is golden brown on all sides, 3 to 4 minutes. Taste the fritter and if necessary, add more flour or liquid to the batter.
4. Fry the remaining batter, working in batches and letting the oil regain its heat between each batch. Once the fritters float to the top and are lightly colored after about 3 to 4 minutes, remove them with a slotted spoon, drain them briefly on paper towels, and serve immediately with lemon wedges.

Wine notes: For sparkling or white wine lovers, this is a match made in heaven. The briny, sweet flavors of the fritters serve as the perfect contrast to fruity but dry lighter whites as well as fruit-driven bubbly. Either way, the acidity in the wine will bring out the fresh sea taste of the dish.

**White:** Soave from Veneto; Gavi from Piedmont; Friulano or Sauvignon from Friuli-Venezia Giulia; Pinot Bianco from Trentino-Alto Adige

**Sparkling:** Trentino or Trento from Trentino-Alto Adige; Prosecco from Veneto; Franciacorta from Lombardy

# Luccio al vino rosso

## PIKE WITH RED WINE

Pike is a firm fish that flakes when you cook it. For alternatives, see page 230.

**SERVES 4 TO 6**

- 2 lb pike fillets
- Kosher salt and freshly ground black pepper, as needed
- All-purpose flour, as needed
- ½ cup (1 stick) unsalted butter, plus more as needed
- 12 baby carrots, peeled and halved crosswise
- 18 small cipollini or pearl onions, peeled
- 9 baby turnips, peeled and halved
- 1 cup red wine
- 2 thyme sprigs
- 2 bay leaves
- 2 tbsp minced lemon zest and flat-leaf parsley mixed together
- Fish Broth (page 238), as needed

1. Preheat the oven to 325 degrees F.
2. Season the fish fillets with salt and pepper and then coat them with flour.
3. In a large ovenproof sauté pan, heat the butter over medium-high heat until foamy. Shake the excess flour from the fillets and sauté until golden brown, 2 to 3 minutes on each side.
4. Remove the fillets from the pan and set aside. Add the carrots, cipollini or pearl onions, and turnips to the pan. Sauté the vegetables until they start to get color, about 6 minutes, and then add the fish back to the pan.
5. Add the wine, thyme, and bay leaves. Bring to a simmer, and then place in the oven and bake until the fish is cooked through and the flesh is opaque, about 5 minutes.
6. Transfer the fish to plates. Remove the herbs from the sauce in the pan and adjust the consistency of the sauce by adding some butter or broth, reducing it if necessary.
7. Pour the sauce and the vegetables on top of the fish and sprinkle the zest-parsley mixture on top. Serve at once.

---

Wine notes: With this hearty fish dish, you've got a choice of robust white wines or lighter reds. If you want to emphasize the delicacy of the pike, choose a white. If, however, you want to echo the more complex flavors of the sauce, you can build a bridge by selecting a red.

**White:** Roero Arneis or Chardonnay from Piedmont; Chardonnay or Pinot Grigio from Veneto, Trentino-Alto Adige, or Friuli-Venezia Giulia; Chardonnay from Sicily; Fiano di Avellino or Greco di Tufo from Campania

**Red:** Valpolicella from Veneto; Chianti from Tuscany; Grignolino, Dolcetto, or Freisa from Piedmont; Montepulciano d'Abruzzo from Abruzzo

# Naselli in bagna verde

## HAKE IN GREEN BROTH

Serve this with steamed potatoes and the vegetables of your choice.

**SERVES 4**

- 1¼ to 1½ lb hake fillets
- Kosher salt and freshly ground black pepper, as needed
- All-purpose flour, as needed
- 6 tbsp extra-virgin olive oil
- 2 garlic cloves, lightly crushed
- ¼ cup white wine
- 1 cup water
- ½ cup minced tarragon, parsley, oregano, and mint leaves, minced together

1. Season the fillets with salt and pepper and then coat them in flour.
2. In a medium sauté pan, heat the olive oil and garlic over medium-high heat. Add the fillets and sauté until lightly colored on both sides, about 3 to 4 minutes total.
3. Add the wine and let evaporate completely. Add the water and the herbs.
4. Cover the fish fillets and let them cook until they are cooked through and the flesh is opaque, about 5 minutes.
5. Adjust seasoning with salt and pepper, remove the garlic, and serve the fish with all the sauce. The sauce should be a beautiful green from all the herbs with a brothy consistency.

Wine notes: Here, we're looking for fish and herb-friendly white wines. A dry but fruit-driven white with perhaps a touch of spice makes for an exciting marriage of food and wine.

**White:** Gavi from Piedmont; Soave Classico from Veneto; Friulano or Sauvignon from Friuli-Venezia Giulia; Traminer (Gewürztraminer) or Sylvaner from Trentino-Alto Adige; Vermentino di Gallura from Sardinia

# Orata con patate e capperi

## SEA BREAM WITH POTATOES AND CAPERS

Sea bream is a popular fish in Europe, but it is not as common in the United States. Try it if you can find it, but if not, substitute a firm white fish like snapper or sea bass.

**SERVES 4**

- One 2-lb orata (sea bream), cleaned and scaled
- Sea salt, as needed
- 1 or 2 rosemary sprigs
- 4 or 5 small Yukon gold potatoes (1¼ lb)
- 1 bay leaf
- Pinch of dried oregano
- 2 tbsp salted capers, rinsed
- 4 plum tomatoes, peeled, seeded, and chopped
- ½ cup white wine
- 6 tbsp extra-virgin olive oil, plus more for serving

1. Preheat the oven to 350 degrees F.
2. Season the fish inside and out with salt, and place the rosemary in the cavity.
3. Slice the potatoes ⅛ to ¼ inch thick and place in a single layer in a baking dish large enough to fit the fish.
4. Place the fish on top of the potatoes, and sprinkle with the bay leaf, oregano, capers, tomatoes, and white wine. Drizzle with the olive oil and cover with foil.
5. Bake until the fish is cooked and the potatoes are tender, about 15 minutes.
6. Remove the orata from the pan. Place the potatoes on a serving platter and place the fish on top. Lightly reduce the liquid on the stovetop and pour over the fish. Drizzle with extra-virgin olive oil and serve.

Wine notes: This is a simply delicious dish, and when it comes to wine, put the accent on that simplicity. A dry white wine, relatively light in body and with soft fruit flavors, will contrast with the briny and salty flavors of the fish and capers and bring out the garden flavors of the tomatoes and herbs.

**White:** Salice Salentino Bianco or Chardonnay from Puglia; Falanghina from Campania; Vermentino di Sardegna from Sardinia; Trebbiano d'Abruzzo from Abruzzo; Gavi from Piedmont; Soave Classico from Veneto; Sauvignon Blanc from Tuscany; Sauvignon or Friulano from Friuli-Venezia Giulia; Pinot Bianco or Pinot Grigio from Trentino-Alto Adige

# Sardine in casseruola

## BAKED SARDINES

Baked sardines is a typical preparation in many regions in Italy, and the flavors included in this recipe are typical for the southern cuisine.

**SERVES 4 TO 6**

20 sardines (about 2½ lb)

¼ cup extra-virgin olive oil

4 plum tomatoes, peeled, seeded, and diced

Kosher salt, as needed

1 cup plain dry bread crumbs

1 tsp dried oregano

3 tbsp chopped flat-leaf parsley leaves

1 garlic clove, finely chopped

2 tbsp pecorino

2 tbsp white wine

1. Preheat the oven to 400 degrees F.
2. Clean the sardines and remove the heads if you prefer (see page 50). Rinse and dry the sardines, and place them in a baking dish large enough to perfectly fit all the sardines in one layer. Drizzle with the extra-virgin olive oil and sprinkle with the diced tomatoes. Season with salt.
3. Mix the bread crumbs with the oregano, parsley, garlic, and cheese. Moisten the bread crumb mixture with the white wine and sprinkle all over the sardines.
4. Bake until the sardines are cooked and the bread crumbs are crisp and golden, about 10 minutes. Serve hot.

Wine notes: The aromatic bread crumbs create a perfect foil for the delicate flavor and texture of the sardines, and the tomatoes provide a kick of acidity. The wine should also be fairly delicate and refreshing, but with enough structure to stand up to the earthy baked characteristics of the dish. Medium-bodied whites or light- to medium-bodied sparklers will pair beautifully.

**White:** Vermentino di Gallura from Sardinia; Falanghina from Campania; Gavi from Piedmont; Soave Classico from Veneto; Verdicchio from Le Marche; Friulano from Friuli-Venezia Giulia

**Sparkling:** Prosecco from Veneto; Franciacorta from Lombardy

# Sgombri con piselli

## MACKEREL WITH PEAS

Mackerel is an affordable fish commonly found in the Italian fish market. It is prepared in many ways. Here is a recipe suitable for making in the spring, when fresh sweet peas are available.

**SERVES 4 TO 6**

- 2 mackerel (about 1½ lb each)
- 5 or 6 green onions, peeled and sliced
- 6 tbsp extra-virgin olive oil, plus more for brushing
- 4 plum tomatoes, peeled, seeded, and diced (fresh or canned)
- ½ cup water
- Kosher salt, as needed
- 1 cup shelled fresh peas
- 2 tbsp coarsely chopped mint leaves

1. Preheat the oven to 350 degrees F.
2. Fillet the fish by running the knife blade from the head to the tail along the bones. Remove any small bones with tweezers.
3. In a pan large enough to fit the fillets, sweat the onions in the olive oil until translucent and tender, about 3 minutes. Add the tomatoes and cook for 3 minutes. Add the water.
4. Season the fish with salt, brush with some extra-virgin olive oil, and place the fish fillets skin side up on top of the tomatoes. Place the pan in the oven and bake for about 10 minutes, until the fillets are cooked through.
5. While the fish is cooking, cook the peas in an abundant amount of salted boiling water until tender but still firm.
6. When the fish is ready, remove the fillets from the pan and set the fish aside. Add the peas and the mint to the pan, and cook over low heat for 2 minutes to heat the peas and flavor the sauce. Serve the sauce over the fish fillets.

Wine notes: The briny flavors of the mackerel and the fresh, sweet flavors of peas and aromatic mint combine with dry, fruit-driven Italian whites or sparkling wines that are light enough to savor the nuances of flavor while still adding a refreshing acidity to encourage another bite of food, another sip of wine.

**White:** Inzolia from Sicily; Vermentino di Gallura from Sardinia; Vermentino or Sauvignon Blanc from Tuscany; Falanghina from Campania; Soave Classico from Veneto; Friulano or Sauvignon from Friuli-Venezia Giulia

**Sparkling:** Prosecco from Veneto

# Tonno alla ghiotta

## SICILIAN-STYLE TUNA STEAKS

This flavorful dish from Sicily reflects an Arab influence and incorporates the sweet-sour flavors from raisins, capers, pine nuts, and olives.

**SERVES 4**

Four 5-oz tuna steaks

Salt and freshly ground black pepper, as needed

6 tbsp extra-virgin olive oil

2 tsp minced garlic

1 cup sliced yellow onions

4 or 5 plum tomatoes, peeled, seeded, and chopped

¼ cup raisins

⅓ cup pine nuts

3 tbsp salted capers, soaked in water for 10 minutes and drained

3 tbsp minced pitted green olives

2 tbsp chopped flat-leaf parsley

2 tbsp chopped basil

1. Season the tuna with salt and pepper.
2. In a large sauté pan, heat the oil with the garlic over medium-high heat. Add the tuna and sauté, turning the steaks once, until golden on both sides, 3 to 4 minutes total. Remove the tuna and set aside.
3. In the same pan, sweat the onions over low heat, stirring frequently, until translucent, about 3 minutes. Add the tomatoes and cook for 5 minutes longer.
4. Add the raisins, pine nuts, capers, olives, parsley, and basil, and put the tuna back into the pan.
5. Cover with a lid and let slowly cook over low heat until the tuna is done, about 6 minutes.
6. Serve the fish with the sauce poured over the top.

Wine notes: Where to start? The intense, almost meaty flavor of the tuna steaks makes this a "crossover" dish when it comes to pairing with wine. True, a full-bodied white would match that intensity and create a compelling contrast for the sauce, but so would a dry rosé—still or sparkling—and a light- to medium-bodied red. Try serving a small glass of white and another of red or rosé, and see how the dish—and the wines—change.

**White:** Inzolia or Chardonnay from Sicily; Vermentino di Gallura from Sardinia; Fiano di Avellino or Greco di Tufo from Campania; Verdicchio from Le Marche; Pinot Grigio or Chardonnay from Trentino-Alto Adige or Friuli-Venezia Giulia; Chardonnay from Piedmont or Tuscany

**Rosé:** Rosato from Valle d'Aosta or Friuli-Venezia Giulia; Montepulciano d'Abruzzo Cerasuolo from Abruzzo; Lacryma-rosa from Campania

**Red:** Cerasuolo di Vittoria from Sicily; Valpolicella Classico from Veneto; Chianti from Tuscany; Sangiovese di Romagna from Emilia-Romagna; Dolcetto d'Alba from Piedmont; Pinot Nero from Trentino-Alto Adige

**Sparkling:** Franciacorta rosato from Lombardy; Trento rosato from Trentino-Alto Adige

# Involtini di pesce spada

## STUFFED GRILLED SWORDFISH

Salmoriglio sauce is a pungent but simple combination of olive oil, lemon, and oregano. Pass it at the table so that everyone can dress their fish to suit themselves.

**SERVES 4 TO 6**

SALMORIGLIO

**6 tbsp extra-virgin olive oil**

**2 tbsp lemon juice**

**1 garlic clove, lightly crushed**

**1 tbsp chopped flat-leaf parsley leaves**

**1 tsp chopped oregano leaves**

**½ tsp dried oregano**

**2 lb swordfish steaks**

STUFFING

**1 cup minced yellow onions**

**6 tbsp extra-virgin olive oil, plus more for brushing**

**1 garlic clove, minced**

**2 tbsp chopped flat-leaf parsley**

**2 tbsp chopped basil**

**1 tbsp salted capers, soaked in cold water for 10 minutes and drained**

**¾ cup plain dry bread crumbs**

**1 cup shredded provolone (4 oz)**

**Salt and freshly ground black pepper, as needed**

1. Preheat a grill to medium heat.
2. To make the salmoriglio, mix all the ingredients in a bowl.
3. Slice the swordfish into thin slices about ½ inch thick, pound them lightly, and trim the slices into a square shape. Mince the trimmings and reserve to add to the stuffing in step 4.
4. To make the stuffing, sweat the onions in 3 tablespoons olive oil over medium heat with the garlic, parsley, and basil until the onions are translucent, about 3 minutes. Add the capers and the trimmings from the swordfish. Add the bread crumbs and cook for 2 minutes. Remove from the heat and add the cheese. Season with salt and pepper.
5. Place some of the stuffing in the center of each slice of swordfish and roll them up. Place the rolls on skewers and brush with the remaining olive oil.
6. Grill, turning once, until golden brown on both sides and cooked through, 4 to 6 minutes.
7. Serve at once, drizzled with the salmoriglio or served on the side.

Wine notes: Stuffed grilled swordfish skewers drizzled with a fragrant, flavorful salmoriglio provide a delightful mix of the ocean and the earth. The grilled fish provides a sweet flavor and rich texture, while the stuffing and sauce provide a complex but fairly light mix of flavors. Medium- to full-bodied white wines, dry rosés, and refreshing sparklers will all add something different to the dish, but each of the wines will help to harmonize its disparate elements.

**White:** Inzolia from Sicily; Vermentino di Gallura from Sardinia; Falanghina from Campania; Verdicchio dei Castelli di Jesi Classico from Le Marche; Pinot Grigio from Trentino Alto-Adige or Friuli-Venezia Giulia; Gavi from Piedmont; Frascati Superiore from Lazio; Orvieto Classico from Umbria

**Rosé:** Rosato from Valle d'Aosta or Friuli-Venezia Giulia; Montepulciano d'Abruzzo Cerasuolo from Abruzzo; Lacrymarosa from Campania

**Sparkling:** Prosecco from Veneto

# Gamberi in padella con caponata

## PAN-ROASTED SHRIMP WITH CAPONATA

This dish combines several outstanding southern Italian flavors into one harmonious preparation. You could make a double or triple batch of the caponata to have on hand to top bruschetta.

**SERVES 6 TO 8**

### CAPONATA

- 1½ lb eggplant, coarsely chopped
- Salt, as needed
- 1 cup finely chopped yellow onions
- 2 small stalks celery heart, tender part only, finely chopped
- ¼ cup extra-virgin olive oil
- ½ cup Tomato Sauce (page 194)
- 2 tbsp toasted pine nuts
- 2 tbsp raisins
- ¼ cup green olives, pitted and sliced
- 1½ tbsp salted capers, soaked and drained
- 6 or 7 basil leaves
- 1 tbsp sugar
- ¼ cup red wine vinegar

### SHRIMP

- 40 medium shrimp (20/25 count), peeled and deveined
- Salt and freshly ground black pepper, as needed
- 2 tbsp extra-virgin olive oil, plus more for serving
- 3 tbsp chopped flat-leaf parsley leaves

1. To make the caponata, season the eggplant with salt and let it rest for at least 1 hour to leach part of the water out of the eggplant. Drain on paper towels.
2. In a large sauté pan, sweat the onions and celery in 2 tablespoons olive oil over medium-low heat until tender with no color, about 4 minutes. Add the tomato sauce. Cook for 5 minutes longer.
3. In a separate pan, fry the eggplant in 2 tablespoons of olive oil until soft and it has a nice dark color. Add the eggplant to the vegetables, toss to coat, and remove from the heat. Add the pine nuts, raisins, olives, capers, and basil.
4. In a saucepan, bring the sugar and vinegar to a boil. Pour over the caponata in the sauté pan. (The caponata is ready to serve now, or you can store it in a covered jar in the refrigerator for up to 3 days.)
5. Season the shrimp with salt and pepper and coat with olive oil. Quickly sauté in a medium nonstick pan over medium-high heat, turning as necessary, until cooked through, about 6 minutes.
6. Spoon the caponata into the center of the serving plate. Arrange the shrimp around the caponata and dress with the parsley and extra-virgin olive oil.

Wine notes: The shrimp is sweet and the caponata is salty and highly seasoned, so you need some fruit in the dry white wine to accompany the dish. The fruit mediates between the shrimp and the seasoned eggplant, creating an integrated taste experience.

**White:** Inzolia from Sicily; Vermentino di Sardegna or Vermentino di Gallura from Sardinia; Falanghina from Campania; Frascati or Est! Est!! Est!!! from Lazio; Orvieto Classico from Umbria; Gavi from Piedmont; Friulano or Sauvignon from Friuli-Venezia Giulia; Pinot Bianco from Trentino-Alto Adige

# Triglie in guazzetto

## RED MULLET STEW

The fish cooked with the bone in will flavor the sauce more intensely, but the recipe can be prepared with only the fillets as well.

**SERVES 6**

6 red mullets, scaled, cleaned, and rinsed (about 1 lb each)

Salt and freshly ground black pepper, as needed

¼ cup extra-virgin olive oil, or as needed

3 garlic cloves, minced

2 celery heart stalks, finely chopped

½ cup chopped flat-leaf parsley

6 to 8 plum tomatoes, peeled, seeded, and chopped

¼ cup dry white wine

½ cup water

1. Season the fish with salt and pepper.
2. In a large pan that can fit the fish comfortably, heat the olive oil over medium-high heat.
3. When the oil is hot, sauté the fish on one side for 2 minutes, then turn the fish and add the garlic, celery, and parsley to the pan. Cook for 2 minutes longer.
4. Add the tomatoes, wine, and water to the pan.
5. Cover and gently simmer until the fish is cooked through, 5 to 6 minutes depending upon the size. Transfer the fish to plates and serve it with the sauce.

Wine notes: Red mullet, simultaneously sweet and savory, is an extraordinarily wine-friendly fish, especially for medium-bodied dry whites and dry rosés. The fish brings out the fruit in the wine, and the wine brings out the sweetness in the mullet.

**White:** Vernaccia di San Gimignano or Sauvignon Blanc from Tuscany; Pinot Grigio from Friuli-Venezia Giulia or Trentino-Alto Adige; Gavi from Piedmont; Frascati Superiore from Lazio; Orvieto Classico from Umbria; Inzolia from Sicily; Vermentino di Gallura from Sardinia; Falanghina from Campania; Verdicchio from Le Marche

**Rosé:** Rosato from Valle d'Aosta or Friuli-Venezia Giulia; Montepulciano d'Abruzzo Cerasuolo from Abruzzo; Lacryma-rosa from Campania

# Trote ai funghi

## TROUT WITH MUSHROOMS

This recipe is typical in the northern part of Italy, where trout were traditionally available in mountain rivers and porcini foraged in the woods. Typically the trout are cooked whole with the porcini, sprinkled with parsley and garlic, and then drizzled with olive oil.

**SERVES 4**

- 4 trout fillets (about 6 oz each)
- Salt and freshly ground black pepper, as needed
- ½ cup olive oil
- 2 garlic cloves, finely chopped
- 4 tbsp chopped flat-leaf parsley leaves
- 1 lb fresh porcini mushrooms, sliced
- ¼ cup white wine

1. Preheat the oven to 350 degrees F.
2. Season the fish with salt and pepper. Add half of the olive oil to a medium sauté pan over medium-high heat and cook the fish, skin side down, until the skin is crispy, about 3 minutes.
3. Remove the fish from the pan and add the rest of the olive oil, along with the garlic and parsley.
4. Cook for about 2 minutes, and then add the porcini and cook until done, 4 to 5 minutes longer. Add the wine.
5. Add the fish fillets back to the pan and finish cooking them in the oven, about 5 minutes. Serve the fish with the mushrooms and any juices from the pan.

Wine notes: Ah, fresh trout! The sweetness of this freshwater fish coupled with the earthiness of the porcini mushrooms calls for a wine that can serve both stream and soil. Reasonably full-bodied whites, rosés, and sparklers will bring out the fresh flavors of the fish and the earthbound flavors of the porcini.

**White:** Terre di Franciacorta Bianco from Lombardy; Roero Arneis from Piedmont; Greco di Tufo from Campania; Chardonnay from Sicily, Veneto, Tuscany, or Trentino-Alto Adige; Pinot Grigio from Trentino-Alto Adige; Verdicchio from Le Marche
**Rosé:** Rosato from Friuli-Venezia Giulia; Montepulciano d'Abruzzo Cerasuolo from Abruzzo
**Sparkling:** Franciacorta from Lombardy

# Carni

If you think of Italian food only as pasta, you will be surprised at the number of big roasts and braises in this chapter. We offer a number of quick options as well, from sautés that "jump into the mouth" to quick grills. It shouldn't come as a surprise that Italians take full advantage of whatever the season has to offer, from little birds to rabbit, as well as veal, pork, and beef.

# Polenta col sugo di salsiccia

## POLENTA WITH SAUSAGE SAUCE

Sausage is an ingredient that may vary in taste according to the area of Italy you are in. In America, get a good-quality sausage made by your local butcher or another good source where you know it is consistent and not full of chemicals.

**SERVES 4**

1 oz dried porcini mushrooms

1 tbsp olive oil

2 lb Italian sausage, removed from casing

1 small yellow onion, minced

1 celery stalk, minced

½ leek, thinly sliced

1 carrot, thinly sliced

2 tbsp tomato paste

½ cup water

POLENTA

2 qt water

Salt, as needed

2 cups cornmeal (12 oz)

½ cup (1 stick) unsalted butter

½ cup grated Parmigiano-Reggiano (2 oz; optional)

¼ cup coarsely chopped flat-leaf parsley

1. Place the porcini mushrooms in a bowl and pour boiling water over them. Let them soak for 20 minutes, then drain and coarsely chop them.
2. In a saucepan, heat the oil, then add the sausage. Once the fat of the sausage starts rendering, after about 3 minutes, add the onion, celery, leek, carrot, and the porcini, making sure you break the sausage up as it starts cooking. Cook for 10 minutes longer, then mix the tomato paste with the water and add to the saucepan.
3. Stir well, cover, and cook very slowly for 30 to 40 minutes. If necessary, add a little bit of water during cooking to make sure the sauce doesn't stick to the bottom of the pan.
4. To make the polenta, bring the water to a simmer. Add salt and slowly add the cornmeal, making sure you whisk continuously. Simmer gently for about 45 minutes or until the polenta is done, stirring frequently to make sure the polenta does not stick.
5. Remove the polenta from the heat, adjust seasoning, and add the butter and cheese, if using, mixing vigorously until combined.
6. Add the parsley to the sausage mixture. Serve the polenta and sausage together.

Wine notes: This dish pairs beautifully with either a full-bodied white wine or a medium-bodied red. The white will bring out the earthy flavors of the sausage and mushrooms, while that same earthy character of this dish will bring out the fruit in the red wine.

**White:** Verdicchio dei Castelli di Jesi Classico Superiore from Le Marche; Greco di Tufo from Campania; Chardonnay from Veneto, Friuli-Venezia Giulia, Trentino-Alto Adige, or Sicily

**Red:** Valpolicella Classico, Bardolino Classico, or Merlot from Veneto; Chianti from Tuscany; Sangiovese di Romagna from Emilia-Romagna; Dolcetto d'Alba, Dolcetto di Dogliani, Barbera d'Asti, or Barbera d'Alba from Piedmont; Pinot Nero/Pinot Noir or Teroldego Rotaliano from Trentino-Alto Adige

# Maiale al latte

## MILK-BRAISED PORK

This particular simple dish, if done properly, is very tender and delicious. For a good presentation, serve it on the bone, but make sure you ask your butcher to remove the chine before you proceed with the recipe; if you try to slice it when the chine is still in it, it will fall apart. This recipe is a combination of braising and roasting. You may wrap the pork in bacon for a smoky flavor when searing it, or even stud the pork with garlic and sage, or rub it with a chopped mixture of parsley, rosemary, and garlic. This dish is meant to be served with mashed potatoes or braised leeks or even with some cabbage. Other suggestions: braised chestnuts, carrots, Brussels sprouts, turnips, parsnips, or any type of squash. You may also use different cuts of meat such as pork shank or butt, which will also be very delicious.

**SERVES 6**

- 1 bone-in pork loin roast (about 7 lb)
- Salt and freshly ground black pepper, as needed
- 4 rosemary sprigs, chopped
- 4 sage sprigs, chopped
- ¼ cup (½ stick) unsalted butter
- ¼ cup canola oil
- 2½ lb yellow onions, diced
- 2 bay leaves
- 1½ cups dry white wine
- 2 lb Idaho potatoes, peeled and thickly sliced
- 2 qt milk, or as needed

1. Preheat the oven to 325 degrees F. Season the pork with salt and pepper and half of the rosemary and sage.
2. Heat the butter and oil in a large pot over high heat until very hot. Sear the pork well on each side, about 4 minutes per side. Remove the pork and set aside.
3. In the same pot over medium-high heat, sweat the onions until translucent but with no color, about 10 minutes. Add the remaining chopped herbs, the bay leaves, and pork.
4. Add the wine and stir to combine. Add the potatoes, mix well, and then add just enough milk to cover the meat.
5. Cover and bake for about 50 minutes or until the meat is very tender and the internal temperature is 160 to 165 degrees F. During cooking you might have to add a little more liquid if the dish gets too dry.
6. Remove from the oven. Discard the bay leaves, transfer the liquid with the onions, potatoes, and herbs to a blender, and puree. Adjust seasoning, and if necessary reduce the pureed sauce on the stovetop to a creamy consistency.
7. Slice the pork. Each bone is one portion. Serve with the onion-and-potato sauce.

Wine notes: The braising/roasting combo of cooking methods creates a succulent dish that needs a complex white wine or a fruity but rich red.

**White:** Chardonnay from Tuscany, Veneto, Trentino-Alto Adige, Piedmont, or Sicily; Pinot Grigio from Trentino-Alto Adige; Fiano di Avellino from Campania

**Red:** Chianti Classico, Rosso di Montalcino, or Rosso di Montepulciano from Tuscany; Montefalco Rosso or Torgiano Rosso from Umbria; Valpolicella Ripasso from Veneto; Montepulciano d'Abruzzo from Abruzzo; Aglianico del Vulture from Basilicata; Salice Salentino or Primitivo from Puglia; Cerasuolo di Vittoria or Merlot from Sicily; Pinot Noir/Pinot Nero from Trentino-Alto Adige or Valle d'Aosta

Pork rack tied and seasoned for searing

# Agnello scottadito con fave alla romana

## "BURN YOUR FINGER" LAMB CHOPS WITH FAVA BEANS, ROMAN-STYLE

This is traditionally eaten in the spring, from May 1 (a national holiday) through June. We love to enjoy it when favas are young and fresh enough to eat raw or just barely cooked with olive oil and lemon juice.

**SERVES 4 TO 6**

1 cup olive oil

2 garlic cloves, thinly sliced

2 rosemary sprigs, leaves chopped

2 thyme sprigs, leaves chopped

Salt and freshly ground black pepper, as needed

12 to 18 lamb chops (about 3½ oz each)

FAVE ALLA ROMANA

4 lb broad beans in the shell

¼ cup extra-virgin olive oil

½ medium yellow onion, minced

2½ oz pancetta, cut into small cubes

Salt and freshly ground black pepper, as needed

¼ cup dry white wine

½ cup water

½ cup chopped flat-leaf parsley

1. Mix the oil, garlic, rosemary, thyme, and salt and pepper in a large baking dish. Marinate the lamb in this mixture in the refrigerator for at least 4 hours.
2. To make the fave alla Romana, hull the beans and, if very large, peel the surface; the peel is sometimes bitter.
3. Heat the oil in a large skillet over medium heat. Add the onion and cook for about 3 minutes, or until soft but with no color. Add the pancetta and let brown for 2 to 3 minutes longer, until well rendered.
4. Add the beans, season with salt and pepper, and stir. Add the wine and let it evaporate, then add the water and cook for 10 to 15 minutes.
5. Heat a grill to high temperature. Remove the lamb chops from the marinade, dragging them across the edge of the container to remove the excess and grill over direct heat, turning once, until browned on both sides and cooked to medium rare, about 3 minutes on each side.
6. Just before serving, add the parsley to the beans, and serve hot with the lamb chops.

Wine notes: With its rich texture and rustic flavors, this delicious dish will pair well with a medium- to full-bodied red wine that is both elegant and earthy.

**Red:** Torgiano Rosso or Montefalco Rosso from Umbria; Chianti Classico Riserva, Carmignano, Vino Nobile di Montepulciano, or Rosso di Montalcino from Tuscany; Barbera d'Alba, Nebbiolo d'Alba, Gattinara, or Ghemme from Piedmont; Aglianico del Vulture from Basilicata; Cerasuolo di Vittoria from Sicily; Cannonau di Sardegna from Sardinia

# Coscia d'agnello arrostita

## ROASTED LEG OF LAMB

This lamb is cooked for quite a long time and is cooked to medium-well. If you want to serve it medium-rare or medium, just remove the lamb when the inside temperature reaches 120 to 125 degrees F, and then let it rest before you carve it. We love this dish with a simple warm potato salad made with onion, lots of parsley, olive oil, and a splash of red wine vinegar, but any vegetables or starches can go with it.

**SERVES 8**

- 6 lb bone-in leg of lamb roast
- ½ cup honey
- 1 cup chopped mixed herbs, such as thyme, mint, rosemary, marjoram, and flat-leaf parsley
- ¼ cup water
- ½ cup (1 stick) unsalted butter, softened
- 2 tbsp chopped anchovies
- 2 tbsp olive oil
- Salt and freshly ground black pepper, as needed
- 5 garlic cloves, crushed
- 1½ cups chicken Brodo (page 88)
- 1 tsp crushed hot red pepper

1. At least 8 hours or the day before you plan to cook the lamb, trim the leg of excess fat.
2. Mix the honey with the herbs and add just enough water to create a smooth paste. Spread the honey-herb paste all over the lamb, massaging the meat well. Cover and refrigerate for at least 4 hours and up to 24 hours.
3. Mix the butter with the anchovies and set aside.
4. Remove the leg from the refrigerator and season it with the olive oil, and salt and pepper. Create a few cuts around the leg and insert the garlic cloves, spreading the anchovy-butter mixture inside the cuts too. Refrigerate for 4 hours longer.
5. Preheat the oven to 400 degrees F. Place the lamb on a roasting rack.
6. As soon as the lamb is in the oven, turn the temperature down to 275 degrees F and roast it for about 1½ hours, basting occasionally with the pan drippings.
7. Turn the leg over and keep on roasting for 30 to 40 minutes longer or until the internal temperature reaches 130 degrees F; make sure that you keep on basting the leg with the drippings.
8. Cover the lamb with aluminum foil and let it rest for at least 15 minutes before carving. The internal temperature will rise to 135 to 140 degrees F during this time.
9. Meanwhile, prepare the sauce for the lamb. Remove any excess fat from the roasting pan, add the chicken brodo directly to the roasting pan, and scrape up any brown bits on the bottom. Place on the stovetop and boil until slightly reduced.
10. Strain the sauce and season with salt and pepper and hot red pepper. Serve with the lamb.

Wine notes: This hearty dish calls for a full-bodied wine with great character. The impact of the food and wine pairing should create a "second sauce" on the palate.

**Red:** Brunello di Montalcino, Cabernet Sauvignon, Syrah, or Merlot from Tuscany; Barolo or Barbaresco from Piedmont; Taurasi from Campania; Inferno or Grumello, from Lombardy; Sagrantino di Montefalco from Umbria; Nero d'Avola from Sicily

# Cima alla genovese

## VEAL BREAST GENOA-STYLE

This is a typical meat dish from Genoa. It is a classic recipe, but you may omit or add anything you like. You may serve this meat on a hot or cold sandwich, or by itself with mashed potatoes or a salad. On a buffet, it could be your centerpiece to carve as needed.

**SERVES 8 AS A ROAST**

- 8 oz ground pork
- 3 oz mortadella, cut into small cubes
- 3 bread slices, soaked in ½ cup milk, squeezed and broken up
- 3 tbsp grated Parmigiano-Reggiano
- 4 large eggs, lightly beaten
- ¼ cup shelled unsalted pistachios
- ¼ tsp grated nutmeg
- Salt and freshly ground black pepper, as needed
- 3 to 4 lb veal breast, cleaned and butterflied (ask your butcher)
- 4 oz chicken tenders, soaked in Marsala for a few hours
- ¼ cup cooked peas
- 3 hard-cooked eggs, quartered

1. Mix together the ground pork, mortadella, bread, cheese, eggs, pistachios, nutmeg and salt and pepper.
2. Spread the meat filling in the center of the butterflied veal breast. Place the chicken pieces, peas, and eggs randomly over the filling.
3. Using thin butcher twine and a meat needle, sew the extremities of the veal breast so that the filling will not spill out during cooking.
4. Place in a casserole large enough to hold the meat. Add enough water to cover and enough salt to season the water and bring to a gentle simmer. Simmer for about 2 hours, until completely cooked through. Remove the breast from the casserole. Slice and serve warm, or, to serve cold, place on a dish and top with a board or a platter. Put a weight (a few cans of tomatoes, for instance) on top of the board and refrigerate until completely cold before slicing.

Wine notes: If you are serving this veal dish cold in a sandwich or warm with a salad, consider a medium-bodied white or have some fun with a sparkling rosato, which will make it seem as though you added red currants to the dish. If carving the meat for a buffet or serving with potatoes, think about pairing it with a fruity, lighter red.

**White:** Pigato or Vermentino from Liguria; Vermentino from Tuscany; Traminer (Gewürztraminer), Riesling, or Sylvaner from Trentino-Alto Adige; Chardonnay from Veneto, Tuscany, Friuli-Venezia Giulia, Piedmont, or Sicily; Roero Arneis from Piedmont

**Red:** Rossese di Dolceacqua from Liguria; Chianti from Tuscany; Dolcetto d'Alba from Piedmont; Pinot Nero/Pinot Noir from Trentino-Alto Adige or Valle d'Aosta; Montepulciano d'Abruzzo from Abruzzo; Primitivo di Manduria or Salice Salentino from Puglia

**Sparkling:** Franciacorta Rosato from Lombardy; Trento Rosato from Trentino-Alto Adige

# Spezzatino con patate e piselli

## VEAL STEW WITH POTATOES AND PEAS

You may use veal, beef, pork, chicken, or any kind of meat when preparing this dish. For veal stew, choose meat from the shoulder or ask your butcher for advice. Avoid any very tender or lean piece of meat, as it won't be very tasty. You may add any vegetables to the spezzatino, such as baby carrots, turnips, mushrooms, or Jerusalem artichokes. You may omit the tomato paste and add crushed tomatoes also; just adjust the amount of liquid a little to compensate.

SERVES 4

- 2 lb boneless veal round, cut into 1-inch cubes
- Salt and freshly ground black pepper, as needed
- ¼ cup olive oil
- All-purpose flour. as needed
- 1 celery stalk, diced
- 1 carrot, diced
- 1 medium yellow onion, minced
- 2 tbsp tomato paste
- 1 cup dry white wine
- 1 cup veal or chicken Brodo (page 88)
- 1 bundle herb sprigs, such as rosemary, bay leaf, flat-leaf parsley, and thyme
- 2 potatoes, diced (about 1½ lb)
- ¾ cup shelled green peas
- 2 tbsp chopped flat-leaf parsley

1. Season the meat with salt and pepper. In a Dutch oven, heat the oil over medium-high heat, dust the meat with flour, and sear the veal well, making sure all sides are browned, about 8 minutes total. Remove from the Dutch oven.
2. Lower the heat, add the celery, carrot, and onion to the Dutch oven, and sweat them well, about 5 minutes. Add the veal and cook for few minutes, then add the tomato paste and, after 1 minute longer, the wine.
3. Let the wine evaporate, then sprinkle 1 tablespoon of flour on top and combine well.
4. Add the brodo and the herb bundle, cover, and gently simmer for about 1 hour.
5. Add the potatoes and cook for 20 to 25 minutes. Add the peas and cook until done, about 10 minutes longer.
6. Remove the meat from the sauce, raise the heat, and reduce the sauce until the desired consistency is achieved. Adjust seasoning with salt and pepper. Then put the veal back into the sauce, add the parsley, and serve.

**Wine notes:** This delicious stew needs a medium-bodied red wine that enhances the sauce and simultaneously refreshes the palate, encouraging another bite of food, another sip of wine. **Red:** Barbera d'Asti or Barbera d'Alba from Piedmont; Inferno or Grumello from Lombardy; Merlot, Valpolicella Ripasso, or Bardolino Classico Superiore from Veneto; Chianti Classico, Rosso di Montalcino, or Carmignano from Tuscany; Montefalco Rosso or Torgiano Rosso from Umbria; Primitivo di Manduria from Puglia; Aglianico del Vulture from Basilicata; Cerasuolo di Vittoria from Sicily

# Brasato di manzo al barolo con pure di patate

## BRAISED BEEF IN BAROLO WITH MASHED POTATOES

This dish is typical to Piedmont but is made pretty much all over Italy. You will find recipes with different types of wine, no tomato product, or no celery or carrot. Here we try to give you a simple way to prepare it with easy steps. Enjoy it. We like to accompany this with a simple potato puree (recipe follows), but polenta is also a good friend to this wonderful dish. Cipollini, boiled potatoes, mushrooms, and other vegetables may be served with it as well.

**SERVES 4 TO 5**

- 3 lb boneless beef chuck or shank, trimmed
- Salt and freshly ground black pepper, as needed
- ¼ cup olive oil
- 1 medium yellow onion, diced
- ½ carrot, diced
- ½ celery stalk, diced
- 2 tsp tomato paste
- 1¼ cups Barolo
- 1 sachet containing 1 bay leaf, 1 rosemary sprig, 1 thyme sprig, 3 juniper berries, crushed, 1 garlic clove, crushed, 4 whole black peppercorns, and peel from ¼ orange
- 2 cups beef Brodo (page 88), or as needed
- Fresh horseradish (optional)

1. Preheat the oven to 300 degrees F.
2. Season the beef with salt and pepper and, if necessary, tie it into a roast with butcher's twine.
3. Heat the oil in a Dutch oven and add the beef. Sear all sides of the beef until well colored, about 8 minutes total. Remove and set aside.
4. Add the onion to the Dutch oven and sweat for a few minutes, then add the carrot and celery. Add the tomato paste and let it cook over low heat until it has a sweet aroma and a deep color, about 3 minutes.
5. Put the beef back into the Dutch oven and add the wine. Lower the heat and let the liquid reduce by half.
6. Add the sachet and enough brodo to just cover the beef.
7. Cover and bake for about 2½ hours or until fork-tender. Remove and discard the sachet.
8. Gently remove the beef from the Dutch oven. Pass the sauce with vegetables through a food mill and check for consistency. If too thin, reduce by cooking over medium-high heat until it thickens. If too thick, add more brodo. Adjust seasoning with salt and pepper.
9. Remove the twine from the meat, if necessary, and cut into ¼-inch slices. Serve with the sauce on top. If desired, you may grate some fresh horseradish over the top just before serving.

# Potato purée

**SERVES 4 TO 6**

2 lb Yukon gold or russet potatoes

½ cup milk

¼ cup (½ stick) unsalted butter

Salt, as needed

1. Place the potatoes in a large saucepan and cover with cold water. Bring to a boil, then reduce the heat and simmer until tender, 20 to 25 minutes.
2. Drain, peel, and mash the potatoes. Put the potatoes in a large saucepan over medium heat and cook until they dry out a bit, about 1 minute.
3. Heat the milk until warm. Stir the butter into the mashed potatoes and whip. Add the milk and whip again, until nice and creamy. Season with salt.

Wine notes: Barolo in the sauce echoed by Barolo in the glass is a can't-miss marriage of food and wine, but any of these wines, all made from 100 percent Nebbiolo grapes, will pair beautifully.

**Red:** Barolo, Barbaresco, Roero, Nebbiolo d'Alba, or Langhe Nebbiolo from Piedmont

# Costolette alla valdostana

## VEAL CHOPS WITH FONTINA

The best way to prepare this dish is to have some good white truffle on hand and shave some on top just before serving it. As it could be quite expensive you may omit the truffle and simply drizzle a few drops of truffle oil inside the chops when stuffing them with the Fontina cheese. You may also use pork chops for this preparation, and if you want to avoid the butterflying procedure, you may simply cook the chops in butter and sage, and once ready, place a piece of Fontina on top (you may also place a slice of prosciutto or bacon on the chop before the Fontina). Then finish in the oven until the cheese is completely melted. You may serve this dish with wilted spinach (page 23) and potato purée (previous page), or a side of sautéed mushrooms (page 257).

**SERVES 4**

- 4 veal chops (about 14 oz each)
- 6 oz Fontina cheese, thinly sliced
- Salt and freshly ground black pepper, as needed
- 1 cup all-purpose flour
- 3 large eggs, beaten
- 2 cups plain dry bread crumbs
- 6 tbsp (¾ stick) unsalted butter
- ½ cup olive oil
- ½ oz white truffle (optional)

1. Butterfly the veal chops by cutting through them horizontally toward the bone, leaving the bone attached.
2. Slightly flatten the chops and place 1½ ounces of sliced cheese on the inside of each chop.
3. Season the chops inside and out with salt and pepper. Pound the edges together with a mallet, making sure the cheese is sealed inside the chop.
4. Put the flour, eggs, and bread crumbs in three separate shallow bowls. Dust each chop with flour, then dip into the eggs, and then dip into the bread crumbs.
5. Heat the butter and oil in a large skillet. Place the veal chops in the skillet and cook for 3 to 4 minutes on each side, until golden brown. If the chops are very thick, you may finish them in the oven at 400 degrees F, about 15 minutes.
6. If desired, serve with shaved white truffle on top.

Wine notes: The veal chop and the Fontina will be right at home with a substantial white, perhaps with a bit of spice on the palate, or a light- to medium-bodied fruity red. Both whites and reds will complement the flavors of the veal while creating a bracing contrast to the richness of the melted cheese.

**White:** Chardonnay from Valle d'Aosta, Piedmont, Veneto, Trentino-Alto Adige, or Sicily; Pinot Grigio from Trentino-Alto Adige; Greco di Tufo or Fiano di Avellino from Campania; Traminer (Gewürztraminer) from Trentino-Alto Adige

**Red:** Pinot Nero/Pinot Noir from Valle d'Aosta or Trentino-Alto Adige; Dolcetto d'Alba or Dolcetto d'Asti from Piedmont; Merlot, Valpolicella Classico, or Bardolino Classico from Veneto; Teroldego Rotaliano or Lagrein from Trentino

# Costolette di vitello alla milanese

## VEAL CHOPS MILANESE

The best way to eat the classic Milanese is to leave the chop almost as is, without pounding it too thin. When you buy the chops, try to get the center cut of the rack, not the end. Serve with a potato salad simply dressed with olive oil, salt, pepper, and some minced red onion and a salad of arugula with tomato.

**SERVES 4**

4 veal chops (about 14 oz each)

1 cup all-purpose flour

4 large eggs, beaten

3 cups soft white bread crumbs

6 tbsp (¾ stick) unsalted butter

½ cup olive oil

Salt and freshly ground black pepper, as needed

1 lemon, cut into wedges

1. Slightly flatten the chops with a mallet or rolling pin just enough to enlarge them just a little.
2. Put the flour, eggs, and bread crumbs in three separate shallow bowls. Dust each chop with flour, then dip into the eggs, and then dip into the bread crumbs, making sure you press the bread crumbs well into each side of the chop.
3. Heat the butter and oil in a large skillet over medium heat, and when the butter stops foaming, add the veal chops and cook for about 5 minutes on one side, until lightly golden.
4. Turn the chop, season with salt and pepper, and cook for 5 minutes longer, making sure both sides are lightly golden brown.
5. Serve immediately with lemon wedges.

Wine notes: Either whites or reds—both medium-bodied—will work well with this dish. If you want to highlight the sweetness of the dish and the refreshing acidity of the lemon, choose a white. If you choose to focus on the meaty qualities of the chops, look no further than fruity reds.

**White:** Roero Arneis or Chardonnay from Piedmont; Chardonnay from Veneto, Trentino-Alto Adige, Friuli-Venezia Giulia, or Sicily; Verdicchio dei Castelli di Jesi Classico Superiore or Verdicchio di Matelica from Le Marche

**Red:** Grumello from Lombardy; Dolcetto d'Alba or Barbera d'Asti from Piedmont; Valpolicella Classico Superiore, Valpolicella Ripasso, Bardolino Classico Superiore, or Merlot from Veneto; Chianti Classico or Rosso di Montalcino from Tuscany; Torgiano Rosso from Umbria; Primitivo or Salice Salentino from Puglia; Cannonau di Sardegna from Sardinia

# Fegato alla veneziana

## VENETIAN-STYLE LIVER

When you go to your butcher, choose the calf liver that is nice in color and firm, not slimy or smelly, of course. Another quick way to prepare this classic dish is to cook the liver in hot oil in one pan and the onions in another pan. Then combine them and finish with a little olive oil and fresh parsley, without adding any acidity. Serve this with grilled polenta.

**SERVES 4**

¼ cup olive oil

2 medium yellow onions, chopped

1 bay leaf

Salt and freshly ground black pepper, as needed

1 lb calf's liver, thinly sliced and cut into 2-inch pieces

All-purpose flour, as needed (optional)

½ cup dry white wine

¼ cup Chicken Brodo (page 88; optional)

¼ cup (½ stick) unsalted butter, cubed

½ cup chopped flat-leaf parsley

1. Heat half of the oil in a large skillet over low heat and sweat the onions with the bay leaf and a little salt and pepper until cooked but not brown, 10 to 12 minutes. Set the onions aside.
2. Heat another skillet over high heat with the rest of the oil. Dust the liver with a little flour just before you put it in the hot oil, if you wish. Put the liver in the oil and quickly sauté, turning as necessary to color the liver on all sides. This will only take 1 or 2 minutes, due to the very thin cut of the liver.
3. As soon the liver starts to develop some coloring, add the reserved onions and sauté together with the liver over high heat for 1 minute. Add the wine and brodo, if using, and simmer for another minute.
4. Adjust seasoning with salt and pepper, remove the liver and onions from the pan, and top with the butter and parsley. Serve immediately.

Wine notes: Very earthy in flavor but quite delicate in texture, this dish needs a wine that mirrors those qualities. Lighter, fruitier reds will do the trick with this dish.

**Red:** Valpolicella Classico or Bardolino Classico from Veneto; Chianti from Tuscany; Dolcetto d'Alba from Piedmont; Merlot or Pinot Nero/Pinot Noir from Trentino-Alto Adige; Montepulciano d'Abruzzo from Abruzzo; Cerasuolo di Vittoria from Sicily

# Involtini di verza in umido

## STEWED STUFFED CABBAGE ROLLS

This is one of those dishes that every country in Europe claims as its own. This is a simple way to prepare it, and if you feel like it you may add any other flavor to the stuffing. You may use a combination of veal, pork, and beef if you like, or even chicken. You may also substitute brown rice or any grains for the white rice. Serve with potato purée (page 270) or polenta (page 261).

**SERVES 4 TO 6**

- 12 green cabbage leaves
- 1 lb ground beef
- 1 lb loose pork sausage
- ¾ cup cooked rice
- 1 medium yellow onion, minced
- Salt and freshly ground black pepper, as needed
- 2 cups crushed peeled tomatoes
- 1 cup water or chicken Brodo (page 88)
- 2 bay leaves
- ¼ cup coarsely chopped flat-leaf parsley
- ½ tsp chopped oregano leaves

1. Bring a large pot of salted water to a boil and blanch the cabbage leaves for 1 minute or until soft and limp. Remove, drain, and let cool.
2. Preheat the oven to 350 degrees F. Mix the beef, sausage, rice, onion, salt and pepper, and ¾ cup of the crushed tomatoes in a large bowl until combined.
3. Place some of the meat mixture in each cabbage leaf, and roll up to form a package, making sure you close the edges of the cabbage leaves, tucking all sides under.
4. Place the cabbage rolls seam side down in a 9 X 13-inch baking dish. Pour the remaining crushed tomatoes over the top, and then the water or brodo, and then the bay leaves, parsley, and oregano. Cover and bake for about 40 minutes, or until the cabbage is very tender and the filling is very hot.
5. Remove the cabbage rolls from the baking dish, and, if desired, reduce the sauce to a thick consistency on the stovetop. Pour the sauce over the cabbage rolls just before serving.

Wine notes: If serving the cabbage rolls for lunch or as an appetizer at dinner, pair with a white wine or perhaps a sparkler to lighten the dish. If serving as a main course with polenta or potatoes, bring out the medium-bodied reds to match the intensity of flavors.

**White:** Verdicchio dei Castelli di Jesi Classico Superiore from Le Marche; Chardonnay from Piedmont, Tuscany, Veneto, Trentino-Alto Adige, or Sicily

**Red:** Grumello from Lombardy; Dolcetto di Dogliani or Dolcetto d'Alba from Piedmont; Valpolicella, Bardolino, or Merlot from Veneto; Refosco or Merlot from Friuli-Venezia Giulia; Lagrein, Teroldego Rotaliano, Pinot Nero/Pinot Noir, or Merlot from Trentino-Alto Adige; Chianti from Tuscany; Montepulciano d'Abruzzo from Abruzzo; Salice Salentino or Primitivo from Puglia

**Sparkling:** Franciacorta from Lombardy

# Pollo alle olive

## CHICKEN WITH OLIVES

This braised chicken has nice saltiness from the olives that goes well with polenta, potato purée (page 270), or simply boiled potatoes. Make sure you use good-quality olives when preparing this dish.

**SERVES 4**

1 whole chicken (3 to 4 lb, cut into 16 pieces) or 4 lb chicken thighs

Salt and freshly ground black pepper, as needed

2 tbsp olive oil

1 medium yellow onion, diced

1 celery stalk, diced

½ tsp chopped thyme

1 tbsp chopped oregano

2 bay leaves

½ tsp crushed hot red pepper

¼ cup lemon juice

¼ cup orange juice

1 cup chicken Brodo (page 88) or water

½ cup peeled and chopped plum tomatoes, fresh or canned

½ cup small black olives, pitted but left whole, plus more for garnish

¼ cup small green olives, pitted but left whole, plus more for garnish

2 tbsp chopped flat-leaf parsley

1. Season the chicken with salt and pepper.
2. In a Dutch oven over high heat, heat the oil until very hot. Add the chicken, skin side down, and brown well on all sides, about 6 minutes total. Remove and set aside.
3. Lower the heat to medium, add the onion, and cook for about 5 minutes. Add the celery and cook until the vegetables are soft, about 5 minutes longer. Add the thyme, oregano, bay leaves, and crushed hot red pepper and cook for another minute or two.
4. Add the lemon juice and orange juice, and 1 minute later add the brodo or water, tomatoes, olives, and parsley.
5. Partially cover the pan and let cook for 25 to 30 minutes or until tender.
6. Carve the chicken if necessary and serve it garnished with more olives on top.

## OLIVES

Pliny described 15 varieties of olives in his day. Today, there are many more varieties from Italy and around the world.

**MANZANILLO:** These large, rounded oval fruits with purple-green skin have a rich taste and thick pulp. Prolific bearers, they are grown around the world.

**FRANTOIO AND LECCINO:** These cultivars are the principal participants in Italian olive oils from Tuscany. Leccino has a mild, sweet flavor, while Frantoio is fruity, with a stronger aftertaste. Due to their highly valued flavor, these cultivars are also now grown in other countries.

**ARBEQUINA:** This is a small brown olive grown in Catalonia, Spain, that is good for eating and for oil.

**EMPELTRE:** This is a medium black olive grown in Spain, good for eating and for oil.

**KALAMATA (OR CALAMATA):** This large, almond-shaped, black-purple olive comes from Greece. It has a smooth and meat-like taste and is used as a table olive. These olives are usually preserved in vinegar or olive oil. Kalamata olives enjoy protected-designation status.

**KORONEIKI:** This olive originates from the southern Peloponnese, around Kalamata and Mani in Greece.

**PECHOLINE OR PICHOLINE:** This olive originated in the south of France. It is green, medium size, and elongated. The flavor is mild and nutty.

**MISSION:** This type originated on the California Missions and is now grown throughout the state. They are black and generally used for table consumption.

**SICILIAN-STYLE OLIVES:** A medium green color, they are cured in salt brine and preserved with lactic acid. Made from the larger Seville variety, they are crisp and salty.

**GREEK-STYLE OLIVES:** This style is usually made from olives that have been allowed to ripen longer on the tree. They are dry-salt-cured and rubbed with olive oil. They are strong-tasting, black, and wrinkled. Some Greek-style olives are salt-brine-cured and packed with vinegar.

**GAETA:** From Italy, this olive is dry-salt-cured, then rubbed with olive oil. It is black and wrinkled but surprisingly mild. Some styles with this name are brine-cured. They are often packed with rosemary and other herbs.

**NIÇOISE:** This brown to brown-green-black olive comes from France. It is a small, tasty olive with a large pit.

Wine notes: When it comes to wine, chicken is one of the ultimate "crossover" foods, happy to be paired with moderately complex white wines, dry but fruity rosés, refreshing sparklers, or light-bodied, fruit-driven reds. Take your pick.

**White:** Inzolia from Sicily; Falanghina from Campania; Gavi from Piedmont; Pinot Bianco from Trentino-Alto Adige; Sauvignon from Friuli-Venezia Giulia; Soave from Veneto; Albana di Romagna from Emilia-Romagna

**Rosé:** Montepulciano d'Abruzzo Cerasuolo from Abruzzo; Lacrymarosa from Campania

**Red:** Refosco from Friuli-Venezia Giulia; Pinot Nero/Pinot Noir from Trentino-Alto Adige; Dolcetto d'Alba from Piedmont; Valpolicella from Veneto; Chianti from Tuscany; Sangiovese di Romagna from Emilia-Romagna

**Sparkling:** Prosecco from Veneto; Franciacorta from Lombardy; Trento from Trentino-Alto Adige

# Pollo al diavolo

## CHICKEN DEVIL-STYLE

This is a typical dish found in many trattorias. The trattoria is the Italian equivalent of the French bistro: homey restaurants with amazing, simple food, run mostly by families who often live there too.

**SERVES 4**

MARINADE

**1 tsp chopped oregano**

**½ tsp chopped thyme**

**1 tsp chopped rosemary**

**½ tsp kosher salt**

**½ tsp crushed hot red pepper**

**½ tsp freshly ground black pepper**

**¾ cup olive oil**

**¾ cup dry white wine**

**2 tbsp lemon juice or red wine vinegar**

**1 whole chicken (3 to 4 lb)**

PANURIA

**1 tbsp Colman's dry mustard powder (or other strong dry mustard)**

**¼ cup dry white wine**

**½ cup fresh plain bread crumbs**

**¼ cup grated Parmigiano-Reggiano (1 oz)**

**2 tbsp chopped flat-leaf parsley**

**½ tsp chopped garlic**

1. To make the marinade, mix the oregano, thyme, rosemary, salt, hot red pepper, and black pepper with the oil, wine, and lemon juice or vinegar in a bowl and set aside.
2. Remove the wing tips and butterfly the chicken by removing its backbone with a chef's knife or poultry shears. Lay the chicken flat on a work surface with the breast facing up. Press down on the keel bone firmly (the center of the breast) with the heel of your hand to flatten the bird. Make a few incisions, about ¼ inch deep, on the thickest part of the leg, to help make sure the chicken will cook evenly.
3. Place the chicken in a large zipper-top bag and pour three-quarters of the marinade into the bag. Seal and massage it well to rub the marinade into the chicken. Reserve the rest of the marinade for later use. Leave the chicken in the marinade for at least 20 minutes before you proceed, or up to 1 day in the refrigerator.
4. Preheat the oven to 400 degrees F. Place the chicken in a roasting pan skin side up and roast until the internal temperature registers 160 to 165 degrees F, about 40 minutes. Make sure you baste the chicken several times during cooking to keep it moist. Remove from the oven and set aside.
5. Preheat the broiler.
6. To make the panuria, mix the dry mustard with the wine and brush it on the chicken.
7. Mix the bread crumbs, cheese, parsley, and garlic in a bowl. Sprinkle the mixture on the chicken and place it under the broiler to get crisp, 1 to 2 minutes.
8. Remove and carve the chicken, pouring the reserved marinade over the top.

Wine notes: With this spicy dish you're going to want a fruity white, or better yet, the simple, refreshing quality of bubbles, to contrast the heat and cool off your palate.
**White:** Falanghina, Fiano di Avellino, or Greco di Tufo from Campania; Verdicchio dei Castelli de Jesi from Le Marche; Frascati from Lazio; Roero Arneis from Piedmont; Traminer (Gewürztraminer), Müller-Thurgau, or Sylvaner from Trentino-Alto Adige; Inzolia from Sicily; Vernaccia di San Gimignano or Sauvignon Blanc from Tuscany
**Sparkling:** Prosecco from Veneto

# Pollo alla cacciatora

## HUNTER'S STYLE CHICKEN

Different versions of this dish are found all over Italy. We give you different options for adding flavors, so try a few and then see which you enjoy most. We like this dish the day after it has been made, served with polenta on a chilly autumn or winter night.

**SERVES 4**

½ oz dried porcini mushrooms

1 lb mushrooms, such as white mushrooms or any firm type

½ tsp chopped thyme

1 tbsp chopped rosemary

2 tbsp chopped flat-leaf parsley

1 whole chicken (3 to 4 lb, cut into 16 pieces) or 4 lb chicken thighs

Salt and freshly ground black pepper, as needed

2 tbsp olive oil or a combination of unsalted butter and oil

1 medium yellow onion, diced

1 carrot, diced

1 celery stalk, diced

¾ cup chopped green or red bell pepper (optional)

2 bay leaves

1 cup dry white wine

1 cup peeled and crushed plum tomatoes, fresh or canned

½ cup chicken Brodo (page 88) or water

1. Place the porcini mushrooms in a bowl with enough hot water to cover and let soak for about 30 minutes. Drain and chop into small pieces.
2. Remove the stems from the fresh mushrooms and cut them into quarters. Set aside. Chop the thyme, rosemary, and parsley together very finely and set aside.
3. Season the chicken with salt and pepper.
4. In a Dutch oven, heat the oil over high heat. Add the chicken, skin side down, and brown well, turning as necessary to color on all sides, about 6 minutes total. Remove and set aside.
5. Lower the heat to medium, add the onion, and cook for about 5 minutes. Add the carrot, celery, and bell pepper, if using, and cook until the vegetables are soft but not mushy, about 6 minutes longer. Add the porcini, chicken, the chopped herbs, and the bay leaves. After a minute or two, add the wine, and 1 minute later add the tomatoes. Add enough brodo or water to almost cover the chicken.
6. Partially cover the pan and cook for 20 to 25 minutes or until tender.
7. Let rest for at least 1 hour before serving to allow the flavors to develop, but this is even better served the next day. When ready to serve, bring to a boil to heat everything through.

Wine notes: This is another chicken dish that will work well with either white or red wine. If you want to capture the rustic simplicity of the dish, choose a white; it will bring out the basic flavor combinations. To add a bit more complexity and a touch of spice to the dish, pair a dry red wine that features fruits such as red currants or raspberries on the nose and on the palate.

**White:** Vernaccia di San Gimignano, Sauvignon Blanc, or Chardonnay from Tuscany; Albana di Romagna from Emilia-Romagna; Roero Arneis or Chardonnay from Piedmont; Soave Classico from Veneto; Pinot Grigio or Pinot Bianco from Trentino-Alto Adige or Friuli-Venezia Giulia; Chardonnay from Sicily

**Red:** Chianti from Tuscany; Torgiano Rosso or Montefalco Rosso from Umbria; Sangiovese di Romagna from Emilia-Romagna; Barbera d'Asti, Barbera d'Alba, or Dolcetto d'Alba from Piedmont; Merlot, Valpolicella Classico, or Bardolino Classico from Veneto; Refosco or Merlot from Friuli-Venezia Giulia; Pinot Nero/Pinot Noir from Trentino-Alto Adige or Valle d'Aosta; Montepulciano d'Abruzzo from Abruzzo; Salice Salentino from Puglia

# Tagliata al rosmarino

## T-BONE STEAK WITH ROSEMARY

*Tagliata* in Italian means a piece of meat sliced and served with good extra-virgin olive oil and rosemary on top, very simple and easy if you can get a good-quality cut of beef and a great-tasting olive oil. Of course, do not try to substitute dried rosemary for the fresh, because it will not work. You may use New York strip, rib eye, or any tender cut of meat. Serve with roasted potatoes, any roasted vegetables, and any greens or a simple salad. In the summer, it is great served on a bed of arugula with olive oil, lemon juice, and Parmigiano-Reggiano shavings.

**SERVES 2**

- 2 lb T-bone steak, preferably aged (at least 1 inch thick)
- 3 tbsp extra-virgin olive oil, plus more for brushing
- Sea salt and coarsely ground black pepper, as needed
- 1 garlic clove, crushed
- 1 rosemary sprig

1. Brush the steak on both sides with olive oil and season with salt and pepper. Turn the grill to the highest setting and brush the grill with oil.
2. Grill the steaks to the desired doneness: about 4 minutes per side for rare, 5 minutes per side for medium-rare, and 6 minutes per side for medium. If the meat is getting too dark on the outside, you may transfer it to the oven to finish cooking if you wish. Let the meat rest for about 5 minutes.
3. While the meat is resting, in a small sauté pan over low heat combine 3 tablespoons olive oil with the garlic and cook very gently. Once the garlic starts to color, remove it, add the rosemary, and cook for about 1 minute or until the rosemary flavor is infused.
4. When ready to serve, remove the meat from the bone (if you are cooking on the bone) and slice. Place the meat on a plate, pour the oil on top of the steak, and serve immediately.

Wine notes: A good steak, redolent with the aromatics of rosemary, calls for a fine red wine, full-bodied and complex, perhaps with a bit of bottle age. Younger versions of these reds have their charms, too.

**Red:** Brunello di Montalcino, Chianti Classico Riserva, Carmignano, or Morellino di Scansano from Tuscany; Barolo, Barbaresco, Nebbiolo d'Alba, Langhe Nebbiolo, Gattinara, or Ghemme from Piedmont; Inferno from Lombardy; Cabernet Sauvignon from Tuscany, Friuli-Venezia Giulia, or Trentino-Alto Adige; Taurasi from Campania; Nero d'Avola from Sicily; Cannonau di Sardegna from Sardinia

# Ossobuco alla Milanese

## VEAL OSSO BUCO

The translation for *ossobuco* is "bone with a hole." This dish is typical of Milan and is usually served with saffron risotto. You may use more or less tomato depending on how you like it. You may also add some dried porcini mushrooms to the sauce while it is cooking for an earthier flavor.

**SERVES 4**

½ cup olive oil

4 pieces veal osso buco (center cut, about 1½ inches thick)

Salt and freshly ground black pepper, as needed

1 cup all-purpose flour

1 medium yellow onion, minced

1 leek, white part only, minced

2 carrots, diced

2 celery stalks, diced

4 sage leaves, chopped

2 rosemary sprigs, chopped

1 bay leaf

1 cup dry white wine

2 cups peeled and crushed plum tomatoes, fresh or canned

1 cup veal or chicken Brodo (page 88)

1 tsp finely shredded lemon zest

1 tbsp chopped flat-leaf parsley

1. Preheat the oven to 350 degrees F.
2. Heat the olive oil over high heat in a heavy pot large enough to hold the veal.
3. Season the ossobuco with salt and pepper and dredge in the flour.
4. Brown each side of the osso buco in the hot oil, about 10 minutes total. Remove and set aside.
5. In the same pot over medium heat, sweat the onion, leek, carrots, and celery until soft, about 4 minutes. Put the osso buco back into the pot and add the sage, rosemary, bay leaf, and wine. Let the wine evaporate.
6. Add the tomatoes and cook for 1 minute, then add the brodo.
7. Cover and bake for about 2 hours or until tender.
8. Remove the osso buco from the pot, and if desired, reduce the sauce on the stovetop. Serve the osso bucco wih the sauce. Just before serving, sprinkle the lemon zest and parsley on top.

Wine notes: So many classic Italian reds match with this classic Italian dish. You don't want the wine to overwhelm the flavors of the veal and risotto, but at the same time you want a wine that will meet the intense flavors of the osso buco head on. Younger medium- to full-bodied reds will do the job nicely.

**Red:** Inferno, Grumello, or Valgella from Lombardy; Barbera d'Asti, Barbera d'Alba, Nebbiolo d'Alba, Langhe Nebbiolo, Ghemme, or Gattinara from Piedmont; Merlot or Valpolicella Ripasso from Veneto; Chianti Classico, Rosso di Montalcino, Carmignano, Vino Nobile di Montepulciano, or Merlot from Tuscany; Cabernet from Veneto, Friuli-Venezia Giulia, or Trentino-Alto Adige; Aglianico del Vulture from Basilicata; Primitivo di Manduria from Puglia; Cannonau di Sardegna from Sardinia; Cerasuolo di Vittoria, Nero d'Avola, or Merlot from Sicily

# Anatra con mele

## ROAST DUCK WITH APPLES

Although there is no specially prepared sauce to accompany this dish, you should certainly enjoy the pan juices from the roasting pan spooned over the duck.

**SERVES 4 TO 6**

- 1 duckling (about 4½ lb)
- Salt and freshly ground black pepper, as needed
- 2 bay leaves
- Zest of 1 lemon (cut in wide strips with a vegetable peeler)
- 2 celery stalks, chopped
- 1 medium yellow onion, chopped
- 3 or 4 green apples (such as Granny Smith), peeled, cored, and sliced
- ¼ cup grappa or apple brandy

1. Preheat the oven to 375 degrees F. Wash and dry the duck and cut away any excess fat.
2. Season the cavity with salt and pepper and place the bay leaves and lemon zest inside the cavity. To tie the duck, cut a long piece of butcher twine. Use the twine to tie together the ends of the legs and run the twine along the duck and around the wing tips. Pull the twine to tighten it and tie the ends together.
3. In a large pan that can fit the duck just comfortably, sauté over low heat until it has a good golden color and the fat is rendered, 8 to 10 minutes.
4. Place the duck in the oven and roast for 30 minutes. Add the celery, onion, apples, and grappa, stirring to release any drippings there might be. Continue to roast for 20 minutes longer. Turn the oven down to 325 degrees F. Roast the duck until the legs are tender, another 25 to 30 minutes.
5. Remove the duck from the pan and carve into portions. Serve with the apples and pan juices.

Wine notes: Roasted duck with apples is a great match with fruit-driven, spicy whites with rich flavors or with red wines that are happy to play a background role to the rich flavors of the duck. Both whites and reds should feature at least a moderate level of refreshing acidity to pair happily with the apples.

**White:** Traminer (Gewürztraminer), Sylvaner, or Müller-Thurgau from Trentino-Alto Adige; Verdicchio dei Castelli di Jesi Classico Superiore from Le Marche; Chardonnay from Piedmont, Tuscany, Friuli-Venezia Giulia, or Sicily

**Red:** Schiava, Lagrein, Teroldego Rotaliano, Pinot Noir/Pinot Nero, or Merlot from Trentino-Alto Adige; Chianti Classico, Rosso di Montalcino, or Merlot from Tuscany; Bardolino Classico Superiore, Valpolicella Ripasso, or Merlot from Veneto; Sangiovese di Romagna from Emilia-Romagna; Montepulciano d'Abruzzo from Abruzzo; Salice Salentino or Primitivo di Manduria from Puglia; Cerasuolo di Vittoria or Merlot from Sicily

# Coniglio in porchetta

## RABBIT STUFFED WITH PANCETTA AND FENNEL

Here is a stuffed rabbit dish prepared like the common pork preparation. Normally the rabbit is left with the bones in for cooking, but for this recipe we remove the bones from the rabbit first. In this recipe we include a fennel bulb, but a stronger, flavorful wild fennel is more commonly used. You could supplement the fennel flavor here by seasoning the rabbit with some ground fennel seeds.

**SERVES 4 TO 5**

**1 whole rabbit (about 4 lb)**

**Salt and freshly ground black pepper, as needed**

**2 garlic cloves, thinly sliced**

**1 rosemary sprig, leaves finely chopped**

**7 or 8 slices flat pancetta, cut in ¼-inch slices**

**3 tbsp olive oil**

**1 fennel bulb, sliced, fronds chopped**

1. Preheat the oven to 350 degrees F.
2. Bone the rabbit as follows: Cut out the backbone and remove the spine, lay the rabbit flat, skin side down, and then use the tip of a boning knife and make cuts to free the bones of the rib cage. Use the tip of the knife to cut around the bones in the leg and scrape to remove the bones from the flesh. Try not to cut all the way through the skin as you work.
3. Lay the rabbit flat, skin side down, and season with salt and pepper, the garlic slices, and the rosemary. Lay the pancetta over the entire surface.
4. Heat 1 tablespoon olive oil in a skillet over medium-high heat and sauté the sliced fennel bulb for about 1 minute. Transfer to a bowl and mix with the chopped fronds. Let the fennel cool just enough to be able to handle it, and place it in a layer over the pancetta.
5. Roll the rabbit up around the filling and tie with butcher's twine.
6. In a large pan, heat the remaining olive oil over high heat and sear the rabbit on all sides, about 8 minutes total. Transfer to a roasting pan and roast in the oven for about 1 hour.
7. Let the rabbit rest for 20 minutes, then slice and serve.

Wine notes: To cut the richness of the rabbit and pancetta, pair the dish with a robust white. To savor that richness and find a partner for the fennel, think about choosing an earthy, medium-bodied red. To surprise your palate with every sip, try a cleansing sparkling rosato.

**White:** Verdicchio dei Castelli di Jesi Classico Superiore or Verdicchio di Matelica from Le Marche; Chardonnay from Piedmont, Veneto, Friuli-Venezia Giulia, Trentino-Alto Adige, Tuscany, or Sicily

**Red:** Rosso Conero or Rosso Piceno from Le Marche; Nebbiolo d'Alba, Barbera d'Asti, or Barbera d'Alba from Piedmont; Chianti Classico Riserva, Rosso di Montalcino, or Merlot from Tuscany; Sangiovese di Romagna from Emilia-Romagna, Torgiano Rosso from Umbria; Montepulciano d'Abruzzo from Abruzzo; Salice Salentino or Primitivo di Manduria from Puglia; Merlot from Veneto, Friuli-Venezia Giulia, or Sicily; Pinot Nero/Pinot Noir from Trentino-Alto Adige

**Sparkling:** Franciacorta Rosato from Lombardy; Trento Rosato from Trentino-Alto Adige

1. After layering the filling, start gently rolling the rabbit.

2. The roll should be snug but not too tight.

3. Use kitchen twine to tie the roll into a neat package for cooking.

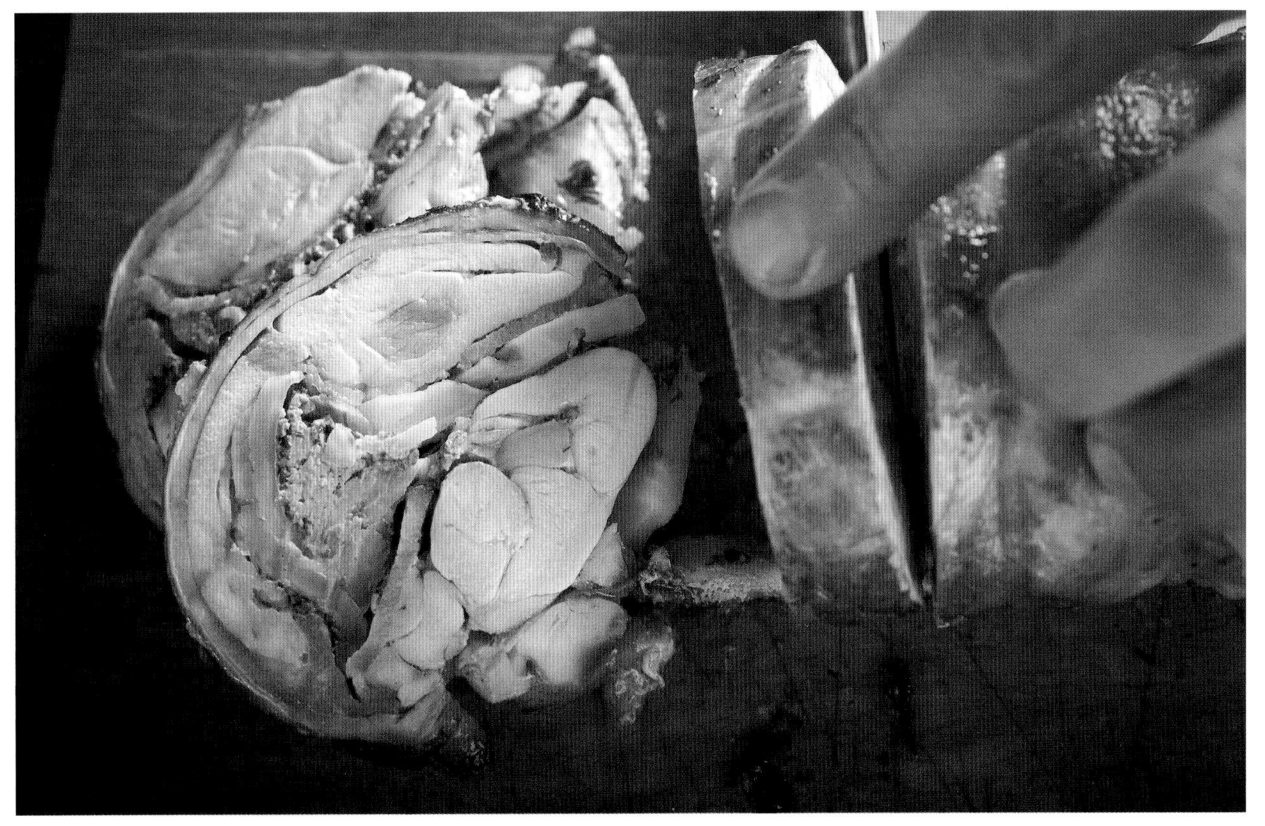

Coniglio in Porchetta

# Coniglio all'ischitana

## RABBIT IN THE STYLE OF ISCHIA

While Ischia is surrounded by water, the region has produced several famous dishes based upon the foods found in its mountainous interior. This dish is traditionally prepared in an earthenware or ceramic casserole, known as a *tegame*.

**SERVES 6 TO 8**

**1 whole rabbit (about 4 lb)**

**Salt, as needed**

**2 rosemary sprigs, chopped**

**½ cup olive oil**

**½ cup dry white wine**

**Chicken Brodo (page 88), as needed**

**5 or 6 plum tomatoes, peeled, seeded, and coarsely chopped**

**1 bunch basil, coarsely chopped**

**½ cup black olives, pitted but left whole**

1. Preheat the oven to 350 degrees F.
2. Cut the rabbit into large pieces by separating the legs from the body: cut through the joint with the tip of a boning knife; cut the hind legs in half by cutting through the joint. Cut away the backbone, and cut the body portion in half to separate the loin and rib sections (use a heavy knife to cut through the bones). Season with salt and the rosemary.
3. In a large pot, heat the olive oil over high heat. Sauté the rabbit until all the pieces have a good golden color on all sides, about 6 minutes total. Add the wine and let it evaporate completely.
4. Add about 1 cup brodo and the tomatoes. Bake for about 40 minutes, turning the rabbit pieces often during the cooking time and adding brodo if it gets too dry.
5. Add the basil and olives and bake for 5 minutes longer. Serve immediately.

Wine notes: To bring out the gaminess of the rabbit, try this dish with any of the white wines listed here. If you want to integrate the flavors of the dish and create a "sauce in a glass," then choose a fruit-driven red.

**White:** Greco di Tufo or Fiano di Avellino from Campania; Chardonnay from Sicily, Piedmont, Veneto, Friuli-Venezia Giulia, or Trentino-Alto Adige; Verdicchio dei Castelli di Jesi Classico Superiore from Le Marche

**Red:** Bardolino Classico Superiore, Valpolicella Ripasso, or Merlot from Veneto; Lagrein, Teroldego Rotaliano, Pinot Nero/Pinot Noir, or Merlot from Trentino-Alto Adige; Chianti Classico, Rosso di Montalcino, or Rosso di Montepulciano from Tuscany; Torgiano Rosso or Montefalco Rosso from Umbria; Aglianico del Vulture from Basilicata; Cannonau di Sardegna from Sardinia; Cerasuolo di Vittoria or Merlot from Sicily

# Bracioline alla messinese

## GRILLED STUFFED VEAL IN THE STYLE OF MESSINA

*Caciocavallo* translates from the Italian as "horse cheese"; some say this southern Italian cheese may have first been made from mare's milk. It is made in much the same way as mozzarella and provolone. You may have seen it hanging up in a deli; it has a distinctive gourd shape.

**SERVES 4 TO 6**

- 2 lb boneless veal top round (in 1 piece)
- ½ cup plain dry bread crumbs
- 3 garlic cloves, minced
- ½ cup chopped flat-leaf parsley
- 2 tbsp grated pecorino
- 2 tbsp olive oil, plus more as needed
- Salt and freshly ground black pepper, as needed
- 4 to 5 oz caciocavallo, cut into sticks (1½ inches long and ¼ inch square)

1. Preheat a grill to medium-high heat.
2. Cut the top round into thin, small slices, about ¼ inch thick, then lightly pound them with a mallet.
3. In a bowl, mix together the bread crumbs, garlic, parsley, pecorino, and 2 tbsp olive oil.
4. Rub the veal pieces with olive oil and season with salt and pepper. Cover both sides of each piece with the aromatic bread crumbs. Place a stick of caciocavallo cheese in the center of each piece and roll the meat around it.
5. Skewer 3 bracioline together at a time onto long metal skewers.
6. Grill for 3 to 4 minutes on each side or until done. Serve immediately.

Wine notes: Grilled, herbaceous veal wrapped around a core of caciocavallo cheese calls for a sturdy but not too "big" red wine—a dry wine with both red and black fruits on the nose and on the palate to bring out the sweetness of the meat and highlight the richness of the cheese.

**Red:** Cerasuolo di Vittoria, Nero d'Avola, or Merlot from Sicily; Cannonau di Sardegna from Sardinia; Aglianico del Vulture from Basilicata; Salice Salentino or Primitivo from Puglia; Rosso Conero or Rosso Piceno from Le Marche; Sangiovese di Romagna from Emilia-Romagna; Chianti Classico, Rosso di Montalcino, Rosso di Montepulciano, or Merlot from Tuscany; Bardolino Classico, Valpolicella Ripasso, or Merlot from Veneto; Lagrein, Pinot Nero/Pinot Noir, or Merlot from Trentino-Alto Adige; Barbera d'Alba or Barbera d'Asti from Piedmont

# Saltimbocca alla romana

## VEAL SALTIMBOCCA

We like to serve this preparation with fried artichokes, which are also typical to this region, or simply with a green salad.

**SERVES 4 TO 6**

- 2 lb boneless veal top round (in 1 piece)
- 10 to 12 sage leaves
- 10 to 12 slices prosciutto
- All-purpose flour, as needed
- ½ to ¾ cup olive oil
- Chicken Brodo (page 88), as needed
- Unsalted butter, as needed

1. Slice the meat about ¼ inch thick, then cut the slices into 2 or 3 smaller pieces. With a mallet, pound the meat to a slightly thinner and even thickness.
2. Place a leaf of sage and a slice of prosciutto on top of each piece. Dredge the meat slices in flour.
3. In a large sauté pan, heat the olive oil over medium-high heat and sauté the meat, in batches if necessary. Start with the prosciutto side down and sauté for 2 minutes on each side. Set aside.
4. Remove any excess oil from the pan and deglaze the pan with the brodo. Reduce the brodo to the desired consistency, then whisk in a small amount of butter.
5. Spoon the sauce over the meat and serve immediately.

Wine notes: This is a delicate preparation of veal that, especially if served with fried artichokes, will need a fruity white wine or that simple but elegant spumante known as Prosecco. The sweetness of the veal and prosciutto will bring out the pleasant background flavors of the wine, and the artichokes will create a fruit salad of flavors in that same wine.

**White:** Frascati Superiore from Lazio; Orvieto Classico from Umbria; Roero Arneis from Piedmont; Soave Classico from Veneto; Pinot Bianco or Friulano from Friuli-Venezia Giulia; Traminer (Gewürztraminer) or Müller-Thurgau from Trentino-Alto Adige

**Sparkling:** Prosecco from Veneto

# Scaloppine al limone

## VEAL CUTLETS WITH LEMON

Many classic dishes in the Italian repertoire are slow-cooked, but this scallopini dish is an exception to the rule. It is quick to prepare and to cook, with a fresh, direct flavor that is bolder than you might expect from just a few simple ingredients.

**SERVES 4 TO 6**

**2 lb boneless veal top round (in 1 piece)**

**Salt and freshly ground white pepper, as needed**

**Zest and juice from 3 lemons**

**All-purpose flour, as needed**

**½ to ¾ cup (1 to 1½ sticks) unsalted butter**

**3 tbsp olive oil**

**Chicken Brodo (page 88), as needed**

**2 tbsp chopped flat-leaf parsley**

1. Slice the meat about ¼ inch thick, and then cut the slices into 2 or 3 smaller pieces. With a mallet, pound the meat to a slightly thinner and even thickness.
2. Dry the meat well, season with salt and pepper, and rub the lemon zest all over it. Dredge the meat slices in flour and shake well.
3. In a large sauté pan over medium-high heat, heat half of the butter and the oil. Cook the meat, in batches if necessary, for 2 minutes on each side. Set aside.
4. Remove any excess oil from the pan and deglaze the pan with the brodo. Reduce the brodo for a couple of minutes and add the lemon juice.
5. Reduce the sauce by half and then whisk in the rest of the butter. Add the parsley and spoon the sauce over the meat.

Wine notes: Believe it or not, when it comes to pairing wine with this dish, the flavor you want to focus on is the lemon. It's important to choose a white or sparkling wine with high enough acidity to complement the lemon, so that the other flavors and textures can emerge in both the food and the wine. **White:** Roero Arneis or Chardonnay from Piedmont; Soave Classico from Veneto; Sauvignon, Pinot Grigio, or Chardonnay from Friuli-Venezia Giulia; Chardonnay or Pinot Grigio from Trentino-Alto Adige; Sauvignon Blanc from Tuscany; Verdicchio dei Castelli di Jesi or Verdicchio di Matelica from Le Marche; Falanghina from Campania; Chardonnay from Sicily **Sparkling:** Prosecco from Veneto; Franciacorta from Lombardy; Trento from Trentino-Alto Adige

# Polenta e osei

## ROASTED LITTLE BIRDS WITH POLENTA

*Osei* translates to mean "little bird." The traditional birds used for this dish were lark, fig-pecker, or thrush, all of which are now protected under endangerment laws. For this recipe, we use quail, which is a close substitute for those dainty songbirds. This preparation is typical of northern Italy, particularly the Lombardy region. Polenta is commonly found at the table served along with this dish.

**SERVES 4 TO 6**

2 qt water

Salt, as needed

2 cups cornmeal

10 to 12 bone-in quail

¾ to 1 cup (1½ to 2 sticks) unsalted butter

2 oz lard or pancetta in 1 piece, cut into large sticks

10 to 12 sage leaves

Chicken Brodo (page 88) or broth, as needed

1. Preheat the oven to 350 degrees F.
2. Prepare the polenta by boiling the water with some salt. Slowly add the cornmeal to the boiling water, while whisking to avoid lumps.
3. Cook the polenta over medium heat for 45 to 60 minutes, stirring often.
4. Meanwhile, wash and dry the birds and season with salt.
5. In a large sauté pan, melt half of the butter with the pancetta over high heat. When the butter is hot, add the birds a few at a time and sauté until they start to get some color, turning as necessary to color them evenly, about 2 minutes total.
6. Put all of the birds into a roasting pan and place the pancetta over the top. Add the remaining butter and sage and place in the oven.
7. Roast the quail, basting frequently with the butter from the pan, until they are done, 8 to10 minutes. If the butter starts to burn, add some of the brodo to the bottom of the pan.
8. Serve the polenta with 2 or 3 birds placed on top and drizzle with the melted butter from the pan.

*When cooking polenta, stir often to avoid lumps.*

Polenta e Osei

Wine notes: To capture the culture of this dish, based on small birds historically found in Lombardy, seek out one of the suggested classic Lombardian red wines, admittedly a bit hard to find. But don't despair, as the other full-bodied Italian reds listed here will deliver great pleasure and a perfect pairing. **Red:** Grumello, Valgella, Sasella, or Inferno from Lombardy; Barbera d'Alba, Barbera d'Asti, or Nebbiolo d'Alba from Piedmont; Chianti Classico Riserva, Carmignano, Morellino di Scansano, or Merlot from Tuscany; Torgiano Rosso or Montefalco Rosso from Umbria; Sangiovese di Romagna from Emilia-Romagna; Cannonau di Sardegna from Sardinia; Cerasuolo di Vittoria or Merlot from Sicily; Merlot from Veneto, Friuli-Venezia Giulia, or Trentino-Alto Adige

# Dolci

Italians have a sweet tooth and have invented hundreds of cookies, cakes, tarts, tortes, and puddings. Gelato is the Italian ice cream, smooth and luscious and perfect to pair with seasonal fruits like peaches or strawberries.

Some of the recipes in this chapter are meant to be enjoyed as an afternoon treat, while others are more elaborate presentations meant to conclude a special family feast or holiday celebration.

# Macedonia

## FRUIT SALAD

The most typical fruits in a macedonia are apples, strawberries, berries of all sorts (except cranberries), bananas, pears, melon, watermelon, figs, and grapes. You may add any type of fruit in season, using more or less sugar depending on taste. For a more exotic touch, try this with mango, pineapple, papaya, kiwi, star fruit, litchi, or pomegranate. Serve with gelato (such as vanilla or hazelnut) or sorbetto (such as lemon or a berry flavor)

**SERVES 6 TO 8**

- 3 lb fresh fruit of any kind
- Juice of 1½ lemons, strained
- ½ cup water
- ¼ cup sugar (optional)
- ¼ cup liquor, such as maraschino, rum, or whatever you like (optional)

1. Core any apples, pears, pineapples, or other fruit that needs it. Peel bananas, melons, mangoes, or kiwis. Remove seeds from any melons, figs, and or papayas. Remove and discard the skin of any pomegranates, if using, and use the seeds whole. Cut any large pieces of fruit into cubes, or use a melon baller to make spheres.
2. Stir together the lemon juice, water, and sugar, if using, until the sugar is completely dissolved, to make a light syrup.
3. Place the fruit in a bowl, mix in the light syrup, and toss well, adding the liquor, if desired, just before serving.

Wine notes: **Sparkling White:** Asti or semi-sparkling Moscato d'Asti from Piedmont **Sparkling Red:** Brachetto d'Acqui from Piedmont

# Tiramisù di pavesini

## CLASSIC TIRAMISÙ WITH PAVESINI COOKIES

Reading any recipe for tiramisù, you will notice that the most common cookies used are ladyfingers. In this recipe, we are using Pavesini cookies, which are similar to a waffle cookie, instead of the more familiar ladyfingers. They are very light and thin, so you need to make more layers to get a taller tiramisù.

**SERVES 6 TO 8**

**6 egg yolks, room temperature**

**½ cup sugar**

**1 lb mascarpone**

**2 oz Kahlúa or dark rum**

**4 egg whites**

**2 packages Pavesini cookies (about 80 cookies)**

**2 cups brewed espresso (or 1 cup American coffee and 1 cup espresso), room temperature**

**Unsweetened cocoa powder, for garnish**

1. Whip the egg yolks with the sugar in an electric mixer until pale, making sure the sugar is completely dissolved.
2. Add the mascarpone and whip for 1 to 2 minutes, until well combined and smooth. Add the liquor and mix well.
3. In a clean bowl, whip the egg whites to stiff peaks. Fold the egg whites into the mascarpone mixture in two or three additions.
4. In a casserole or on a plate with a border that is 6 by 9 inches, spread a thin layer of the mascarpone cream.
5. Soak each individual cookie in the coffee and arrange them very tightly on top of the cream, until covered.
6. Spoon another layer of the mascarpone cream on top, then place another layer of the soaked cookies, and finally spoon another layer of the cream on top to completely cover the cookies. If you like more layers, you can keep on going, making sure you put less cream per layer or increase the amount of cream when you make the recipe.
7. Refrigerate for at least 1 hour or up to 2 days. Dust with a nice amount of cocoa powder just before serving.

*If you can't find Pavesini cookies and want to substitute ladyfingers, you will need about 25 ladyfingers, and probably one layer of them is enough.*

*If you want an even richer consistency, you could substitute 2 cups of whipped heavy cream for the egg whites, or you could add 1 cup of whipped cream in step 3 in addition to the egg whites for an airier consistency, although purists will tell you that it is not the classic original recipe.*

# Panna Cotta

## COOKED CREAM

Different variations on panna cotta can be found throughout many locations, cities, and restaurants. This version has a slightly sour taste given by the buttermilk, which cuts a little into the sweetness and makes the flavor more interesting. Good accompaniments to this dessert are any fresh fruit, chocolate sauce, caramel sauce, coffee sauce, saba (also called vin cotto), aged balsamic vinegar, or chestnut honey.

**SERVES 6 TO 8**

- 1 envelope (2¼ tsp) unflavored gelatin
- 2 tbsp cold water
- 2¾ cups heavy cream
- 1 vanilla bean, scraped
- ¾ cup sugar
- Pinch of salt (optional)
- 1½ cups buttermilk

1. Place the gelatin in a bowl and add the cold water, stirring briefly to ensure the granules are completely moistened, and let it bloom for 10 to 15 minutes, until soft.
2. Combine the heavy cream, vanilla bean, sugar, and salt, if using, in a saucepan. Warm the mixture over low heat to dissolve the sugar, making sure the mixture does not simmer.
3. Add the bloomed gelatin into the warmed heavy cream and stir until completely blended (the gelatin may tend to sink, so be sure to scrape the bottom and sides of the pan to make sure it is well incorporated). Let the cream sit until it is room temperature, and then blend in the buttermilk and strain.
4. Evenly divide the panna cotta among individual serving cups, or use a pudding mold if you prefer to unmold it and present it on a platter.
5. Refrigerate until firm, at least 4 and up to 24 hours.
6. Serve the panna cotta directly in individual molds if desired. Or unmold them by tipping the mold upside down onto the plate and allowing the panna cotta to slowly fall out on its own. Then lift away the container and serve.

*You may infuse the cream as it heats with coffee beans, different types of herbs, or spices.*

*To change the texture and make it even more interesting, you may also want to try replacing ½ cup of the heavy cream with a good sheep's milk ricotta (pureed until very smooth first).*

# Zabaglione

## ZABAGLIONE

The classic way to enjoy this dessert is to serve it warm as soon as it is made, either on its own or with cookies, berries, or seasonal fruits. However, if you prefer, chill it and then fold in some whipped cream for a different way to enjoy this simple, adaptable dessert.

SERVES 4

4 egg yolks

¼ cup sugar

½ cup Marsala

1 cup heavy cream, for whipping (optional)

1. In a bowl set over barely simmering water, whisk together the egg yolks, sugar, and Marsala.
2. Whisk constantly until thickened and glossy, 5 to 7 minutes. Make sure you don't overcook it or it will scramble.
3. Serve at once as a warm custard.
4. For a cold dessert, transfer the bowl to an ice water bath and stir occasionally until the mixture is cool. Transfer to the refrigerator and chill completely, about 1 hour. If desired, whip the heavy cream to medium-stiff peaks and fold the whipped cream into the sabayon. Spoon into molds or glasses, and serve as a mousse.

*Use any of several different wines from Madeira to Vin Santo, Prosecco to Port, or different liquors, such as Kahlúa, Grand Marnier, or Sambuca instead of the Marsala to flavor the dessert. A pinch of freshly grated citrus zest would also be a nice touch. Mint or any type of dessert herb may be added at the end for garnish.*

Wine notes: **White:** Vin Santo or Moscadello di Montalcino from Tuscany; Recioto di Soave from Veneto; Picolit from Friuli-Venezia Giulia; Malvasia delle Lipari from Sicily **Sparkling White:** Asti or semi-sparkling Moscato d'Asti from Piedmont **Sparkling Red:** Brachetto d'Acqui from Piedmont

# Affogato al caffè

## COFFEE-DROWNED GELATO OR ICE CREAM

*Affogato* means "drowned," and in this case, the gelato is drowned by espresso. Our version includes a coffee-infused gelato that is worth the effort, but to be honest, the fastest way to create this simple but delicious dessert is to pour 1 or 2 shots of very hot and very strong freshly brewed espresso over vanilla gelato. Top with some whipped cream and dust with some grated dark chocolate or cocoa powder, or maybe some grated orange peel. Serve with biscotti or any type of dry Italian cookies.

**SERVES 6 TO 8**

2 cups milk

1 cup coffee beans

1 vanilla bean, scraped, or 1 tsp vanilla extract

¼ cup brewed strong espresso

6 egg yolks

¾ cup sugar

½ tsp powdered instant coffee

2 cups heavy cream

Freshly brewed espresso, for serving (1 or 2 shots per serving)

Unsweetened cocoa powder, as needed, for garnish

1. In a 3-quart saucepan, bring the milk to a boil with the coffee beans and the vanilla bean, if using.
2. Remove from the heat and add the espresso.
3. Whip the yolks together with the sugar in a large bowl until light yellow ribbons form.
4. Add half of the hot milk, and then add this back to the remaining milk. Let the mixture steep at room temperature for 1 hour.
5. Strain the mixture into a clean pan and cook over low heat without boiling until the mixture coats the back of a spoon thickly, about 5 minutes. Stir in the vanilla extract, if using, and the coffee powder. Cover and chill for at least 2 and up to 8 hours.
6. Whip half of the cream to medium peaks and incorporate it into the custard mixture. Transfer to an ice cream machine and freeze according to the manufacturer's instructions. Transfer to a container and let the gelato ripen in the freezer at least 4 hours before serving. It will last in the freezer for up to 1 week.
7. When you are ready to serve, brew espresso. Whip the rest of the heavy cream to medium peaks and set aside.
8. Scoop the frozen gelato into a glass and pour the espresso over the gelato. Top with a dollop of whipped cream and serve with some cocoa powder sprinkled on top (and a straw that you can use to drink the coffee).

# Torta della nonna con pignoli

## GRANDMA'S CAKE WITH PINE NUTS

This dessert is quite popular all over Italy, and has been duplicated to the point that the commercially produced version has given a bad reputation to this wonderful and delicate dessert. The difference between them lies in the flavor of a fresh pastry cream flavored with lemon zest and pine nuts baked into the top layer. You will have about 16 ounces of dough left over, which may be used for cookies or for another tart.

**MAKES 1 CAKE; SERVES 8**

FILLING

**6 egg yolks**

**⅔ cup sugar**

**3 tsp vanilla extract**

**5 tsp sifted all-purpose flour**

**2 cups milk**

**2 tsp lemon zest**

DOUGH

**1 cup (2 sticks) unsalted butter, cut into small pieces**

**3½ cups sifted all-purpose flour**

**1 cup sugar**

**4 tsp almond flour (finely ground almonds)**

**2 tsp baking powder**

**½ tsp salt**

**1 tsp lemon zest**

**3 large eggs**

**2 tsp vanilla extract**

**1 tsp water, as needed, plus 1 tbsp**

**½ cup pine nuts or as needed to cover the cake**

**Confectioners' sugar, for serving**

1. To make the filling, whisk together the yolks, sugar, and vanilla in a bowl. Add the flour.
2. In a saucepan, heat the milk, and then gradually add the milk to the egg-flour mixture, making sure it is well incorporated. Transfer the mixture to the saucepan and cook over low heat, stirring until the mixture comes to a boil. Cook for 1 minute, and remove from the heat and stir in the lemon zest. Cool the cream on top of a bed of ice or in the refrigerator, covering the top directly with plastic wrap to prevent a skin from forming.
3. To make the dough, use a pastry cutter or two table knives to cut the butter into the flour, sugar, almond flour, baking powder, salt, and lemon zest, working just until the mixture resembles coarse meal. Blend in 2 of the eggs and the vanilla, and knead gently until a workable dough forms; if necessary, add the 1 teaspoon water. Divide the dough into 3 pieces (two should be about 16 ounces each, and the third should be 12 ounces; reserve one of the 16-ounce pieces in the refrigerator or freezer for cookies or a tart).
4. Preheat the oven to 350 degrees F.
5. Butter a 10- or 11-inch round springform pan. Press or roll one of the 16-ounce pieces of dough to fit into the pan. Spoon the filling into the tart shell, leaving a ¼-inch border around the edges.
6. On a floured surface, roll out the remaining dough piece into an 11- to 12-inch circle. Lay this over the filling and pinch the edges of the dough together to seal.
7. Make an egg wash by beating the remaining egg with the remaining 1 tablespoon water. Brush the surface of the dough with the egg wash. Use a fork to make several slits on the top. Sprinkle the pine nuts on top and bake until golden and the center is set, 35 to 40 minutes.
8. Cool on a wire rack before dusting with confectioners' sugar, slicing, and serving.

Wine notes: **Sparkling White:** Asti or semi-sparkling Moscato d'Asti from Piedmont
**White:** Vin Santo or Moscadello di Montalcino from Tuscany; Picolit from Friuli-Venezia Giulia
**Sparkling Red:** Brachetto d'Acqui from Piedmont; Lambrusco from Emilia-Romagna

# La sbriciolata

## RICOTTA COOKIE TART

This dish is similar to a very crumbly cookie-type cake (that can actually also be made into cookies) called *sbrisolona*. But this has an inside of fresh ricotta and chocolate chips, a great texture and flavor combination.

**SERVES 6 TO 8**

FILLING

**2 cups ricotta**

**½ cup sugar**

**1 tbsp Strega liqueur**

**½ tsp vanilla extract**

**⅓ cup coarsely chopped dark chocolate**

DOUGH

**3 cups all-purpose flour**

**1 tsp baking powder**

**⅔ cup sugar**

**Pinch of salt**

**½ cup (1 stick) unsalted butter, diced and softened**

**2 large eggs**

**¼ tsp vanilla extract**

**Confectioners' sugar, for serving**

1. Preheat the oven to 180 degrees F.
2. To make the filling, work the ricotta with the sugar, Strega, and vanilla by hand in a mixing bowl with a wooden spoon until the ricotta is very creamy and smooth. Fold in the chocolate and set aside.
3. To make the dough, sift the flour together with the baking powder in a bowl; add the sugar, salt, and butter. Slowly "sbriciolate" the dough: This is where the name comes from, and it means using your fingertips to work the butter into the flour, working it until it becomes grainy and somewhat crumbly and sandy.
4. Add the eggs and vanilla. Work it very quickly with your fingertips or a fork, just enough to come together. Make sure you don't overwork this mixture; it should still be crumbly in texture.
5. Lightly flour and butter a 10- or 11-inch round springform pan with sides 1½ inches high. Place a layer of the dough crumbles on the bottom of the pan.
6. Pour the ricotta on top of the crumbles, leaving a border around the edge, and then cover the rest with the remaining dough crumbles.
7. Bake for 35 to 40 minutes, until golden brown.
8. Cool for about 1 hour on a wire rack. Sprinkle with confectioners' sugar and cut into slices.

Wine notes: **Sparkling White:** Asti or semi-sparkling Moscato d'Asti from Piedmont
**White:** Picolit from Friuli-Venezia Giulia
**Sparkling Red:** Brachetto d'Acqui from Piedmont

# Cantucci di pistacchi e ciliege

## PISTACHIO BISCOTTI WITH SOUR CHERRIES

Each region, every city, has its own version of biscotti but cantucci are only from Tuscany. Traditionally, they have no butter, but for a richer flavor you may add some softened butter to the dough, increasing the amount of flour a bit. You may store these biscotti in an airtight container or even freeze them if you want to keep them for a long time. Any type of nuts and flavorings can be added: lemon zest, orange zest, different liquors, cocoa powder, and so forth.

**SERVES 6**

- ¾ cup shelled unsalted pistachios
- 2 cups cake flour
- ½ cup light brown sugar
- ¼ tsp kosher salt
- 1 tsp baking powder
- 2 large eggs
- ¼ cup honey
- ¾ tsp anise extract
- ¼ tsp vanilla extract
- ¼ cup dried cherries, chopped

1. Preheat the oven to 350 degrees F. Coarsely chop the pistachios, and toast them on a baking sheet for 5 to 7 minutes. Set aside to cool. Lower the oven temperature to 325 degrees F.
2. Place the flour, sugar, salt, and baking powder in a bowl. Make a well in the center and add the eggs, honey, anise, and vanilla into the well.
3. Work the eggs to blend, gradually incorporating small amounts of the dry ingredients at a time until the mixture comes together to form a soft dough. Add the pistachios and cherries, gently working them in, using a small amount of additional flour if necessary.
4. Shape the dough into a large log and divide it into two equal pieces. Divide each half into three equal pieces and roll each into a long cylinder about the diameter of an index finger.
5. Line baking sheets with parchment paper. Bake the dough cylinders on the baking sheets until lightly baked but without color, about 20 minutes. Cool for 5 to 10 minutes.
6. Slice the cylinders while still slightly warm on the bias into biscotti, about ¼ inch wide. Turn the oven down to 200°F. Return the biscotti to the parchment-lined baking sheets, cut side down, and bake until dry, about 45 minutes. Cool on a wire rack. The cookies will become very crunchy when cool.

Wine notes: **Sparkling White:** Asti or semi-sparkling Moscato d'Asti from Piedmont

**White:** Vin Santo or Moscadello di Montalcino from Tuscany; Picolit from Friuli-Venezia Giulia

**Sparkling Red:** Brachetto d'Acqui from Piedmont

# Chiacchiere o crostoli

## CARNIVAL "LOVER'S KNOTS"

Serve these delightful fritters warm or cold, with any type of cream. Zabaglione (see page 297) makes a great marriage with this type of fritter. These sweets are great served with dessert wine and are a perfect finale to any festivity or celebration. Even though the name means "knots," and tradition calls for the dough to be formed into knots, you may simply cut it into triangles or any shape you like. You may also add any type of liquor to this dough.

**SERVES 6**

4 large eggs

⅔ cup sugar

⅔ cup (1⅓ sticks) unsalted butter, room temperature

¼ cup grappa or rum

½ tsp finely grated lemon zest

2 cups sifted all-purpose flour

Pinch of salt

1 tsp baking powder

2 to 3 qt olive or peanut oil for frying, as needed

Confectioners' sugar, for dusting

1. Beat the eggs, sugar, butter, grappa or rum, and lemon zest in a large bowl with a whisk until very thick and creamy.
2. Stir in 1½ cups of the sifted flour, the salt, and baking powder. Continue adding flour just until you have a dough that is firm enough to knead; you may not need the full amount. Knead by hand on a lightly floured surface until smooth and elastic. (You can knead the dough in a food processor, in two batches.) Let the dough rest in a covered bowl for 30 minutes.
3. With a pasta machine or by hand, roll the dough into strips measuring 5 inches wide, 3 inches long, and ¹⁄₁₆ inch thick. Lay the strips out on a lightly floured counter.
4. Cut the strips into pieces that measure ½ inch by 5 inches; cut a 2-inch-long slit lengthwise in the center of each one; and then flip one end through the slit to create a knot.
5. Heat the oil in a deep fryer or a deep pot to 350 to 375 degrees F. Fry the dough strips until golden brown, turning once, about 3 minutes. Drain them briefly on paper towels and serve hot, dusted with confectioners' sugar.

Wine notes: **Sparkling White:** Asti or semi-sparkling Moscato d'Asti from Piedmont

**White:** Vin Santo or Moscadello di Montalcino from Tuscany; Picolit from Friuli-Venezia Giulia; Malvasia delle Lipari from Sicily

**Sparkling Red:** Brachetto d'Acqui from Piedmont

# Frollini

## CRUMBLY COOKIES

The word *frollini* refers to anything crumbly or likely to shatter, like this cookie. They are good for an afternoon snack with tea or coffee. The recipe for this cookie is easy to make and easy to vary. To make almond flour, grind about ¾ cup slivered blanched almonds in a blender, pulsing the blender on an off, to a flour-like consistency.

**MAKES 30 COOKIES**

**¾ cup plus 2 tbsp (1¾ sticks) unsalted butter**

**¾ cup confectioners' sugar**

**1 large egg**

**½ cup almond flour**

**1¾ cups all-purpose flour**

1. Preheat the oven to 350 degrees F. Butter and flour a baking sheet.
2. In the bowl of a stand mixer fitted with the paddle attachment, cream the butter with the sugar until white and creamy, about 3 minutes.
3. Add the egg and mix until well combined.
4. Add the almond flour and all-purpose flour and mix just to combine.
5. Spoon the mixture into a pastry bag and pipe the mixture onto the baking sheet in any shapes you like, such as circles, straight logs or sticks, S-shapes, or squiggles.
6. Bake until the cookies are set and barely golden around the edges, about 10 minutes. Let cool on a wire rack.

Wine notes: **Sparkling White:** Asti or semi-sparkling Moscato d'Asti from Piedmont
**White:** Vin Santo or Moscadello di Montalcino from Tuscany; Picolit from Friuli-Venezia Giulia; Malvasia delle Lipari from Sicily
**Sparkling Red:** Brachetto d'Acqui from Piedmont or Lam-brusco from Emilia-Romagna

# Bunet all'astigiana

## CRÈME CARAMEL FROM PIEDMONT

This dish is similar to the well-known crème caramel, but it is flavored with cocoa and amaretti cookies, a cookie typical in the Piedmont region.

**SERVES 6**

CARAMEL

**1 cup sugar**

**¼ cup water**

CUSTARD

**¾ cup amaretto cookie crumbs (2 oz)**

**⅔ cup sugar**

**4 large eggs**

**⅓ cup unsweetened cocoa powder**

**1 cup milk**

**1 cup heavy cream**

**Zest of 1 lemon**

1. Preheat the oven to 350 degrees F. Fill a large cake pan or roasting pan halfway with water and place it in the oven to preheat. (The pan needs to be large enough to hold six 4-ounce custard cups or soufflé molds.) Have the molds near the stove when you begin to cook the caramel.
2. To make the caramel, stir the sugar together with the water in a saucepan and cook, shaking or swirling the pan but not stirring, over medium heat until golden brown, about 4 minutes. (Once the sugar starts to turn golden, it will cook fast, so be careful not to burn it.) Pour a bit of caramel immediately on the bottom of each mold, enough to cover the bottom.
3. To make the custard, crumble the amaretti cookies between your hands into a bowl.
4. In a separate bowl, mix the sugar with eggs, then add the cocoa and mix well until everything is well incorporated.
5. In a saucepan, bring the milk, cream, and lemon zest slowly to a boil over low heat. Remove from the heat immediately.
6. Add the milk mixture to the egg mixture, a little at a time to prevent the heat from the milk from scrambling the eggs. Mix well to incorporate. Strain the milk-egg mixture, using a fine-mesh strainer, into the bowl with the cookies.
7. Fill the molds with the mixture. Carefully place the molds into the hot water inside of the pan. Bake for about 50 minutes. If they start to get color on top, cover with a sheet of foil. After baking, transfer the molds from the pan to a wire rack and let cool. Refrigerate the molds before serving.
8. To serve, run a knife around the outside of the custard to loosen from the mold, and flip the mold upside down onto a plate.

Wine notes: **Sparkling White:** Asti or semi-sparkling Moscato d'Asti from Piedmont **Sparkling Red:** Brachetto d'Acqui from Piedmont

# Gelato fior di latte

## "FLOWER OF MILK" GELATO

This is a simple gelato, very versatile; enjoy it plain, with fresh fruit, or to accompany a cake. This gelato is often used in the preparation of affogato al caffè, where the gelato is covered with brewed espresso and topped with whipped cream.

**MAKES 1 QUART**

2 cups milk

2 cups heavy cream

1¾ cups sugar

1 tbsp light honey

½ tsp vanilla extract

1. Heat the milk and cream in a large saucepan over medium heat, then add the sugar and honey and stir to dissolve. Add the vanilla extract.
2. Strain through a fine-mesh sieve into a glass or metal container. Cool the gelato base over an ice water bath or in the refrigerator, stirring from time to time. When completely chilled, pour into an ice cream maker. Process according to the manufacturer's instructions.
3. Transfer to a container and freeze for about 2 hours before serving.

*To make a stracciatella gelato, before freezing, slowly drizzle melted bittersweet chocolate into the mixture and blend gently to incorporate. Make sure the chocolate is not warmer than 85 degrees F when you add it.*

# Babà

A babà is a sweet, yeast-raised cake that has a rich golden color from the quantity of eggs added to the dough. The baked cake is soaked in a rum syrup, giving the cake a luscious texture. Serve it topped with whipped cream and fresh fruit.

**MAKES 1 CAKE OR 14 INDIVIDUAL CAKES**

BABÀ

**2¼ cups all-purpose flour**

**5 tbsp unsalted butter**

**4 large eggs**

**2 tbsp sugar**

**1 envelope active dried yeast**

SYRUP

**½ cup water**

**½ cup rum**

**1⅓ cups sugar**

GARNISH

**Whipped cream, lightly sweetened and flavored with lemon zest as needed**

**Fresh fruit, chopped or sliced, as needed**

1. To make the babà, mix the flour, butter, eggs, sugar, and yeast in the bowl of a stand mixer fitted with a dough hook on low speed until evenly blended, about 2 minutes. Increase the speed to medium and beat until the dough is smooth and elastic, but still rather soft, another 2 minutes.
2. Preheat the oven to 350 degrees F.
3. Scrape the dough into an oiled babà mold or tube pan for a single large cake, or into 14 timbales (or muffin tins), filling them about half full. Let the babà rise, covered, until doubled in volume and filling the molds to the top, about 1½ hours.
4. Bake until the top is golden brown, 30 to 35 minutes for a large babà or 10 to 12 minutes for individual ones. Remove from the heat and reserve.
5. Meanwhile, to make the syrup, combine the water, rum, and sugar in a saucepan and simmer over medium heat until all the sugar is dissolved.
6. Remove the babà from the oven and let them cool for 10 minutes, then unmold the babàs and transfer them, upside down, to a platter or baking dish while they are still warm. Use a skewer to poke holes in the large babà. Place the large cake or individual cakes on a platter and then pour about half the rum syrup over the cakes. Let the cakes absorb the syrup for about 20 minutes, then turn the cakes over and pour the remaining syrup over them. Cover the cakes and let them absorb the syrup, about 1 hour.
7. Serve with whipped cream and fresh fruit.

Wine notes: **Sparkling White:** Asti or semi-sparkling Moscato d'Asti from Piedmont

**White:** Vin Santo or Moscadello di Montalcino from Tuscany; Picolit from Friuli-Venezia Giulia; Recioto di Soave from Veneto; Malvasia delle Lipari from Sicily

**Sparkling Red:** Brachetto d'Acqui from Piedmont

# Strudel di mele

## APPLE STRUDEL

This dessert comes from the northern part of Italy, from the regions closest to the Alps and most directly influenced by German and Austrian cooking.

**MAKES 1 STRUDEL; SERVES 6**

### STRUDEL DOUGH

**1¼ cups all-purpose flour**

**3 tbsp olive oil**

**⅔ cup water, as needed**

### FILLING

**2½ cups cored, chopped apple**

**2 tbsp sugar**

**1 tsp ground cinnamon**

**¼ cup pine nuts**

**½ cup seedless raisins**

**Zest and juice of 1 lemon**

**¼ cup (½ stick) unsalted butter, melted**

**½ cup plain dry bread crumbs**

**Confectioners' sugar, for dusting**

1. To make the strudel dough, knead the flour, oil, and water together until the dough is smooth and elastic. Let the dough rest for 1 hour.
2. To make the filling, mix the apple, sugar, cinnamon, pine nuts, raisins, lemon zest, and lemon juice in a bowl.
3. Heat half of the butter in a small skillet and toast the bread crumbs in the butter. Set aside.
4. Preheat the oven to 350 degrees F. Butter a baking sheet.
5. Lightly flour a large work surface and start rolling and stretching the dough with a rolling pin, trying to maintain a square shape. When the dough is about 1/16 inch thick, put both hands underneath the dough and use the back of your hands to stretch the dough until it becomes as thin as a sheet of paper. Let the dough rest for a few minutes between stretches so that it won't spring back.
6. Cut the dough into a rectangle about 20 × 18 inches and transfer to a clean cloth towel. Brush the dough lightly with the remaining melted butter, sprinkle with the bread crumbs, and place the apple mixture along one side of the dough.
7. Using the towel, roll the dough around the apple, then roll the strudel onto the baking sheet. Brush with more butter on top and bake until the dough is crisp and golden brown, about 20 minutes.
8. Sprinkle with confectioners' sugar, slice, and serve while warm.

# Crostata di amarena

## SOUR CHERRY CROSTATA

A crostata is a jam tart, made with *pasta frolla*, the Italian version of shortbread dough.

**MAKES 1 TART; SERVES 10 TO 12**

CHERRY JAM

**2 lb pitted sour cherries, fresh or frozen**

**3¼ cups sugar**

**Juice from ½ lemon**

PASTA FROLLA

**1½ cups all-purpose flour**

**½ cup confectioners' sugar**

**½ tsp baking powder**

**½ tsp finely grated orange or lemon zest**

**½ cup (1 stick) unsalted butter, cold, cut into small cubes**

**1 large egg**

**Few drops heavy cream, as needed**

1. To make the jam, combine the cherries with the sugar and lemon juice in a saucepan. Cook until the mixture reaches 120 degrees F.
2. Pulse the mixture in a food processor to blend the jam. Refrigerate until ready to use.
3. To make the pasta frolla, in a food processor combine the flour, sugar, baking powder, and citrus zest. Add the cold butter cubes and toss lightly to coat. Pulse until the butter is the size of small peas.
4. Add the egg and pulse to moisten the dough until it begins to come together.
5. Turn the dough out onto a lightly floured board and knead by hand. If the dough is too dry, add a few drops of heavy cream. Shape into a small disk, wrap, and chill thoroughly for at least 3 hours or overnight.
6. Preheat the oven to 350 degrees F.
7. Divide the dough into two pieces and roll between two sheets of plastic wrap to a thickness of ⅛ inch, about 10 inches in diameter.
8. Lay one piece of the dough into an 8-inch tart pan and fill with the cherry jam. Roll out the rest of the dough and cut into strips ½ inch wide. Place the strips on top of the tart, creating a diamond pattern.
9. Bake the tart until the dough is golden brown, about 40 minutes. Cool completely on a wire rack before slicing and serving.

Wine notes: **Sparkling White:** Asti or semi-sparkling Moscato d'Asti from Piedmont
**White:** Vin Santo from Tuscany; Picolit from Friuli-Venezia Giulia; Recioto di Soave from Veneto; Malvasia delle Lipari from Sicily
**Sparkling Red:** Lambrusco from Emilia-Romagna; Brachetto d'Acqui from Piedmont

# Torta di pere

## PEAR CAKE

This is a simple cake that is good for breakfast or an afternoon snack. Bosc pears are a good choice because of their lower water content. Make sure they are perfectly ripe. This cake is also good when made with apples.

**MAKES 1 CAKE; SERVES 10 TO 12**

- 1¼ cups all-purpose flour
- ½ cup cornstarch
- 1 tsp baking powder
- ½ tsp ground cinnamon
- ½ cup plus 2 tbsp (1¼ sticks) unsalted butter
- 1 cup sugar
- 4 large eggs
- 2½ cups pears cut into large chunks

1. Preheat the oven to 350 degrees F. Lightly butter and flour a 10-inch cake pan.
2. Sift together the flour, cornstarch, baking powder, and cinnamon.
3. In the bowl of a stand mixer fitted with the paddle attachment, cream the butter with the sugar until light in color and consistency, about 3 minutes. Add the eggs, one at a time, and mix until incorporated. Add the sifted flour mixture and mix until well incorporated.
4. Fold in the pears by hand, and pour the batter into the cake pan.
5. Bake until a toothpick inserted in the center comes out clean, about 50 minutes,. Cool on a wire rack.

### Wine notes:

**Sparkling White:** Asti or semi-sparkling Moscato d'Asti from Piedmont
**White:** Picolit from Friui-Venezia Giulia; Recioto di Soave from Veneto
**Sparkling Red:** Brachetto d'Acqui from Piedmont

# Castagnole

## CARNIVAL FRITTERS

This is a little one-bite cookie that, like many fried cookies in Italy, is typically prepared during the carnival time in February.

**MAKES ABOUT 30 COOKIES**

- 2½ cups all-purpose flour
- ⅓ cup sugar
- 6 tbsp (¾ stick) unsalted butter
- ½ tsp baking powder
- 1 tsp mixed orange and lemon zest
- ¼ cup Marsala
- Peanut or olive oil for frying, as needed
- Confectioners' sugar, for dusting

1. In the bowl of a stand mixer fitted with the paddle attachment, mix the flour, sugar, butter, baking powder, and citrus zest. Blend in the Marsala. Mix until smooth, about 2 minutes.
2. Remove the dough from the bowl and shape into small balls about ½ ounce each and about ½ inch in diameter.
3. Heat the oil in a deep fryer or deep pot to 350 degrees F. Cook the castagnole, in batches, until they have a dark color, about 3 minutes.
4. Drain on paper towels. Dust with confectioners' sugar and serve warm.

Wine notes: **Sparkling White:** Asti or semi-sparkling Moscato d'Asti from Piedmont
**White:** Vin Santo or Moscadello di Montalcino from Tuscany; Picolit from Friuli-Venezia Giulia; Recioto di Soave from Veneto; Malvasia delle Lipari from Sicily
**Sparkling Red:** Brachetto d'Acqui from Piedmont; Lambrusco from Emilia-Romagna

# Amaretti morbidi

## SOFT AMARETTI COOKIES

Amaretti are crunchy almond cookies typical throughout the Piedmont region. The name itself translates to "little bitter ones." The version here is typical in the south of Italy, and the cookies are soft instead of dry and brittle. Bitter almonds, the traditional flavoring for these cookies, cannot be sold legally in the United States, so we've substituted almond extract.

**MAKES ABOUT 30 COOKIES**

- 1⅓ cups sugar
- 12 oz shelled raw almonds
- ¼ tsp pure almond extract
- 1 tsp orange zest
- 2 egg whites
- 1 tbsp honey
- Confectioners' sugar, as needed

1. Preheat the oven to 375 degrees F. Lightly butter and flour a baking sheet, or line it with parchment paper.
2. In a food processor, grind the sugar with the almonds until reduced to a cornmeal-like texture. Add the almond extract and orange zest and pulse a few times to incorporate, then transfer the mixture to a bowl.
3. Add the egg whites and honey, and mix well until incorporated.
4. Form the mixture into balls about ½ ounce each with a diameter of about ½ inch and roll them in confectioners' sugar.
5. Place the balls on the baking sheet and, with the thumb and index fingers of both hands, lightly press the amaretti balls in on both sides to make a rough pyramid shape.
6. Bake for 8 to 10 minutes, until lightly colored but still soft inside. Cool on a wire rack.

Wine notes: **Sparkling White:** Asti or semi-sparkling Moscato d'Asti from Piedmont

**White:** Vin Santo or Moscadello di Montalcino from Tuscany; Picolit from Friuli-Venezia Giulia; Recioto di Soave from Veneto; Malvasia delle Lipari from Sicily

**Sparkling Red:** Brachetto d'Acqui from Piedmont

# Brutti ma buoni

## "UGLY BUT GOOD" COOKIES

These cookies are famously "ugly" because they look kind of rough and crumbly. You make them from only three ingredients—sugar, egg whites, and hazelnuts—but the flavor is outstanding.

**MAKES ABOUT 30 COOKIES**

2 egg whites

¾ cup sugar

1¼ cup skinned hazelnuts, coarsely chopped

1. Preheat the oven to 300 degrees F. Line a baking sheet with parchment paper.
2. In the bowl of a stand mixer fitted with the whip attachment, whip the egg whites at medium speed, adding the sugar a little at a time. When all the sugar is incorporated, keep whipping at high speed for another few minutes, until the whites are stiff.
3. Mix the hazelnuts into the egg white mixture.
4. Transfer the mixture to a saucepan and cook over low heat until it starts to come away from the sides of the pan, about 10 minutes.
5. Portion each cookie with a spoon onto the baking sheet.
6. Bake until the surface of the cookies is golden brown and looks dry, about 45 minutes. Cool completely on a wire rack before serving or storing in airtight containers for up to 3 days.

Wine notes: **Sparkling White:** Asti or semi-sparkling Moscato d'Asti from Piedmont

**White:** Vin Santo or Moscadello di Montalcino from Tuscany; Picolit from Friuli-Venezia Giulia; Recioto di Soave from Veneto; Malvasia delle Lipari from Sicily

**Sparkling Red:** Brachetto d'Acqui from Piedmont

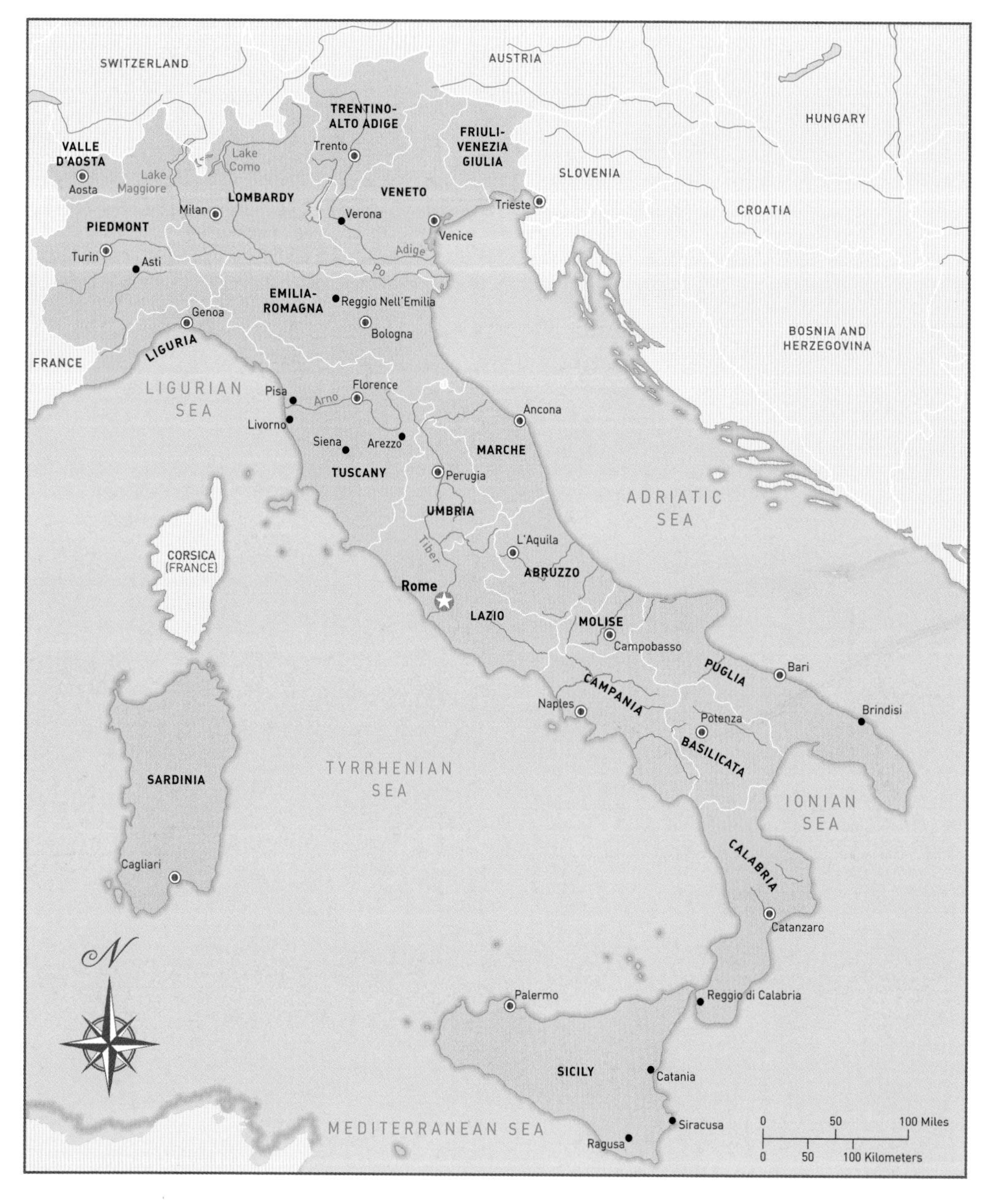


## Northern Italy

Butter, cream, olive oil, lard, Parmigiano-Reggiano; boiled and braised meats: pork, beef, veal, venison, liver, turkey; speck, prosciutto (San Daniele), mortadella, coppa; freshwater fish and seafood, eel, scampi, salt cod; wheat, corn, rice, beans, risotto and polenta, pasta (ravioli, fettuccine, lasagne, tagliatelle, tortellini, agnolotti, bigoli), gnocchi; apples, pears, cherries, radicchio; cabbage, potatoes, tomatoes, asparagus, beets, onions, peas, porcini mushrooms; white truffles, saffron, caraway, horseradish, paprika, balsamic vinegar

## Central Italy

Olive oil, lard, sheep's milk cheese; melon, citrus, tomatoes; Lacinato kale (or black cabbage), spinach, fennel, artichokes, peas; chestnuts, walnuts; freshwater fish, seafood, snails, dried cod; herbs, pesto, wine, black truffles, porcini mushrooms, peperoncini; farinata, unsalted bread, white beans, lentils; pasta (spaghetti, rigatoni, bucatini, egg-based fettuccine, ravioli, maccheroni, spaghetti alla chitarra, pappardelle), crêpes; meats (grilled, roasted, fried, spit-roasted): beef, game, lamb, pork, poultry, rabbit; fish stews and chowders

## Southern Italy

Olive oil, sheep's milk cheese, buffalo mozzarella; citrus, tomatoes, fennel, potatoes, eggplant, mushrooms; chestnuts, hazelnuts, almonds; wheat, couscous, beans; pizza, flatbread (carta da musica); fresh and dried pasta (spaghetti, penne, vermicelli, rigatoni, orecchiette); freshwater fish, sardines, anchovies, tuna, swordfish, oysters, mussels; sausage, lamb, goat, pork, venison; wine, raisins, peperoncini; marzipan, saffron, cinnamon, honey, sweets

# Index

Page numbers in *italics* indicate illustrations

# N



# O



# P

## Q



## R



## S